The Girl Who Killed A Nation

WHEN WORLDS COLLIDE

A TRUE STORY

by Treive Nicholas

Whittles Publishing

Whittles Publishing Ltd,
Dunbeath,
Caithness, KW6 6EG,
Scotland, UK

www.whittlespublishing.com

ISBN: 978-184995-596-6

Dedicated to

Phyllis Rogers, Elizabeth Nicholas, Sarah Neal, Clare Nicholas, Hannah Nicholas, Estela Nicholas, Sabina Nicholas, Heather Nicholas and Penelope Nicholas.

And to Simon Mqamelo (1962–2024).

CONTENTS

Acknowledgements

I doubt if this book would have been started had I not stumbled upon *Frontiers: The Epic of South Africa's Creation and the Tragedy of the Xhosa People* by the late Noel Mostert. His storytelling inspired me so much that for the last five years I've been travelling around South Africa and the UK, diving into books and writing my version of events. It is a pity fate prevented us from meeting so I could show my appreciation.

Writing *The Girl* has been little short of an adventure at times, with many highs and lows. After flapping around enthusiastically but inefficiently on my own in the countryside of the Eastern Cape, I happened upon the Border Historical Society. They recognised a lost but kindred soul before taking me under their wing. Not only did they take me on *vakashas* (adventures / trips) to find isolated historical sites, but they were a great source of challenge and discussion, all in all a mine of knowledge on amaXhosa and colonial history. So, to Patrick Hutchison (Hutch), Mike Kenyon and William Martinson, thanks for the warmth and sincerity of your friendship. I'll never look at a hard-boiled egg the same way again.

For me to better understand 19th-century amaXhosa history it quickly became apparent that I needed to appreciate the indigenous people's relationship with their ancestors. This was clearly pivotal to the decision-making processes of the tribal seniors, spiritual leaders and ordinary people. I have to thank Simon and Jane Mqamelo for their patience explaining this facet of amaXhosa culture to me. Once the penny dropped, I was able to look at amaXhosa history through a very different lens, one that made past events a great deal more logical.

Jaco Schreuder was a superb host ferrying me around Cape Town, while Stephen Fick was more than accommodating when I went in search of Nongqawuse's grave a couple of times.

When my travels took me to Whittlesey in Cambridgeshire, Sue and Ken Palmer went out of their way to open St Mary's Church and show me various artefacts and places associated with Harry Smith. Their help enabled me to tie together the loose ends of my story.

Ingeborg Pelsen was a godsend. Her measured advice about the South African publishing landscape and her negotiating skills helped me navigate so many obstacles, most I couldn't even see.

As part of my research to familiarise myself with contemporary views on Xhosa culture I read Mercy Nqandeka's *Don't Upset ooMalumee*, so it was a great pleasure to have her review my manuscript. As we seemed to hit it off, she was a natural choice to write the foreword, for which I am grateful. Her offer to provide a translation into isiXhosa was enthusiastically received. I'm sure you'll agree that she sets the just right tone from the start.

As you shall read, my research for this book often meant I ignored my domestic responsibilities, to bury my nose deep into a book or journal. On other occasions I might scoot off to remote parts of the Eastern Cape for a couple of weeks in pursuit of historical sites, to better understand their 19th-century secrets. I am grateful to my wife Clare for her patience and empathy – it means a lot to me. She also spent many hours reviewing and editing the manuscript. Thank you so much.

Thanks go to the following institutions for giving me permission to include images in this book: the National Library of South Africa, Western Cape Archives and Records Service, Alamy Ltd, StoryboardThat, The Royal Green Jackets (Rifles) Museum, St Mary's Church in Whittlesey and the *Daily Dispatch*.

Getting a book published is quite a project. It needs someone to share your passion in your story and commit to the all the logistics. So, I'm grateful to Keith Whittles (Whittles Publishing) and Magdaleen Snyman (NB Publishers) who have taken my story from raw text to the bookshelves of the UK and South Africa respectively. En route, Caroline Petherick did a marvellous job with her incisive observations and wordsmithing to help refine and enhance the manuscript.

Finally, I need to acknowledge my mother, who was really the one who taught me to read. For me as a child, words on the page seldom made much sense, and it was hugely frustrating. Thank you for the gift of reading.

Foreword

By Hombakazi Mercy Nqandeka,

Author of *Don't Upset ooMalume! A Guide to Stepping Up your Xhosa Game*

When I received an invitation to review *A Girl Who Killed a Nation,* a story about Nongqawuse, I felt a prickling sensation at the crown of my spine. It wasn't just irritation; it was a weariness that stemmed from seeing African stories often mishandled by western writers approaching them from a skewed, entitled and culturally insensitive perspective. These narratives typically paint Africans as defeated, story-less objects, reinforcing colonialist viewpoints. Moreover, within Xhosa culture, Nongqawuse's tale is seldom discussed, as it is buried beneath layers of multifaceted trauma, shame and famine. It's a story that seems to have been collectively agreed to be sealed away, avoiding the reopening of old wounds and the reliving of past tragedies.

However, upon briefly perusing this book's table of contents, a sense of relief washed over me. There was a palpable shift in perspective, one that did not blame or attack my people for Nongqawuse's fate but approached the story with curiosity and clarity. It felt like a breath of fresh air, sparing us from the trauma and shame of reliving our people's pain.

The author, Treive Nicholas, intrigued me with his background, having spent considerable time in Mthatha and Transkei. His perspective on Nongqawuse's story is not about hammering the last nail into a rotten coffin but rather about reopening it to uncover overlooked evidence. His mission, upon returning many years later, was to understand a story that had sparked his curiosity and to bring it to life through diligent research.

Nongqawuse's story, as many of us know, revolves around her prophecy urging the killing of cattle, which ultimately brought calamity upon the amaXhosa, and how she received this prophecy has remained a mystery, tucked away by our ancestors and elders. Treive, however, hasn't shied away from exploring the possibilities. His narrative is not one-sided, blaming Nongqawuse and the amaXhosa. Instead, he delves deep into the historical context and the colonial systems that may have led to her demise.

He bravely lifts the veil on the grotesque colonial policies that oppressed and stripped the natives of their land, cattle and rights. Treive's pilgrimage to Gxarha River, the site of Nongqawuse's prophecy, was marked by respect and reverence for the people, spirits and nature surrounding it. Throughout his journey, he questioned the greed and selfishness that drove the conquest of the amaXhosa by the British, refusing to shy away from calling things what they were.

Treive's language is not condescending but respectful, especially when discussing kings and elders. He views the cattle-killing not as a standalone event but as a symptom of deeper underlying issues. His respect for Nongqawuse has challenged my perception of her. While she had previously been dismissed as a footnote in amaXhosa history, Treive's portrayal of her compels me to reconsider her as a young girl burdened with a message that would devastate her people.

His pilgrimage from the Gxarha river, the site of the prophecy, to Nongqawuse's grave in Alexandria (Eastern Cape), speaks volumes about his search for her spirit, perhaps in the hope of understanding her side of the story. Reviewing this book has granted me a newfound appreciation for Nongqawuse, viewed through a lens of grace and respect.

Well done, Treive!

IsiXhosa version of the Foreword

Xa ndandifumana isimemo sokuphononongа incwadi 'A Girl Who Killed a Nation' elibali ngoNongqawuse, ndaziva ndinento enyuka emqolo iyokuthi finini entanyeni. Ibingekokucaphuka nje, kodwa ibikukudikwa kukubona amabali ethu eAfrika ebaliswa kakubi, egqwethwa ngendlela engahloniphi nkcubeko ngabantu baseNtshona. Basoloko ke beyityibela iAfrika nje ngabantu abahluphekayo, abangakwazi kubalisa mabali abo, aba babhali basoloko bebalisa ngathi ngeembono zobukoloniyali. Ngaphezukoko ke emaXhoseni, ibali lika Nongqawuse asinto kufane kuthethwe ngayo, yinyewe eyangcwatywa ngapha kokuhlazeka, iintlungu kunye nendlala eyathi yeza nesisihika-hika. Libali ongade uthi mhlawumbi kwavunyelwana ukuba lingcitywe mba, lingaze liphinde livulwe, sisilonda esambandwayo ngenxa yobuzaza baso.

Kodwa ke emva kokuba ndiyiphengululе le ncwadi ukusukela kwisiqulatho, ndeva ndikhululeka noko. Indlela umbhali athetha ngayo ngenkcubeko nabantu ichubekile, akabekityala okanye ahlasele amaXhosa ngesehlo sikaNongqawuse, kodwa kuyavela ukuba ngumntu onomdla wokwazi. Ndaziva ngathi ndiphefumla umoya omnandi kuba ke umbhali lo akahlikihli tyiwa nxebeni.

Umbhali lo uTreive Nicholas, undikhwankqisile ngemvela phi yakhe, ukhe wahlala kwidolophu yaseMthatha. Uluvo lwakhe kwibali likaNongqawuse alubetheleli sikhonkwane sokugqibela kumkhombe wakhe osowuwohlolokile, koko uyawuvula, ukhangela ubungqina obungazange bujongisiswe.

Uthe akubuya emva kweminyaka emininzi, wenza njalo ekwiphulo lokuphanda, lokuqonda nokuvusa ibali elathi lamnika umdla.

Nje ngokuba abaninzi bethu besazi, ibali likaNongqawuse lingombono wakhe owawubongoza abantu ukuba babulale iinlomo zabo, nto leyo yeza nentlekele kwisizwe samaXhosa siphela. Kodwa ke indlela awawufumana ngayo lo mbono useyimfihlo ebumlingwarha ebonakala ngathi yasongwa yabekelwa kude ngababephambi kwethu. uTreive ke uphononongа esisehlo ngokungafihlisiyo, ekhangela nawuphi na unobangela walo mbono. Akajongi cala nye ke kuphando lwakhe, akagxeki maXhosa, koko wemba nzulu kwimbali nendima eyadlalwa ngoondlebe zikhany'ilanga kwesisehlo.

Utyhila umkhusane kwizenzo ezoyikekayo zokucinezelwa kwabantu bomthonyama bebulawa, bethathelwa umhlaba, iinkomo zabo nokucudulelwa kwamalungelo abo. uTreive ke wathatha uhambo oluya kumlambo iGxarha nalapho kukholeleka ukuba uNongqawuse wawufumana khona lo mbono. Olundwendwelo lwakhe luphawulwa ngembeko nentlonipho egqithileyo kubantu abakhoyo nabangasekhoyo, nakwimimoya nendalo ejikeleze lo mlambo. Koluhambo uzibuza ngokurhwaphiliza, nokuzicingela okwakuqhuba amaNgesi kwiimfazwe zokuphuca amaXhosa. Isimbo sakhe sokubhala

xi

asisebenzisi lwimi ludelelayo koko uyahlonipha ngakumbi xa ethetha ngamakhosi, ookumkani nabadala. Esi sehlo sokubulawa kweenkomo akasijongi nje ngesehlo esizimele geqe, koko usinxulumanisa nobunzulu bezinto ezakhokelela kuso. Intlonipho yakhe kaNongqawuse iyishukumisile indlela endicinga ngayo mayela nelibali. Libali elikude esingafane sive ngalo, kodwa emva kokufunda le ncwadi, ndiziva ndinomdla wokwazi ngcono ngoNongqawuse, intokazi eyayithwaliswe umyalezo owathi wonakalisa isizwe sonke.

Uhambo lukaTreive ukusuka kulambo iGxarha ukuya e-Alexandria kwalapha eMpuma Kapa, nalapho wangcwatyelwa khona uNongqawuse lubalula umdla wakhe wokukhangela nokuqonda umoya wale ntokazi. Ukuphonononga le ncwadi kundenze ndamhlonipha ngcono uNongqawuse.

Ngxatsho ke Treive!

Pronunciation of isiXhosa Words

In this book you are going to read about the Xhosa people of the Eastern Cape. Whilst there are many different clans, they all speak a dialect of isiXhosa. One of the distinct characteristics of this language is the inclusion of various clicks. A poem or song delivered in isiXhosa really is a thing of great beauty. Here's a nice example, https://www.youtube.com/watch?v=dCx436UneF8. Through social interaction, geographic proximity and commercial engagement it is believed the Xhosa people assimilated these clicks into their language from the Khoisan people of the Cape. (Those people were once known as Bushmen and Hottentots, but today these names are considered inappropriate.)

As you read *The Girl who Killed a Nation* you will come across a number of people, objects and places with isiXhosa names. I suspect you'll try to pronounce them in your head. So I've provided a basic idea of the principal clicks and linguistic characteristics, although there are other subtleties and nuances that I'm not qualified to address. In some places, I've compared isiXhosa pronunciation with English.

It is worth noting that isiXhosa is a phonetic language. Although there are exceptions, just say what you read to begin with.

Let's start with the letter x, as in the word Xhosa. With your mouth shut, place your tongue at the top and side of your mouth, against your side teeth. Open your mouth quite quickly, draw air in and you should hear your first click. The sound is moderated by the next letter, particularly a, e, i, o and u. For Xhosa, try X-hosa. You'll read about the Gxara River a few times, so the click of the x is followed by the clear enunciation of the 'ah' sound. This YouTube video (https://www.youtube.com/watch?v=Trq_gIe1v04) should help if you want to give it a go. Near the end of this section is another link, taking you to the clicks I describe next.

Q is an altogether different click, and is particularly important as it appears in the name of the book's principal character, a girl called Nongqawuse. Place your tongue firmly on the roof of your mouth and snap it away rapidly. Shape your mouth depending on the vowel sound that follows. So for Nongqawuse, you say Nong-qa-wuse. Some people stress the e at the end, others don't.

The final click is c, which I always feel is expelled from the front of your mouth. Place the tip of your tongue at the top of your mouth, resting on the back of your front teeth. Draw breath in while opening your mouth to enounce a quite sharp sound. The town of Centane crops up a few times in this story, so remember to include the click – Cen-tan-e.

A couple of other pointers to help. The letter r is often a guttural sound, generated at the back of the mouth, and is particularly the case where it is followed by h. The name of Chief Sarhili is a good one to practise with.

Ph and th are frequent letter combinations, but they do not deliver the f and th sounds of the English language. Instead, each letter is spoken separately. For example, King Phalo's name is said P-ha-lo, with not an f in earshot. The regional town of Mthatha should be said M-t-ha-t-ha.

YouTube (https://www.youtube.com/watch?v=VKOQ1pw3AJQ) will give some useful pointers on pronunciation, so make sure your tongue and mouth are warmed up and ready to be tested.

For isiXhosa speakers this will all seem rather too simplistic, but hopefully it will help you if you are unfamiliar with this wonderful-sounding language.

TIMELINE OF PRINCIPAL EVENTS

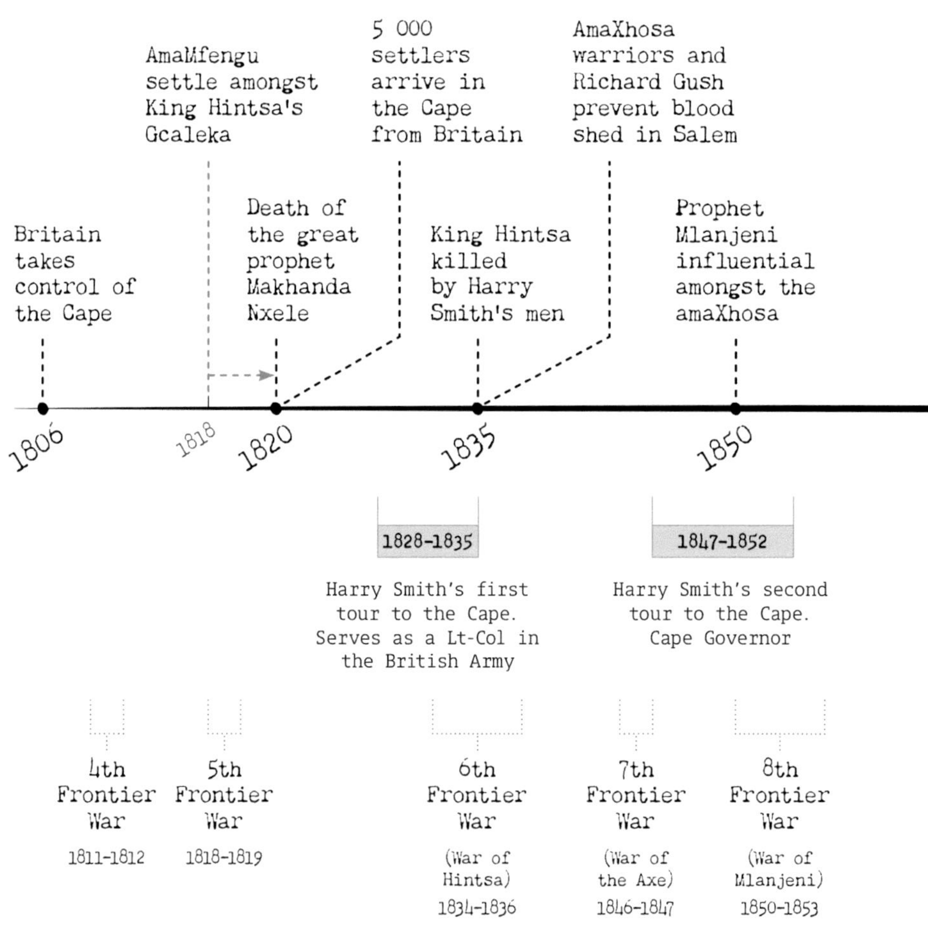

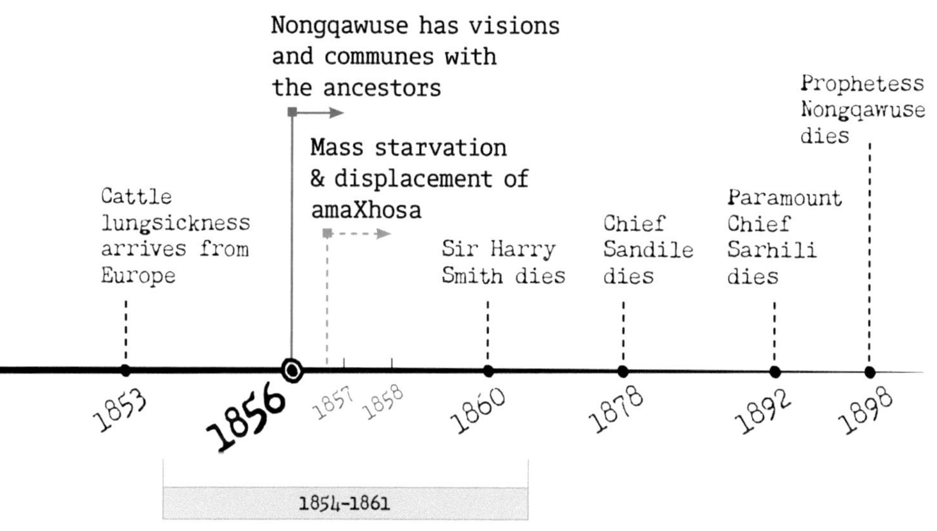

9th Frontier War

(Wedding Feast War)

1877-1878

INTRODUCTION

A word about the title of this book, *The Girl Who Killed a Nation*. It is deliberately provocative, and is the antithesis of what I believe. I am in fact tipping my cap to a play written by H.I.E. Dhlomo in 1935, called *The Girl who Killed to Save: Nongqause the Liberator.* Both titles can't be true – or can they? That is the unsolved conundrum we are about to address.

The Dead Will Arise: Nongqawuse and the Great Cattle-Killing Movement of 1856–7 by Jeff Peires is considered a seminal book on the subject – measured, culturally sensitive and well researched. He concludes his work with 'Even if no further information can be obtained, it must be possible to write of Nongqawuse from other perspectives than mine.' So I have taken up the challenge. This book is my perspective on the subject. I hope my light touch makes the story accessible to you.

On that note, I would like to stress that I am not a historian in any shape or form. If anything, I am a traveller that likes re-telling interesting stories – in this case a historical one – that I've encountered on my wanders. I've blended my physical exploration of South Africa, conversations with experts and reviews of numerous books, videos, journals and learned papers by proper historians. They've done the spadework in the archives. My background is in science, so I'd like to think I bring an objective critical eye to the subject matter, focusing more on evidence than just hearsay. But you can be the judge of that.

Referencing has been kept to a minimum, but a bibliography offers you an opportunity to source original material and explore the whole subject in more detail. Reading any of these, you may spot facts I've missed and so come to different conclusions from mine. As you are about to find out, there are many varied interpretations of 19th-century history of the Eastern Cape. Much of it is gripping, often harrowing – but none of it is dull.

I wrestled with nomenclature when writing this book. For example, there are considerable variations in the spelling of isiXhosa words, particularly the names of people and places. Don't be surprised if you find that some of the principal characters have different spelling when you reference other sources. This includes the prophetess Nongqawuse, who is at the heart of this book; elsewhere, such as on her gravestone, you will find her name written as Nongqause. Similarly, there are different spellings of Chief Sarhili, including Kreli, an anglicised version used in by colonials in the 19th century.

Town names are not straightforward either. In recent years many have thrown off their European titles (which acknowledge 19th-century monarchs, military leaders and colonial politicians) to reflect their indigenous heritage. Examples in the Eastern Cape include Port Elizabeth, Grahamstown and King William's Town, now Gqeberha, Makhanda and Qonce respectively. When I refer to these places, I lead with their isiXhosa name followed by the old European name. Some towns, however – Salem, Alexandria and Port St Johns – are still referred to by their European name.

Witch doctors are mentioned many times, and are an important component of the story you are about to read. Today they are described as traditional healers and medical practitioners. But there is something about context I am trying to convey. In addition to their medical roles, in the 19th century they were used extensively by the chiefs and his councillors to 'smell out' undesirables and members of the clan not adhering to tradition or the authority of the seniors. In this capacity the so-called witch doctor was an administrator of justice who identified people for punishment, including torture and execution. They were a means by which the chief could control not just ordinary people but also seniors / headmen that represented a political threat to his authority by, for example, becoming too wealthy in cattle.

Writing this book, I've been mindful of the many cultural sensitivities associated with the people and events I describe. Dealing with past and present sensibilities has had its challenges, so advice has been taken frequently to ensure that respect has been maintained all around. In the interests of accuracy and conveying the mood of the time, several insightful quotations from the 19th century have been included. At times the language can be abrasive and rude by modern standards.

On that note, join me on my travels from Europe to South Africa and back several times, to explore a profound and deeply spiritual 19th-century African story. Things are not quite what they seem. Hold on tight and keep your mind open.

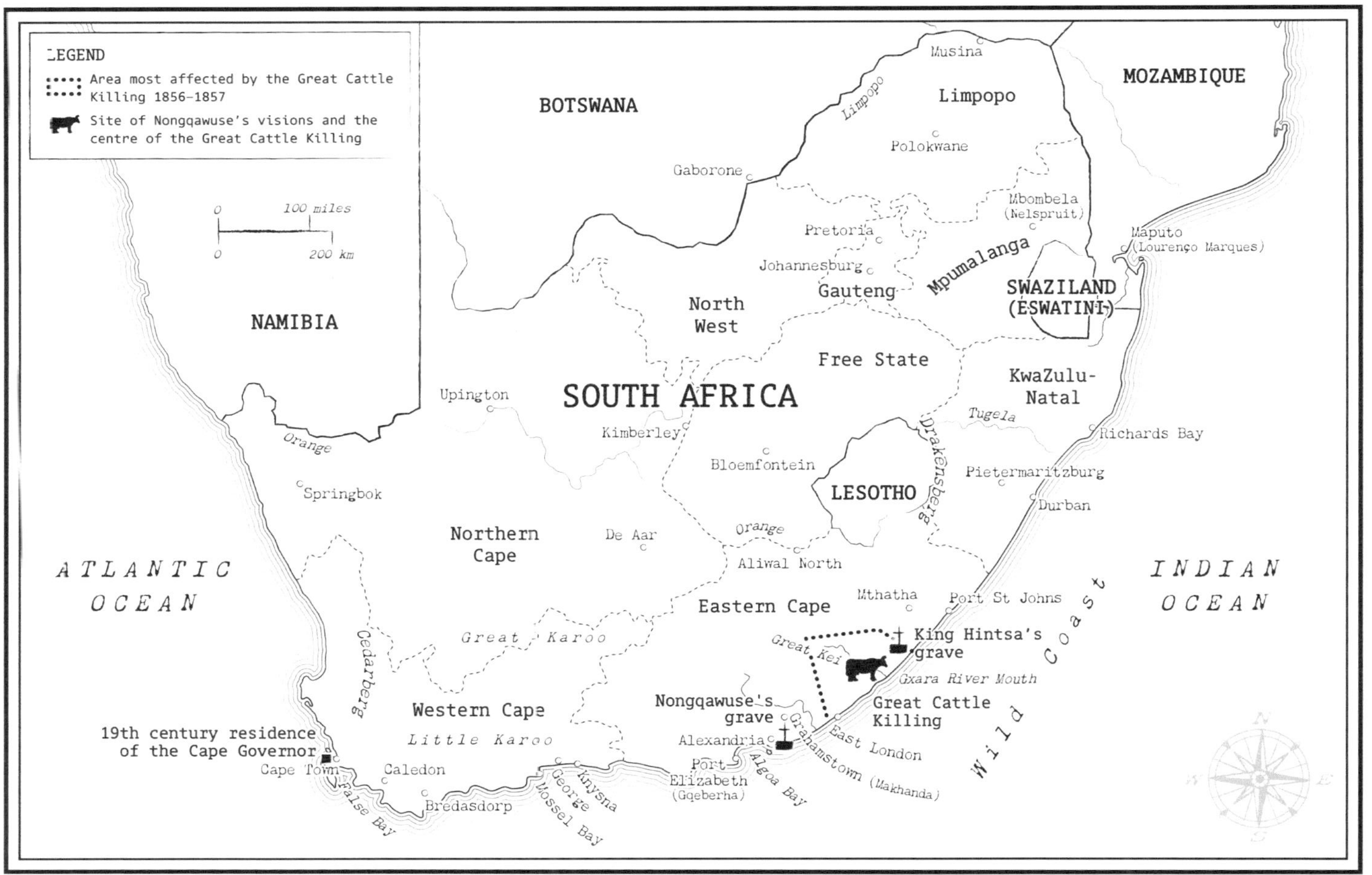

Map 1. South Africa, highlighting the Eastern Cape, the Wild Coast and the principal sites visited.

1: TINDER AND SPARKS

'The reason we are a broken nation today is on account of this girl.'

Brother of King Sarhili, 1910

I'm not much of a reader. I have always found it excessively hard work. In fact, reading out loud in front of other people would have been my Room 101 experience, just as rats were for Winston Smith in Orwell's *1984*. In short, when I had to balance the pleasure of learning with the effort of unscrambling the words, I used to find reading a chore. This meant I was often very selective about what I read, steering clear of anything too voluminous or loaded with clever words and convoluted phrases. American authors appealed to me more than British writers. The Yanks didn't seem to beat about the bush so much with their writing; they were more direct and didn't try to seem clever. Their form and function seem balanced about right, to my way of reading.

However, despite my previous difficulties with the written word, in July 2018 I found myself ordering a copy of *Frontiers* by Noel Mostert, a hardback tome stretching to over 1,300 pages. *Thirteen hundred pages!* A real bargain at just £3.98 from some book warehouse who knows where in the world. It was a monster of a book, weighing in at a hefty 4 lb 7½ oz or, for the metrically minded among you, 2.03 kg. This was the first book I'd owned that presented me with the real risk of a musculoskeletal injury or a broken toe. I was about to embark on a literary marathon, full of numerous clever words and phrases many of which I feared might bamboozle me. Having completed the Great North Run a couple of times, I knew that stamina would be needed to conquer my literary marathon, and I'd have to be prepared to hit 'the wall' at some point before the end. Could I get from page 1 to page 1,355 of *Frontiers*? The task was no less daunting.

The full title of my literary adversary was *Frontiers: The Epic of South Africa's Creation and the Tragedy of the Xhosa People*. Just from the title, I'm sure you can tell I wasn't in for a bit of Jilly Cooper or Jeffrey Archer pulp fiction, littered with equestrian romances and the shenanigans of earthy London detectives. No, *Frontiers* was a detailed description of the history of the Eastern Cape in South Africa up to the late 19th century, focused on one of the principal tribal groups that are broadly called Xhosa people. They in fact consist of numerous clans and groups, all speaking a dialect of isiXhosa. As I had worked in the Eastern Cape with several different clans of Xhosa people some 40 years earlier, I had a particular personal interest. In previous months I'd been reading a number of books about the history of South Africa, with a view to forming a more balanced perspective, one that included the story of the non-European indigenous people. Many of those books told the country's story by giving priority to the settlers and expanding European populations, principally from the Netherlands,

Portugal, Great Britain, Germany and France. Even from this very biased perspective, I found myself increasingly gripped by the subject, and early on in my reading it was evident to me that there was in fact a wealth of knowledge and understanding about the history of the indigenous people, including their peaceful interactions and numerous bloody conflicts with repeated waves of European settlers. Books trying to tell a more balanced or at least fuller story did exist. From a cursory look at the indexes of these books, *Frontiers* kept popping up. So, in order to better understand the history of the Eastern Cape and the amaXhosa, I needed to overcome my aversion to large books.

Much to my surprise, I found myself galloping through the pages, highlighting and marking names, phrases and pages in pencil, and sticking coloured tabs in various places of significance. Margins were littered with personal thoughts, observations and asterisks, and more than a few exclamation marks. I was riveted, sneaking off to have a quick read whenever I could, ignoring the fact that the lawn was getting overgrown and weeds were sprouting out of the gravel driveway. Like an errant teenager wanting more Xbox or Nintendo time, I ended up having to negotiate with my wife for extra reading time: 'If I cut the hedge, can I read for an hour afterwards?'

The book was like a huge canvas painted by one of the greats – the sort you see in the National Gallery, the Prado or the Louvre. It told an epic story, covering hundreds of years of strife, involving many different racial groups, vast geographical areas and larger-than-life characters of all races, many of whom were literally shaping the future of South Africa. Imagine mixing up Shakespeare, Cervantes, Dickens and Marquez – that's how it read. Marquez's *One Hundred Years of Solitude* may be a dreamy mixture of surrealism and imagination, but this pales into insignificance compared to the factual history of the amaXhosa and the Eastern Cape of South Africa. I found that many of the characters in that history, including witch doctors (often called indigenous or traditional healers today) and ghost-like figures hovering over water, murderous soldiers and mercurial prophets, had more than a hint of *Macbeth* about them. The Bard would have had a field day if he'd known about this crucible of strife and mystery.

The thrust of the story concerned the migration of the Bantu people from the Great Lakes at the centre of Africa, reaching the area of modern-day South Africa between 300 and 900CE. The amaXhosa were part of this Bantu migration, first as pastoralists and second as shifting cultivators in the Eastern Cape over hundreds of years before coming into contact with the European settlers who were spreading out rapidly from Cape Town. Initial encounters between the two groups started in the early 18th century but, largely because of conflict over land and livestock, serious fighting began in 1779 and intensified, leading to a series of nine wars over exactly 100 years. These are known as the Frontier Wars, Wars of Dispossession or Xhosa Wars. By 1879 the European settlers, governed by the British, had in effect taken full control of the whole Cape region from Cape Town almost to the border of Natal. By 1894, with the annexation of Pondoland, the border had reached Natal. At this point the non-European people of the Cape were under the control of Europeans based in Cape Town and London, lock, stock and barrel, to use the vernacular.

The philosophy, purpose and energy of 19th-century Europeans in the Cape seemed to be that of 'manifest destiny', a term used by John O'Sullivan, a columnist and editor in the USA at more or less the same time. The term captures the Europeans' apparent sense of divine appointment to 'civilise' and subjugate indigenous peoples – and, in the process, take everything they had. O'Sullivan promoted the idea to justify expansion linked to nationalism. The phrase captured the popular imagination, and was used to justify the most egregious presumption, arrogance and greed.

In South Africa, the amaXhosa and the Khoisan lost a great deal in the process of resisting the advances of European settlers. Much of the land they had traditionally occupied fell under the ownership of advancing settlers. Livestock, their principal source of wealth, became badly diseased from exposure to outside disease; the colonial administrators restricted their freedom of movement; and traditional chiefs and councillors were prevented from implementing the laws they had shaped over hundreds of years to govern their own people. For the privilege of falling under the control of the Cape Government and the British sphere of influence, the amaXhosa were required to pay taxes, which forced to them to seek employment on the emerging industrial or infrastructure schemes run by European settlers rather than subsist on the proceeds of the land and their cattle, as they had done for centuries.

Because of the duration of the nine Frontier Wars, and the loss of life and large amounts of land, the animosity between the amaXhosa and the European settlers in and around emerging towns like Makhanda (Grahamstown) and Qonce (King William's Town) intensified, so that by the mid-1800s the white residents were openly proclaiming the need to 'exterminate' the amaXhosa.

The animosity was mutual. Many amaXhosa wanted the European settlers off their land, to return home across the sea, from where the sun goes down, never to be seen again. The situation was dire. Decades of interaction marked by frequent and intensifying conflict had meant the loss of trust and the collapse of respect, tolerance and understanding.

I had known some of this ugly and contentious history of the Frontier Wars before I read Mostert's book – but he added a whole level of detail and a different perspective, including that of the indigenous amaXhosa. I found it utterly absorbing. And so, while I motored my way through the book, continuing to ignore my neglected garden and the persistent cries of my wife to 'put the damned book down', I had to admit she had a point. But after three weeks the end was in sight – I had reached page 1,165, with only 135 to go. In half-marathon terms, it was the equivalent of reaching the final stretch.

But I was in for a rude surprise.

Everything suddenly changed as I turned a page. What I had thought would be a familiar tale of gradual colonial encroachment suddenly segued into the most unbelievable story of hallucination, blind faith, mass delusion. Here was an extraordinary story of what unshakeable belief can do, manifesting in a tragic series of events. It was a volatile and mercurial mixture of mystery and fact, past and present. The tale involved the clash of indigenous and Christian beliefs, solar abnormalities, kings, chiefs, colonial governors, poor rural people, ancestral spirits, black Russians, witchcraft, lots of cattle, cultural upheaval, death and most importantly, a teenage girl – one who shaped history.

I had stumbled on the story of Nongqawuse, an *igqirha eliligogo* (seer). Or, should I say, I had stumbled on the incredible story of the Great Cattle Killing of 1856–57, also called the Cattle Killing Delusion, or the Cattle Killing Suicide or numerous other variations on this macabre theme. Whichever way you interpret it or dress it up, it was a colossal tragedy. At its most succinct, the story is this: based on the advice of a teenage girl, Nongqawuse, her tribal group, the amaXhosa people, slaughtered most of their cattle (more than 400,000), a result of which 40,000 or more of the amaXhosa people starved to death. About 150,000 were displaced and forced off their land, as starvation drove them to seek refuge or employment among neighbouring tribes or in white-owned enterprises in the Cape. It was as puzzling as it was horrific. Was this horrendous event a zeitgeist for the amaXhosa in the mid-19th century?

In the words of Reverend Tiyo Soga, a 19th-century writer, translator and composer of hymns, 'My poor infatuated countrymen have committed suicide.'

The amaXhosa nation was gravely ruptured by the Great Cattle Killing. Weakened so badly, the people, the king and the nation fell victim to further colonial exploitation that changed them for ever.

I felt like I'd uncovered a secret or a crime scene. Clearly, I hadn't – but I kept asking myself what this was all about, and why I had never heard of these fantastical events before. *Why not?* After all, I had worked in the region and visited South Africa several times. I knew about the Dutch East India Company (VOC) and the 1652 settlement of the Cape by Jan van Riebeeck. The Great Trek of the Boers in the 1830s, the Isandlwana Anglo–Zulu battles of 1879 and the various conflicts between the British and the Boers at the back end of the 19th century were lodged in my subconscious somewhere. I even had a basic knowledge of the struggle for greater equality by the non-white population, leading to the election of Nelson Mandela as the first black President of South Africa in 1994. But I had never heard so much as a whisper about Nongqawuse and the Great Cattle Killing. Added to which, I hadn't a clue how to say her name.

What was it about this story that caught my attention? I'll start with the abridged version. We can explore and unravel it in more detail as we go along, because, in truth, there are many actors, motives and defining events – too many to address in one sitting, so to speak. There are various interpretations of this tragedy, depending on who you ask. The aficionados of this period of amaXhosa history all offer a slightly different emphasis. This, then, is my personal perspective and understanding of Nongqawuse and the Great Cattle Killing of 1856–57.

I'll set the scene. The local amaXhosa people from the Eastern Cape had suffered badly after losing the Eighth Frontier War, or the War of Mlanjeni, 1850–53. Using well-coordinated guerrilla tactics in the mountains and thick bush, they had taken on the colonial forces, European settlers and clans displaced by the Zulus, called amaMfengu or Fingoes. Think of the latter as refugees. The result was a particularly bloody and vicious war, with an estimated 16,000 amaXhosa and 1,400 European lives lost. It was an uncompromising economic as well as military war, with London advocating the 'starving-out' system, supported by a scorched-earth policy. To this carnage can be added ongoing livestock theft, hunger, destruction of farms, huts and crops, and unspeakable atrocities by both sides. Some settlers and representatives of the British Crown were even calling for the extermination of their enemy.

Added to this was the drowning of hundreds of army reinforcements with the sinking of HMS *Birkenhead*, bound for Algoa Bay from Cape Town. In the corridors of Westminster there was resentment about the £2–3 million cost to the British taxpayer of another war in its South African colony.

The causes of the Eighth Frontier War are many and varied, but the tinder had been dry and the sparks to ignite it plentiful. In the words of the renowned amaXhosa chief and distinguished military leader Chief Maqoma, 'Our people steal oxen and cows, but the government steals with the pen.' All trust and respect had been eroded. After seven earlier Frontier Wars, the amaXhosa had been forced further east, off traditional pastures, and were struggling to survive at now high density on poorer land. Colonial military forts, roads and settler towns punctuated the landscape, disrupting amaXhosa life. Drought, too, had reared its ugly head.

Matters were exacerbated by the arrival in 1847 of the British army officer Lieutenant-General Sir Harry Smith, aged 60, for his second stint in the region. This time he was Cape governor and high commissioner, the highest-ranking colonial positions. His first posting in the Cape had ended unceremoniously in 1835, after various formal enquiries had been undertaken about his part in the murder of an amaXhosa king. As this story unfolds we shall bump into Smith many times. But by 1847, and following a posting to India, where he earned the title 'Hero of Aliwal', all had been forgiven by the great and the good in Britain – namely Queen Victoria and the

Duke of Wellington. Smith was back with vigour, and immediately set upon personally humiliating and undermining the amaXhosa – their chiefs, their social status and their traditions. His insensitive, vulgar and bombastic behaviour was relentless and deeply corrosive. AmaXhosa leaders even called him the 'King Killer'. Arguably, he was the spark that lit the tinder and the start of the Eighth Frontier War. Pushed to their limits, the amaXhosa declared '*Ilizwe lifile*' ('The land has died') as a signal to re-engage in conflict. We shall bump into Smith many times as this story unfolds.

To make things worse, cattle – one of the principal sources of food for the amaXhosa, their primary measure of wealth, and of great spiritual significance – were dying in their thousands from lung disease, a type of bovine pneumonia introduced from Europe in the early 1850s via Gqeberha (Port Elizabeth). This was perhaps the final straw on the proverbial camel's back.

These were now deeply distressing and uncertain times for all echelons of amaXhosa society, from the aristocracy and ruling classes, such as Paramount Chief (in effect, King) Sarhili (called Kreli by the colonialists), to his subjects of modest means and influence, who inhabited lands stretching from approximately Gqeberha (Port Elizabeth) in the west to the Amathole Mountains in the north and the Mbashe River to the east. Importantly, the Gcaleka were the senior branch of the Xhosa people, so their chief would need to be consulted on all significant matters, in particular about going to war against the colonialist. As we shall find out, this had proved very significant for King Hintsa when he had refused to go to war but had agreed to hide the spoils of war, namely settler cattle and horses.

Despite winning the Eighth Frontier War or War of Mlanjeni (1850–53) and subsequently bringing the amaXhosa chiefs onto the payroll of the British administration, headed by the Cape governor, Sir George Grey, his field magistrates and many settlers in the Eastern Cape were on edge – especially those in the area called British Kaffraria and Transkei. All was not well. Something was afoot, but what? There were mutterings about a prophetess and strange visions.

If this were a mere tragic drama, we would now start with Act I, Scene I; kings, senior chiefs, minor chiefs, myriad ancestors, herds of cattle, ordinary amaXhosa people, witch doctors, prophets, the Cape governor, field magistrates, military officers, missionaries and colonial settlers take their places in the wings, ready for the curtain to part. Enter from stage right, Nongqawuse. Things were now about to change dramatically and irrevocably, and not as anyone could have foreseen.

At that time, 1856, Nongqawuse was a dishevelled teenager, about 15 years old. She lived in a village near the mouth of the Gxara River on the Wild Coast, close to the Great Kei River, about 100 kilometres north of the modern city of East London in the province now known as the Eastern Cape (then known as the Cape Colony). The

Indian Ocean was an expansive and omnipotent backdrop to the events that unfolded.

One day while protecting her uncle's crops from birds, she wandered down to a pool with her younger friend, Nombanda. From the water, or possibly from the reeds or bushes on the opposite bank, she was approached by two mysterious men whom she took to be ancestral spirits. They spoke to her. They said that the amaXhosa needed to make great sacrifices by killing all their cattle, destroying all their maize and refraining from the evil practice of witchcraft. It was to be a type of purification from all that had gone wrong, with sacrifices reaping reward. Once this had been done, the strangers insisted, great things would happen. The tribe's ancestors, including former kings and prophets, would rise united from nearby rivers and ocean as the New People, led by a Christlike figure called Sifuba-sibanzi or the 'Broad-Chested One'. Most importantly, they would help to drive all the European settlers and the amaMfengu into the sea, vanquishing them forever. From the testimony of the 17-year-old William Gqoba, who was nearby when these momentous events unfolded, the strangers specified to Nongqawuse, 'You are to tell the people that the whole community is about to rise again from the dead.'

The white people, the strangers declared, would be sent back to where they had come from before they had taken any more of the amaXhosa land, or undermined their customs and destroyed their indigenous livelihoods any further. For support, the ancestors would have the help of the black Russians who were waiting not far offshore. (This interesting aspect of the prophecy may have been derived from stories the amaXhosa had heard of the British struggling against the Russians in the Crimean War. Since the Russians were enemies of the British and had recently killed the ex-Cape governor, Cathcart, they were assumed by the amaXhosa to be black.) In return for making this great sacrifice of destroying their livelihood – cattle and maize – the amaXhosa people would be liberally rewarded by the resurrected ancestors. Herds of fresh, healthy cattle would ascend in abundance from the underworld, maize crops would be replenished, and household and farming tools would be replaced by new ones. In short, it was a rebirth. The good times would return. The traditional amaXhosa way of life would be restored, without the interference of Europeans, with their bibles, guns, diseases, money, prudish attitude to nakedness, loathing of red clay body decoration, disapproval of marriage traditions and all the rest.

People who did not participate would be severely punished by becoming subjects of Satan (in other words, Sir George Grey, the Cape governor).

Armed with this incredible news, Nongqawuse and Nombanda returned to the village to convey what they had heard. Initially, there was scepticism and ridicule from the villagers, who accused the young seers of making the whole thing up. So the girls returned to the river the following day. Once more the strangers appeared, insisting that the girls convey their message of sacrifice, resurrection and salvation to the elders of the community. Nongqawuse returned home and repeated the message to her uncle, Mhlakaza, who was also her guardian. After she had described the men, Mhlakaza recognised one of them as his dead brother and became convinced that she was telling the truth. A day or two later, he went down to the river and met with the spirits himself, who gave him the same message.

Now things went up a few notches. Mhlakaza sent word to King Sarhili at his Great Place in Hohita. The king was cautious at first, and in the next few weeks went through phases of doubt and belief as he asked repeatedly for details about the messages from the strangers via the prophetess. At one point he went to the Gxara River himself, to meet with Nongqawuse and her uncle Mhlakaza, and to satisfy himself that the ancestors were indeed waiting to return with fresh cattle and a better future once the prescribed sacrifices had been made. He listened, in person, to the reassuring messages of the ancestors, who were somewhere in the murky distance.

Sarhili, from the royal house of Tshawe and a popular leader of the amaXhosa people, was steeped in a culture that revered the ancestors. Like most amaXhosa at the time, he was accustomed to communicating with those in his own family who had died years earlier, who gave guidance on everyday events and occasionally forecast the future. Often this guidance would be given through an *iGqirha* (a spiritual leader, a traditional healer and diviner able to interpret dreams and liaise with the ancestors), but it was also common for people to receive messages through their dreams. We should note, however, that at this time King Sarhili was a troubled man, carrying the heavy burden of seemingly intractable personal and political challenges. As we shall explore later, he was desperate for solutions, and perhaps primed to believe a message that offered a radical solution combined with great personal and communal sacrifice. So he adhered to tradition and the guidance of his ancestors.

Within a few days, King Sarhili began killing his cattle, leading by example. He sent messengers to all lesser chiefs in settlements across the region to inform them of the sacrifices and to instruct them and their people to do the same. He made demands repeatedly that all cattle should be killed, all maize crops should be destroyed and all witchcraft should be driven out. Failure to do as required, he insisted, would prevent the ancestors from returning, along with their black Russian allies, to drive out the European settlers once and for all.

And so began an orgy of cattle killing and crop destruction lasting from approximately April 1856 to February 1857, covering many thousands of square kilometres of the East Cape (see Map 1, p.xvii). The slaughter and wasting of maize was interpreted as a trial of faith and loyalty towards traditional amaXhosa society and the ancestors. In fact, the issue of whether or not someone believed and participated in this mass sacrifice took on great significance, revealing where the individual or household stood in relation to tradition and the chiefs. The mass destruction of their livestock gained huge momentum amongst the so-called Believers (*amathamba*, 'soft ones', or 'submissives'), who went so far as to hold celebrations in anticipation of the great events to come. It rapidly became a movement that was impossible to control, either by the chiefs or the colonial administrators. It had a momentum and direction of its own.

Fifteen per cent of the amaXhosa population in the region, however, resisted the demands of the movement and were sneeringly labelled Unbelievers (*amagogotya*, 'stingy ones', or 'the unyielding'). As one of the Unbeliever chiefs put it, 'How can it be that our fathers come to talk about killing cattle to a mere girl who has nothing to do with cattle?' He concluded by asking, 'Why do our fathers not talk directly with us? Such a thing can never be.'

The Unbelievers' lack of faith often led to physical attacks on their person, destruction of their property and theft of their livestock – especially as hunger set in. Huge schisms opened up in amaXhosa society between the Believers and the Unbelievers. The animosity and tension ratcheted up further when Nongqawuse insisted that the prophecies would be prevented from realisation by the Unbelievers' refusal to do as their ancestors asked. The ancestors, she said, were just waiting for their conditions to be fulfilled. This greatly concerned the committed Believers, who saw the Unbelievers' lack of faith as the principal obstacle to the return of the ancestors who would usher in a better future, free of diseased cattle, witchcraft and colonial rule.

Families were divided on the issue; fathers, sons, husbands, wives and siblings sometimes took opposite views. Chiefs took different stances. Some, like Chief Sandile of the Ngqika, wrestled with the conundrum, really struggling to decide – was he in or out, a Believer or Unbeliever? It was a tough call, and the stakes were high, but in the end he accorded with the prophecies. Neighbours fell out. Villages disagreed. Should they really make such risky sacrifices based on the claims of an unconventional teenage girl from the Gxara River and her uncle, Mhlakaza?

One of the leading Believers was Chief Mhala, whose Unbeliever son, Chief Smith Mhala, refused to make the sacrifices asked of him. He famously said, 'They say I am killing my father – but I would kill him before my cattle.'

The divisions were many and deep.

There were several disappointments when the prophecy failed to materialise in line with the lunar cycle, including in June and August 1856, and January 1857. Each time a new date was set, the idea was propagated that the ancestors' return would be marked by spectacular solar events: in one version two suns would rise, and in another the sun would rise in the east, turn blood-red and return to set in the east. After several disappointments, the final date was set for 16 and 17 February 1857. This was the moment. By now, hundreds of thousands of cattle and other livestock had been slaughtered or eaten. The maize stores were empty and the fields were uncultivated, as planting had been prohibited. There was no going back, no Plan B.

Long before the appointed date, however, the amaXhosa were feeling the pinch. Hunger was widespread, and many began to starve, living off scraps, bark and roots to stay alive. The first reported deaths from the Great Cattle Killing movement occurred in October 1856. Those still alive literally tightened their belts. But spirits were still high amongst most Believers, who held fast to the conviction that soon their faith would be amply rewarded. A brighter future beckoned for the committed ones, or so they thought.

On the designated days of 16 and 17 February 1857, it was said, two suns would rise, or one would rise, turn red, and return the way it had come, and there would be a great storm, so staying safely indoors was advised. Despite the starvation which had arisen in the regions where cattle had been slaughtered earlier, many people, where stocks remained, were still desperately slaughtering their cattle, having been won over to the side of the Believers.

As the days approached, anticipation grew, until finally, on the morning of the 16th, the amaXhosa awoke to find the sun in its usual solitary position and its usual colour, showing no abnormalities in behaviour. It rose, reached its zenith and set in the west, as usual. The following day turned out to be just the same. None of the prophecies came to fruition. It was a monumental disaster. And so, for many, the event took on the name of the Great Disappointment.

Mhlakaza was alleged to have died of starvation during this time, while Nongqawuse fled north up the coast before being arrested and taken away by the colonial forces, largely for her own protection. Many of the Believer chiefs were arrested by the colonial magistrates and sent to Robben Island, just off Cape Town, as punishment for promoting the prophecies. Some chiefs, like King Sarhili, slipped through the net, then headed north up the Wild Coast and lay low and out of reach amongst the neighbouring Bomvana clan. He was a broken man, worried about the suffering of his people and shamed for his part in promoting the fallacy. His remorse, pleas for forgiveness and requests for help from the Cape governor fell on deaf ears.

For many ordinary amaXhosa, the nightmare was really just starting, as starvation intensified to the point where they lacked the strength to walk to seek help. People collapsed and died by the roadside on the way to a colonial settlement or town in search of food. The old and the young were early casualties. Cannibalism was reported, even within families. Vultures hovered overhead, waiting for the easy pickings. If the starving people reached colonial settlements, the provision of food and support was limited, and in exchange for assistance, many were transported elsewhere in the

Cape Colony, where they were required to work on government schemes such as road building.

Many Unbelievers, who had heeded the governor's advice and resisted the temptation to follow the instructions of the prophetess, were also in a poor way, with their cattle stolen and crops destroyed by the desperate and angry Believers. Most of all they wanted colonial protection from the attacks, but they received little or no reward or sympathy for their loyalty to the colonial administration, which they felt they had demonstrated by refusing to bend to the pressures of the majority. They pleaded for help, but this, too, fell on the governor's deaf ears.

Nongqawuse (right) and Nonkosi (another prophetess, see Chapter 11, the prophets theory) photographed in 1858, after their arrest for their part in the Great Cattle Killing and similar prophecies. (With permission of Alamy Ltd.)

It is estimated that as a result of Nongqawuse's prophecies, the Great Cattle Killing, the Cattle Killing Delusion, the National Suicide, or however you dress it up, 400,000 livestock (most of the amaXhosa cattle) were slaughtered as a sacrifice, and 40,000 or more amaXhosa subsequently died of starvation and related causes. Many more were displaced from their homes, and large areas of the Eastern Cape became depopulated as the starving accepted paid work elsewhere in the Cape in order to survive.

After resisting the physical migration of thousands of European settlers over two centuries, the tighter administrative control by magistrates and the military might of the British Empire, the amaXhosa, a proud branch of the Bantu people, were all but broken. So it seemed, at first sight, that it was not the bullets and cannon fire of Europeans that determined their fate, but a maverick teenage girl from the Gcaleka clan. But I had questions. Did this one young girl, all on her own, really cause the death of a nation, the amaXhosa of the Eastern Cape, by starvation? Or were her prophecies more symptom than cause, pointing to larger, more pernicious issues beyond her control? I could not help feeling that her visions may well have been a reaction to the pressure of relentless European encroachment, and indicative of tensions between traditional conservatives and more progressive elements in amaXhosa society. I was convinced that there was more to this than meets the eye. It seemed that the Believers and Unbelievers might almost represent different views of the future, different attitudes to change – not just about the Cattle Killing prophecies, but about life in general. The Believers might be seen as the more conservative elements in amaXhosa society at the time, valuing tradition and loyalty to the king and his wishes. The Unbelievers may have been the progressives – people more willing to adopt practices introduced by the settlers, and less bound by culture and tradition.

The simple explanation for the tragedy – that these were gullible people too easily swayed by supernatural solutions to real-world problems – seemed too easy, too pat. I felt like a clairvoyant who'd stumbled upon a murder scene where the body, murder weapon and suspect were all neatly presented *in situ*, like an open and shut case. You know what I mean, like a game of Cluedo: Colonel Mustard, in the drawing room, with a lead pipe. It all seemed a little too formulaic, too clean-cut to reflect what might have really happened in 1856. While this episode of history was quite mesmerising and shocking, I felt I couldn't leave it there. Stones needed to be overturned. I was porous with curiosity.

In this translation of a Xhosa poem from Jeff Peires' *The Dead Will Arise* (Indiana University Press, 1989) and Helen Bradford's *Not a Nongqawuse Story: An anti-heroine in historical perspective* (Cape Town: HSRC Press, 2007), the finger of blame was directed squarely at Nongqawuse, with lines such as 'who killed our nation' and 'but she was telling a lie'. The die was clearly loaded.

Oh! Nongqawuse

The girl of Mhlakaza

Who killed our nation

She told the people, she told them all, she told

Them all that the dead will arise from their graves

Bringing joy and bringing wealth.

But she was telling a lie.

On this day, then, indecency descended,
For the maiden of Scatter stood up,
She even appeared on the river bank,
She returned carrying the problem in her mouth,
She reported to men.
Those who have never been told what to do by a promiscuous woman.
That in itself was an omen,
The curse upon the nation of Xhosa,
A female gets up
Saying she has spoken with the ancestors …
There is an omen in that handsome woman,
The maiden with pendulous breasts:
Except on that day when they were large and protuberant,
Because a marriageable maiden had started to emerge from maidenhood
And yet even if it were so
The omen killing the innocent nation of Phalo
Will enter through her.

The original poem in isiXhosa.
Hayi uNongqawuse
Intombi kaMhlakaza
Wasibulala isizwe sethu
Yaxelela abantu yathi kubo bonke
Baya kuvuka abantu basemangcwabeni
Bazisa uvuyo kunye ubutyebi
Kanti uthetha ubuxoki
Kulo mhla ke lehl' inyala,
Kuba yem' intombi kaMhlakaza,

Iba ngakuvela phezu komlambo,
Ibuy' ingxak' iyiphethe ngomlomo,
Ibikel' amadoda.
Int' ezingazanga zeva ngedikazi.
Yayilishobo kwaloo nto,
Ukuqalekiswa kwesizwe sikaXhosa,
Kusuk' umntw' ebhinqile
Ath' uthethile namanyange…
Nalishoba kuloo nzwakazi,
Intomb' emabele made:
Kuloko loo min' ayezizibhungu,
Kub' intombi yayiqal' ukuz' ebuntombini.
Yathi kanti noko kunjalo
Ishoba lokubulal' umzi kaPhal' ungenatyala
Liya kungena ngayo

My first reading of the Great Cattle Killing left me stirred, and I was eager to learn more. However, I closed the book with a sigh, knowing that whatever explanations Mostert had in store would have to wait. The more pressing matters of emptying the dishwasher and cutting the lawn demanded my return to the present. Besides, my sharing of endless facts about the story of the amaXhosa people and mysterious sightings on the Gxara River over 160 years ago was not going down especially well at the family dinner table. Glazed looks suggested that for the time being I'd better return to reality – or our safe and sanitised version of it.

2: WHO NEEDS A MAP?

'Stop desiring a bone (to gnaw) when you are toothless.'

'Yeka uku-tanda ihleza unge-namazinyo.'

Xhosa proverb: Rev. J.H. Soga, The Ama-Xosa. Life and Customs, 1931

Much to my utter amazement, some 18 months later, in January 2020, I found myself on the verge of signing a contract to have a book published, based on my time as a teacher in the Eastern Cape of South Africa in 1980. The publishers and I were haggling over a few details, but I was delighted to see the deal would be sorted in a matter of days.

That was the easy bit.

As part of the contract, the publishers stipulated that they needed some more copy, and I could sense that the conclusion of the book needed rewriting; it was just too shallow, even by my standards. There was something missing from the draft manuscript, but I wasn't sure what it was. Fortunately for me, my long-time friend Steve knew the answer. In fact, he had known the answer many months earlier, even before I had identified an issue.

'You need to go back to where you taught in 1980. There's stuff in your head you haven't resolved in the last 40 years, despite trying.'

'Well, maybe …'

'It's been weighing heavily on your shoulders. Just book a flight and go. Then you'll be able to finish your book properly.'

He had a point. My wife certainly thought so. And perhaps I could learn a bit more about the Cattle Killing while I was in South Africa.

So that's what I did, especially as there was an added urgency. News was growing daily of a nasty disease from Wuhan in China that was spreading globally, with eggheads and grave professorial types suggesting it might turn into a deadly pandemic. Without much planning and forethought, I booked a two-week trip to Mthatha in the Eastern Cape, via Johannesburg.

I made sure to pack some reading about Nongqawuse. Her story and the Great Cattle Killing were still vivid in my mind. But instead of using up a sizeable portion of my luggage allowance with Mostert's *Frontiers*, I opted for the slimmer and more definitive *The Dead Will Arise. Nongqawuse and the Great Xhosa Cattle-Killing Movement of 1856–7* by Professor J. B. Peires. This paperback weighed in at a modest

1lb 2½ oz, so it presented a much lower risk of musculo-skeletal injury while reading at 32,000 feet, with a Bloody Mary and packet of peanuts in hand.

Johannesburg is a large busy metropolis with broad criss-crossing motorways, glass-clad business parks and heavy industrial complexes. Mthatha, by contrast, is a small provincial town in the Eastern Cape, about an hour south of Jo'burg by jet plane. It was notable for two reasons. Up until 1994 and the removal of apartheid, it had been the capital of the Bantustan of Transkei, a so-called homeland for millions of black people of Xhosa heritage. Second, it had been the home town of Nelson Mandela before he left to receive a university education, set up a law practice and lead the Black Liberation struggle. His villages of birth (Mvezo) and upbringing (Qunu) were just down the road.

I used to know Mthatha quite well when I worked there as a teacher, 40 years earlier. But evidently, tide and time wait for no one, including me. Back then its name had been Umtata, and now just about everything else had changed too, from what I could hear, see and smell. What had been a sleepy backwater was now heaving with people and traffic. Rural buildings were scattered randomly across the undulating landscape to the horizon. In the town centre there were advertisements for big consumer brands such as KFC, coffee bars and mobile phone networks. As I sat in my hire car in a long traffic jam on my way from Mthatha airport to my hotel, a large advertising hoarding with the beaming face of a government minister told me how lucky everyone was and how things were getting better. I remember thinking that might be a bold statement.

As the traffic backed up and vehicle horns sounded, I had to accept I was going nowhere fast. I needed to chill, get a little more in tune with the rhythm of my surroundings. Emergency vehicles were zipping in and out of junctions, sounding their sirens, and it was getting warm. Time to turn up the AC. I reminded myself that I wasn't in the UK or big bustling Jo'burg – I was in Mthatha, deep in the Eastern Cape. So I listened to my heart a little more, or should I say my stomach? Giving in to the earthy roadside smell of burning charcoal and wood from street vendors, I handed over 15 rand to an elderly woman for a grilled mielie (maize cob), charred to a tee. Replete with warm, nutty-tasting mielie, I chucked the denuded cob onto the passenger seat. Now I felt I'd arrived.

My accommodation at Ebony Lodge was fabulous, a large, converted colonial-type bungalow with nice polished wooden floors and whitewashed walls and all that. Back in the 1980s, set in its manicured, spacious garden, it would have been one of the nicest houses in town. I had driven past it several times some four decades earlier. Better still, the front of house staff took a bit of a shine to me, allocated me the best room in the hotel (No. 2 in case you ever visit) and took it upon themselves to make sure I didn't 'get into trouble'. They stressed this daily, and they stressed, too, the fact I wasn't like other English people they'd had as guests. Apparently, I wasn't wearing the customary white socks with sandals, and I spoke a lot to just about anybody. I think it was a compliment – anyway that's the way I took it. They insisted that I was not to walk through Mthatha, as the risk of being attacked was too high. This I doubted. I used to do it all the time. But just to make the point, the front of house manager and her husband were attacked the next day while out shopping, in broad daylight, despite carrying a loaded revolver. Neither was I allowed to visit the local township of Ngangelizwe, an old haunt of mine. That was considered way out of bounds, a definite no-no, just too risky. I deliberately ignored this advice, and then recounted my visit to Ngangelizwe to them over an evening beer. They weren't impressed, and told me so. I also used the opportunity to ask them and other guests about Nongqawuse and the Great Cattle Killing. This drew a quite different response.

After dusk, sitting on the restaurant porch sipping our beers and other tipples of choice, our conversation about Nongqawuse and the Great Cattle Killing started to engage quite a few people: staff, visitors and other guests. Even a highly respected judge from Durban joined in. To my surprise, the best informed were a couple of French women passing through, on their way to the Cape. They were reading a book on the history of South Africa by a French scholar, and they were able to offer quite a few opinions on the subject, which they did enthusiastically. What surprised me, though, was the lack of awareness of this monumental 19th-century event amongst many of the South Africans. I shouldn't have been that surprised, though, I suppose, as I had encountered a similar lack of understanding from the people I'd spoken to in Jo'burg. Many knew next to nothing, and just a handful had a limited knowledge of the facts. Facts? Now, that was turning out to be an unfortunate word to use, as it was clear that there were different interpretations of what had happened, and most did not reflect well on Nongqawuse. Facts, so it began to emerge, were thin on the ground. My sympathetic attitude to her role in amaXhosa history did not appear to be universally shared, not even by the French tourists. Words like irresponsible, reckless, stupid and manipulated were being bandied about to describe the way she had started and incited the Cattle Killing movement. After all, look what had happened as a result!

Someone was of the opinion that the whole catastrophe had been deliberately instigated and supported by the British and the Cape governor as a cynical way of finally defeating their enemy, the amaXhosa. I had read that theory as well. Food for thought. I put it in the metaphorical file labelled TBC.

By now, the electricity supply at the hotel was becoming predictably erratic. Electricity outages – load shedding as they were euphemistically called – appeared to have become a part of South African culture, but irritating nonetheless, and were frequently the topic of small talk or rants about government incompetence. The lights might suddenly go off for 30 seconds, 30 minutes or 3 hours. Some power cuts were even scheduled, so people could work around them. To add to the atmosphere, it started raining heavily, so there arose a heady fragrance of moist African soil, tobacco smoke and beer. Those of us who had moved out into the gardens retreated to the protection of the restaurant's canopied porch to continue chatting. As the conversation flowed this way and that, first covering Nongqawuse and then the ubiquitous concerns about South Africa's crime rate and corruption, I could sense that this evening had the potential to become a late boozy night. That wasn't on the cards for me, even though I was being encouraged to share one more round, and another one, I suspected. I had decided to head off the next day to the Gxara River, in search of the real Nongqawuse and the site of her prophecies in 1856. The last thing I needed was a thick head and a late start.

I was up bright and breezy the next morning while it was still dark outside. I packed lightly, with a small rucksack, but included my Nikon SLR camera and a copy of Professor Peires' book about the Cattle Killing movement. I chucked my stuff in my lovely white Nissan Almera, which I had washed the day before.

At this point I should make it clear that I had no map, and the GPS device I'd rented was about as much use as a chocolate fireguard. Neither of these things bothered me at 6 am; I had browsed Google Maps the day before and mentally logged in my head how to travel cross-country from the town of Gcuwa (Butterworth) to Qolora on the Wild Coast, a stone's throw from the site of Nongqawuse's visions and prophecies. With a Google Maps estimated drive time of two and a half hours, I could be there by mid-morning. Someone had suggested that it might be a little tricky taking that route without a map, especially after heavy rain. Instead of listening, I invoked my standard *modus operandi* when travelling, saying to myself, 'I'll worry about that when I get there'– a capricious mixture of naïvety, excessive optimism and arrogance. I know you're thinking that this is a foolhardy and headstrong approach, and now, sitting here at the safety of my desk typing away, I can't disagree. But most of the time, in most of the places I'd visited, over several decades – Brazil, Sri Lanka, Cuba, Oman, to name just a few – it had got me by. Why change the habit? You could almost guarantee there'd never be a dull moment, and you could invariably expect the unexpected.

Loaded with a full tank of petrol, I passed through the hotel's security gates and headed south-west on the N2 out of Mthatha. The early morning air was still and calm as I soaked up the views of the verdant rolling hills, dotted with villages and rectangular mielie plots. It felt good to be travelling, with a loose plan and very few constraints. I was confident of finding the Gxara River, the site of Nongqawuse's mysterious visions, by mid-morning, no sweat. After about 110 kilometres and an hour and a bit on the main road, I remembered to hang a left on the outskirts of Gcuwa (Butterworth). As long as I pointed the car south and west-ish I'd reach Centane and then the aptly named Wild Coast, at Qolora. What could go wrong?

Map 2. February 2020: Road trip in the Eastern Cape to find the site of Nongqawuse's visions.

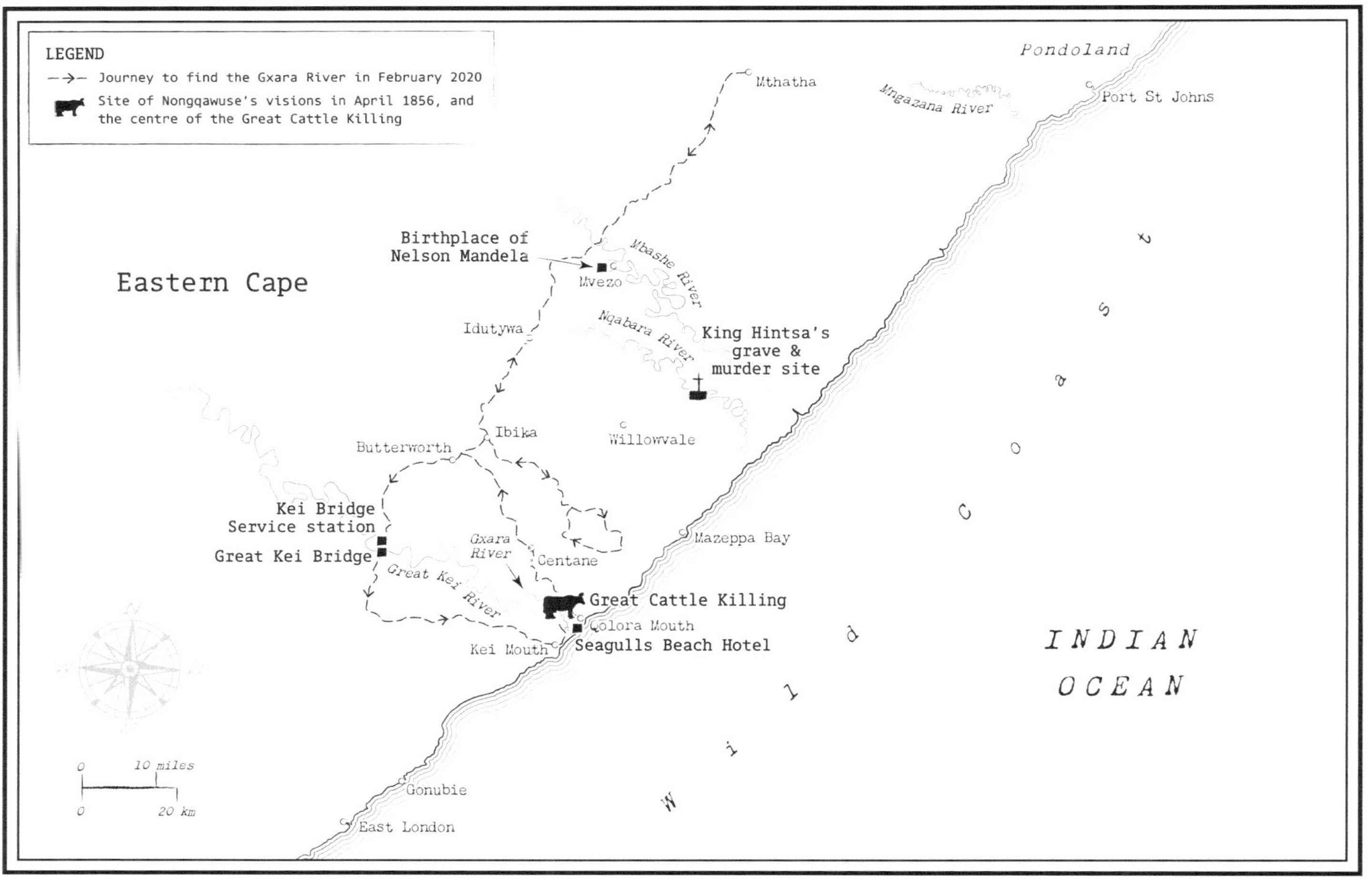

The moment I turned off the N2, things changed. The road surface deteriorated to a potholed metalled mess and then a dirt track, which was what I had expected. All quite normal. But what I hadn't expected was that the road would be littered with the remnants of smoking barricades made of wood, tyres and other rubbish. They were constructed like a chicane, so that any vehicle had to travel at a snail's pace to navigate them safely. Broken glass was liberally scattered over the road, too. It looked like the site of civil unrest and protests. Then I remembered that there'd been mention of this on the local news. The debris was all part of a protest by local people against the poor or non-existent provision of basic utilities like water and electricity.

The idea put me on edge. Back in the mid-1980s I'd been caught up in civil unrest on the streets of Paris. Despite being a tourist at the time, I'd witnessed at close range how things could quickly turn nasty.

So I navigated the smouldering obstructions cautiously, observing the damage to the road. I didn't want to stop; I just wanted to get out of there. I made sure my car doors were locked. A couple of kilometres down the dusty road I was forced to stop, as several classes of older students, many sporting T-shirts supporting the African National Congress (ANC) and Jacob Zuma (the former president), walked down the middle of the road, chanting and singing. Ordinarily, I'd have stopped, made friends and taken photographs of these young people with their exuberance and brightly coloured clothes, but on this occasion I did not. Now, after seeing the scorched tarmac and protesters' barricades down the road, I was nervous and unsure, concerned for my personal safety. It was 40 years since I'd been anywhere near this neck of the woods, and my self-preservation meter told me to keep the doors locked, smile and slowly move on. Which I did, but I was annoyed at myself. I'd chickened out. I was to curse my decision by the time I was less than 5 kilometres down the road.

Soon, the road started to fork a few times, and I had to make uneducated guesses about which one to take. Road signs to familiar places like Centane or Qolora were scarce to non-existent, and I regretted not having a map of any sort. It was already very clear that this jaunt was going to be a little more challenging than indicated by Google Maps. 'Bloody internet,' I mumbled to myself a few times.

To compensate for my navigational deficiencies, I took in the arresting scenery. There were huge vistas of grassland highlighted by round, hexagonal and rectangular homes capped with straw, or red-painted corrugated iron roofs. Occasionally, a *rondavel* (traditional round thatched house) could be seen abandoned and undignified, the mud walls collapsing under the strain of rain, sun, wind and neglect. After a while the topography changed to steep valleys covered with dense woods and sculptured by fast-running rivers. Many times, the views were simply stunning, and I repeatedly had to get out to take a few shots. While the drive was not exactly going to plan, I placated myself with the thought that I was inadvertently familiarising myself with much of the countryside that had been under the stewardship of King Sarhili at the time of the Great Cattle Killing. Only a few months later I learned that the area I was erratically criss-crossing had been the setting of the ninth and final Frontier War (1877–78), also called the War of the Wedding Feast. I was being educated by the landscape, although I didn't realise it at the time.

In addition to deficient signposting, my journey was being hampered by livestock. Innumerable herds of cattle and goats straying across the dirt roads acted like traffic-calming devices. There was no option but to slow to cattle and goat speed until they deigned to step aside. This I had expected. I hadn't expected the road surface deteriorating even further. My pristine white Nissan Almera was now struggling, badly at times. I was regretting not renting a 4×4 vehicle. Being tight with my money at the rent-a-car desk in Mthatha airport now felt like a false economy. But I wasn't at the car rental concession, able to trade up to a suitable vehicle. No, I was properly lost. The battered and fading signpost at the roadside indicated I was somewhere near the Gcaleka Clinic, but that didn't help one jot. Where was Qolora? Which road headed in the direction of Centane? What I wanted was a sign that helped, not taunted.

At other times, the suspension made an unholy metallic bang as we hit a channel in the road or an unexpected stone hump or a dip in the road. I wasn't enjoying myself, and was concerned about damaging the car. As I soldiered on, water from the previous night's downpour started to add to the entertainment. Skirting the occasional puddle and stream was okay, until I caught sight of a pond just ahead, a chocolate-coloured muddy sump covering the whole road, about 10 metres long and 5 metres wide. From the various skidding tyre marks in the mud and grass it was obvious other vehicles had struggled to cross it. In fact, without seeing anyone else cross it I had no idea how deep it was, and out here I did not want to flood the engine, no way. It was still early in the day, and there were very few people about.

So, decision No. 1, do I attempt to cross the mini-lake in front of me? I got out of the car for a visual inspection, walking timidly around it to the other side. I prodded the mud with my shoe. It looked and felt gelatinous. Not very encouraging. Nonetheless, I decided, I was going to give it a go, but my confidence was not high.

Decision No. 2, how should I tackle it? I reversed a couple of metres, wound the windows down for a clear view, pointed the car at the right-hand side of the daunting aquatic obstacle, put my foot on the accelerator and went for it. I reckoned that I needed momentum, and it turned out that I did.

Exactly two-thirds of the way across, the car lost most of its impetus, thwarted by the water and the glutinous mud. Concerned that I might get stuck, I floored the accelerator, which did the trick and I edged forward painfully slowly, the wheels spinning frantically. But now I couldn't see where I'd got to as the windscreen was opaque with mud and soil. I was driving blind. In the process, the tyres had sprayed mud all over the car from the front headlights to the boot. Worse still, having wound the front windows down to improve my view, my camera, my glasses, the rucksack, the upholstery on the front and back seats, the steering wheel and the dashboard were generously slathered with mud, too.

Oh shit! This was one hell of a mess. It looked as though I'd driven my clean hire car through a chocolate fountain. I'd stopped enjoying my little adventure. I was losing track of time; the outside temperature was now rising with the reducing cloud cover, and I was motoring through my litre of drinking water. Fruit and biscuit reserves were low too.

I was beginning to wonder if the Paris to Dakar rally was this difficult.

I wiped the windscreen clean-ish with the world's biggest handful of tissues and carried on, promising myself to turn around if things didn't improve. They didn't. I went up this road and then that one, and then back to the same one again. People repairing the road looked on – amused, I assumed – as they watched me pass the same place several times. I was tired from having to concentrate on the rough track so much, and now the fuel gauge caught my attention. I'd used up so much petrol charging around, getting absolutely nowhere, that it was dipping ominously closer to empty. I might even run out of fuel if things carried on in the same vein, and I'd be stuck out here for God knows how long. Besides, I'd not the slightest idea where the nearest petrol station was, except back where I'd just come from. What a balls-up.

I'm not a quitter, but I quit and threw in the towel. I did a reluctant four-point turn and headed back exactly the way I'd come over the last few hours. The rocky and aquatic obstacles were no less challenging on the return leg of the trip, but at least my abused Nissan and I knew what to expect. We'd formed a sort of partnership – let's say, an understanding. If I promised to stop abusing her, she consented to keep going. The windows were now firmly up as we tackled the large puddle a second time. The AC was up to the maximum setting. My plan to arrive at Qolora by mid-morning was blown out of the water and I was seriously wondering if I was even going to reach it. Should I head back to Mthatha, tail between my legs or head west, to the Great Kei Bridge and cut down to Kei Mouth?

My smart alec *modus operandi* of 'I'll worry about it when I get there' didn't seem so bloody clever at that moment. A modicum of planning and a less cavalier approach might have avoided all this. So by the time I'd navigated the protest-related obstacles and rejoined the N2, Plan B had solidified in my head. I would head west, first through Gcuwa (Butterworth) and then on to the Great Kei Bridge. I was going to tackle this challenge, come what may, and find Nongqawuse's pool, even if I arrived at midnight.

It was midday by the time I pulled into the swanky service station at the Great Kei River Bridge. My supposed two-hour journey by road had taken six hours, and I was still miles away from Qolora and the Gxara River. I was tired and in a very sour mood, so I headed straight for the fast food burger bar and ordered their largest, dirtiest burger, with fries and coke. Ketchup was applied liberally. This vulgar fast-food extravaganza was going down the hatch, tout suite.

Strangely, I felt a lot better after my little indulgence and bought myself a road map from the shop. It wasn't ideal for the job, but it was certainly better than nothing. The squiggly lines indicated the alternative route to Qolora, via Kei Mouth and a ferry. If the travel gods bestowed their favours on me, I reckoned I could reach my destination in an hour and a half or so.

The mouth of the Great Kei River on the Wild Coast, en route to find the site of Nongqawuse's visions.

I'm pleased to report that the rest of the trip to Qolora was free of obstacles, and I reached the mouth of the Great Kei River on a clear warm afternoon, with a comforting breeze coming upriver from the Indian Ocean, only a few hundred metres away. This was a significant place in my search for Nongqawuse, the first time I'd visited a spot associated with the Cattle Killing. It was here, and at other places along the coast, that the ancestors and the healthy cattle had been predicted to rise out of the water to drive away the European settlers – once all the existing cattle had been slaughtered, witchcraft driven out and maize spoiled.

It was also the location where HMS *Geyser*, a British steamship, had got into difficulty in late 1856, and turned back after its support vessel had capsized. At the time, the amaXhosa viewed the approach of the *Geyser* as a possible colonial attack. The capsizing of the support vessel ended with the *Geyser* chugging out of the Kei River back to port. This seemingly minor event had caused great excitement; Nongqawuse's followers took it as a sign, confirmation that the ancestors, including the late Xhosa King Hintsa (killed by the British in 1835), were really helping them and undermining the colonial power. A victory! In the eyes of many the prophecies were coming true, sure evidence that the ancestors would return to save the amaXhosa, their cattle, their land and their traditions. News of the event spread far and wide, causing great excitement, and fuelling the people's commitment to the Cattle Killing movement.

My tired Nissan and I travelled across the mouth of the Great Kei River on a rather basic ferry or pontoon, scrambled off the other side and up a slope towards our destination. Within minutes I was in Qolora on the Wild Coast, being greeted warmly by the security chap at the gates of the Seagulls Hotel. He took one look at the car and asked politely if I would like it washed … I confirmed that I most certainly would.

My mud-covered hire car on the pontoon crossing the Great Kei River, near the Gxara River. Thankfully my tortuous 7½-hour road trip was coming to an end.

A car journey that should have taken two and a half hours, according to the algorithms and digital knowhow of Google Maps, had in fact taken me more than seven and a half. Seven and a half bloody hours! I'd planned to be exploring the Gxara River by mid-morning, and it was now early afternoon. I was cross with myself, tired and more than a little tetchy. Fortunately, the warm afternoon sun and the views of sandy beaches and the Indian Ocean calmed me down a little as I headed for the hotel reception.

3: NATURE'S CATHEDRAL

'Dying and rising, as the moon does.'

'Umafa evuka, njenge nyange.'

Xhosa proverb: Rev. J.H. Soga, *The Ama-Xosa. Life and Customs*, 1931

The Afrikaans woman at reception smiled and listened sympathetically as I described my little sojourn from Mthatha. As I hadn't booked in advance, I was concerned that there might not be any room at the inn. But there was no problem, and I could get their super-duper low daily rate, with breakfast included; and a braai (BBQ) was scheduled for the evening. So now, with a sea view, access to the swimming pool, and a bar on site, my search for Nongqawuse was looking up at last.

I took the opportunity to explain that I'd come to visit the Gxara River to explore the area associated with the Cattle Killing of 1856–57. I was trying to sound knowledgeable but I think I came across as more of a groupie, shallow but keen, which was probably quite accurate. The give-away was my inability to say the prophetess's name. I'd yet to hear anyone say it properly in isiXhosa, but I was sure the q in the middle of the name was going to cause all sorts of linguistic challenges. Also, it was becoming clear that the friendly receptionist couldn't or wouldn't pronounce her name either, so we danced around the subject, referring to her as 'the prophetess'.

With great enthusiasm and no fear of contradiction, I explained that I intended to head off immediately to the Gxara River to explore. To make my point, I dug out an A4 photocopied map of the area from Professor Peires' book. The receptionist suggested it might be better if I used the services of a guide, and as I had ignored most good advice since I'd arrived in South Africa, I thought it best to listen for a change.

Trevor Wigley, she explained, was a local expert on the subject of the prophetess and the Cattle Killing, running tours for people from all over the world. This sounded very encouraging. I had never expected to find a tour or a guide.

'When would you like to go?' she enquired.

'Now, please,' I replied.

'Now? Trevor is probably booked up and already out. I know he's fully booked tomorrow.'

'Can you find out … please?' I asked politely, putting on my best hangdog look.

A young man joined us in reception, the owner's son, I think. He was very friendly, but sceptical about my chances of getting a tour with Trevor that afternoon. He, too, told me that Trevor was booked up in the days ahead and asked if I could wait a couple of days.

No, I could not.

My luck, that day, changed. The gods and ancestors now appeared to be on my side. Out of sympathy, I guess. The receptionist handed me the telephone, with Trevor on the other end. His enthusiasm was muted, and he was trying to put me off needing a tour now. I think he'd done enough work for the day and wanted a siesta, so I invoked the 'I've flown 13,000 kilometres to be here' and 'It would mean a great deal to hear your expert opinion' cards. I stressed that I was writing a book about Transkei, and how I really wanted to add a chapter about Nong … I caught myself just in time, and saved myself the embarrassment of trying to say 'Nongqawuse' out loud to an expert. I defaulted to 'the prophetess' instead.

To my surprise, my grovelling and pitiful flattery worked, and he confirmed that he would be there in an hour. Since I was writing a book, he'd give me the fuller tour. But I hadn't fooled him into thinking that I was an academic or expert. 'Groupie' still felt like the best description.

Sure enough, a red Toyota pickup with 'Trevor's Trails' emblazoned across the side turned up within the hour. Trevor was a tall white chap, mellow and with a few years on the clock. His colleague, Carlos Nkonki, was a younger local chap, wearing a conspicuous Tourist Guide badge in the colours of the national flag. I hopped in the back of the cabin and we were off. We had a race against the fading afternoon light.

Carlos Nkonki showed me around the Gxara River where Nongqawuse had started the Cattle Killing prophecy. He challenged my thinking with searching questions and statements.

I felt a mixture of excitement and a little nervousness that expressed itself in a torrent of questions. For the first time ever I was with experts, and I had a backlog of things to ask. Best of all, I heard Nongqawuse pronounced properly, in isiXhosa, and sure enough, there was a strong verbal click in the middle, a distinct feature of the local language. As I feared, it was a real tongue twister. As we drove along to the Gxara River, Carlos led the way with my elocution lessons, trying not to laugh at my verbal garbage. In the end, I recorded his pronunciation on my phone and promised to work on pronouncing her name back at the hotel. In his mild-mannered way, Trevor started pointing out various landmarks, winding down his window and whipping the backsides of cattle with his leathery sjambok, a stick and whip made of animal hide, whenever they got in the way of the Toyota. A short distance from the sea and hotel, we were on higher undulating grassland, with only an isolated tree here and there, and the occasional local village prominent on the horizon. As he steered the pickup off the metalled road onto a grassy dirt track towards the Gxara River valley, they both pointed to the top of the slopes in the distance to indicate Nongqawuse's village, where remains of her house could still be found. Then we suspended the chitchat as Trevor dropped the Toyota into four-wheel-drive mode, and Carlos hopped out to guide us, one metre at a time, over a steep-ish section of boulders and rock.

As we drove, the landscape gently transformed from mud and boulders to a flat river valley floor. Lush grass was interspersed with a mixture of bushes and trees no more than 10 metres high that grew denser towards the river's edge, where they were met by a thick carpet of reeds, aquatic grasses, silt and the muddy river itself. It all felt serene and welcoming in the late afternoon sunshine. By marked contrast, on the other side of the valley, only a few feet away across the river, a steep cliff rose, with a light-coloured rock face visible between the lush tropical vegetation or jungle. Layer upon layer of palm trees, cactus, strelitzia and agave competed for space, fighting to outgrow each other for light. The leaves, trunks and branches presented a huge variety of exotic shapes and sizes, some curved, some serrated, some flat and some corrugated. It was nothing less than a verdant green cacophony, and they all danced, fluttered and swayed to the tune of a gentle Wild Coast breeze.

The Gxara River valley where Nongqawuse had her visions. I was deeply moved by the beauty and tranquillity. It felt like I was in Nature's Cathedral.

I was already familiar with the Wild Coast, from Pondoland in the north down to Bomvanaland, not so very far away. Without exception, it was all visually striking – the rock formations, the estuaries, the vegetation and the schools of dolphins playing offshore. As I used to say, anyone could take a good photograph along this stretch of coastline. But here, at the very site of Nongqawuse's visions in 1856, my senses were even more heightened. It felt special, and just to emphasise that feeling, as I got out of the pickup, a large fish eagle arose from the reeds some 60 metres away. Up it flew, sharply, quietly and purposefully, into a cloudless sky towards the estuary and the Indian Ocean. Soon it was a silhouette. As I turned to ask Carlos about the eagle, a kingfisher darted in front of us, its radiant colours flashing like an electrical spark.

Was this a sign? Was the mystical power of the Gxara River revealing itself to me in the shape of these magnificent birds? I was certainly in awe of the place, but mysticism and spirituality were well out of my sphere of understanding and comfort. By now, Carlos and Trevor could see I was in my own little world, thinking, touched by the area's sheer natural beauty and mindful of its huge significance in Xhosa history. They let me wander about by myself, up and down the river's edge, in and out of the bushes, and down to a junction of two streams. Now and then I might ask a question, and my companions would point to the spot reputed to be Nongqawuse's bathing place or something similar. The water level was low the day I visited, but I could see how high it swelled with rainfall and tides.

My photocopied map of the Gxara River valley from Peires' book about Nongqawuse was proving very helpful, enabling me to orientate to the key sites. But I hadn't made provision for sweat from my perspiring forehead and hands soaking into the paper. Soon, it was salty damp, and started to fray and curl.

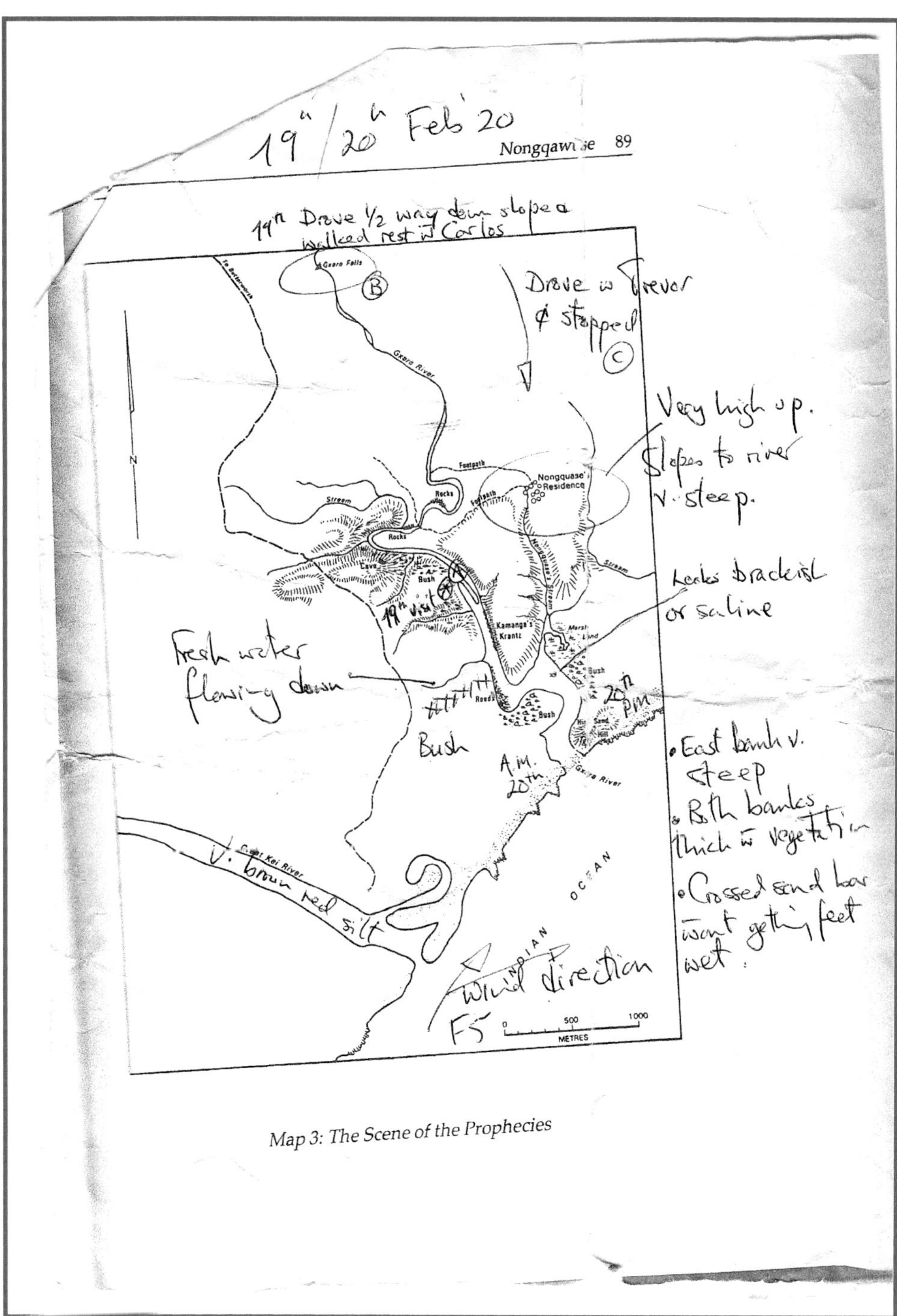

My photocopied map of the Gxara River was very useful but soon frayed with my sweat and rough handling. (With permission of Professor Jeff Peires.)

Wonderfully lush vegetation on the banks of Gxara River, much as it would have been in the 1850s.

At first I was taken by the intensity and variety of vegetation and the tranquillity of the gentle river, weaving its way between large boulders liberally scattered in the ambling water. Then I became attuned to the ambient sounds that complemented them. The Gxara River was turning into a sensual as well as spiritual experience. White noise was the principal theme, the friction and flapping of leaves, and an orchestra of wildlife filling the strings and woodwind sections. These included crickets, frogs and assorted insects and birds. There was also the flow of the river against rock and, ever so faintly, we could just hear the sound of the Indian Ocean, ebbing and flowing, waves crashing against a sand bar.

If this is how it had felt to Nongqawuse and her friend Nombanda in April 1856 as she tended her uncle's crops by the Gxara River, is it any wonder she had visions and heard from her ancestors? I started to see and feel how out-of-the-ordinary things might easily have happened here. It was rather like being in an old cathedral or magnificent amphitheatre – I felt an inner calm, spiced with a sense of awe and respect for things I did not understand. You would have to be pretty thick-skinned or emotionally numb not to be touched by the place. The last time I'd felt that way was in the eastern crypt of Canterbury Cathedral at the burial site of Thomas Becket, the 12th-century martyr murdered by four knights for displeasing Henry II. Standing passively beneath Sir Anthony Gormley's depiction of Becket, a floating human model made of welded old roof nails, I remembered feeling overwhelmed by the spiritual and historical significance. Similar emotions engulfed me at the site of prophetess's visions.

Back in 1856, could large *khamanga* trees and palm branches reflected in the water have given the impression of ancestors or herds of cattle just below the surface? Could voices, the sound of hooves, clattering horns and bellowing of cattle be imagined from the diverse sounds of nature? Might thick reeds, shadows and low tree branches have given the young girls flashes of ephemeral images? Perhaps an unrestrained, more dextrous mind could easily have seen, felt and sensed what might elude a duller mind like mine.

I was glad I'd made the trip, despite the best efforts of the region's roads to thwart me. Trevor and Carlos now asked if I wanted to see more. More? Of course! Where next? The waterfall? We needed to get back in the Toyota, head back out of the Gxara River valley and go upstream, first by tarmacked road and then on gravel track, to a heavily forested flat outcrop overlooking the river.

The waterfall dropped some 18–20 metres off a straight lip on to a flat rocky platform below, and a few metres downstream the water fed a large pool. The water was not clear, but tinged brown-red, like the runoff from a peat bog. Here, Trevor informed me, is where Nongqawuse allegedly came to bathe. If that were true, the young woman certainly had good taste. She would have bathed surrounded on three sides by tall grey cliffs. The angular craggy rock was decorated as generously as any artwork from a modern art gallery. Random splashes of orange and jet-black lichen were dramatically framed by assorted trailing green vegetation sprouting from perilous toeholds in the cracks. The top of the cliffs were crowned by the same lush jungle vegetation we'd seen at our first stop.

I couldn't help thinking that the cascading river surrounded by strident vegetation and muscular topography were a cipher for telling Nongqawuse's story. Collectively they embraced so many intimate secrets.

Carlos and I walked down a stony path to the top of the waterfall. Once again, I was captured by the visual beauty and the variety of natural sounds, as I tried to imagine if and how the waterfall might have featured in the creation and consolidation of the ideas that led to the Cattle Killing movement and the decimation of the amaXhosa people.

Standing on the bare rock at the top of the waterfall, the river only centimetres from my shoes, I asked Carlos why he thought the prophecies of Nongqawuse had failed. Why had the ancestors, with support from the Russians, not returned with healthy cattle laden with grain and new household implements? After so much communal sacrifice and the slaughter of hundreds of thousands of cattle, why hadn't the wretched European settlers been driven into the sea? We knew that Nongqawuse had had reassurances several times from the ancestors at the Gxara River. After her initial encounter with the two strangers, there had been many more communications in this area with the spirits about the return of the New People with new cattle. Even King Sarhili, the leader of the Gcalekas and most senior amaXhosa person in the region, had stated that he'd heard and seen mysterious things in the presence of the prophetess. In fact, there was an irony to my question. Today was exactly 163 years and one day since the Great Disappointment, the final date predicted by Nongqawuse when the momentous events were supposed to have happened. What had prevented this becoming the greatest moment in amaXhosa history, rather than a disaster?

I'd asked in a slightly rhetorical, academic kind of way, not expecting an assured answer. You know how overconfident lecturers and teachers ask big open questions, with a view to stimulating their students' grey matter – it was that sort of question. I'd added a bit of theatrics into the mix. Not for one minute did I think there was a plausible answer. But that's what I got.

It was the Unbelievers, according to Carlos. The *amagogotya,* the stingy ones, that were the root cause of the problem. He had no doubt. An open and shut case. They'd been disloyal to the chiefs, and selfish, not thinking about the greater good of the community. The Fingoes or amaMfengu, clans displaced by the Zulus, had a lot to answer for, too. They'd resisted in their droves. Selfish. The failure by some amaXhosas to believe Nongqawuse and follow her instructions, and the chiefs in particular, had

Waterfall on the Gxara River where Nongqawuse is believed to have bathed.

prevented the ancestors from returning with all that had been promised. The prophecies had been explicit. *All* cattle had to be slaughtered, *all* maize crops spoiled and *all* witchcraft rooted out. Nongqawuse had stressed repeatedly, over many months, that the ancestors were unhappy at the people for not following their clear instructions, and therefore they would not fulfil their side of the deal. They had been disrespected. At one level it was assuring to hear such a decisive and confident answer. But at another level I was disorientated. In the 21st century, this was not the answer I had been expecting. That said, I'm not sure what I *had* been expecting, but I was thrown by the fact that a knowledgeable person such as Carlos thought that it was the Unbelievers that had prevented the prophecies of Nongqawuse from being realised.

I was still digesting this conversation when Carlos and I met up with Trevor back at the pickup. He thought I was a touch contemplative, which was a pretty accurate insight. I was trying to make sense of the past in the light of what I had seen and heard, but I felt that my upbringing and cultural perspectives were hampering my ability to understand.

'What do you think happened?' Trevor asked.

What did I think had happened? Come to think of it, what did I think? Well, I knew what I *felt*. I felt a little uneasy, my vacuousness and shallow perspectives clearly exposed. So I resorted to a stodgy, rational and deductive mode of thinking, trying to shake off the evocative feelings and emotions elicited by the place. Facts and logic were what I knew best. But denying the impact of my current surroundings and the surreal feelings they induced was an exercise in futility.

'I don't know enough about Xhosa traditions and their beliefs in their ancestors, to be honest,' was the best I could think of. What a poor answer. Was that really the best I could muster?

I tried again: 'Trevor, I don't really know what I think, except that the Gxara River has a very special feeling. I can see and feel why a prophetess might have communications with the spiritual world and ancestors in these surroundings.'

Yep, that pretty much summed it up. At 4 pm on 19 February 2020, that's what I thought. My search or pilgrimage for Nongqawuse was a work in progress, but now I could genuinely imagine how thousands of cattle, their horns clattering together beneath the surface of the pool, together with an army of amaXhosa ancestors, might rise out of its depths and from the waves all along the Wild Coast, drive away the European settlers and restore life to what it once had been. At that moment, in that place, such extravagant events did not feel too fanciful.

The sun was heading towards the horizon. There was not enough daylight time to visit Nongqawuse's village, but Trevor and Carlos were good enough to drive part-way there and indicate where the site was before we headed back to the hotel.

Fired up by my visit to the Gxara River, I spent the next day wandering up and down the coast, exploring rivers and estuaries, often in the company of cattle that milled about on open pastures and on the beach. Swathes of mist that draped across the rocky seashore added yet another visual dimension to the mysterious atmosphere of the place.

Before leaving Qolora, I popped in to see Trevor at his house just down the road from my hotel. I loved it, even from the outside. It spoke of a bohemian spirit. The garden and porch were decorated with whale bones, hanging marine displays and various paraphernalia. Inside it had the air of a hippy bachelor pad, with pictures on the wall of a young Trevor surfing the waves of the Wild Coast. He wanted to show me an academic thesis of poetry about Nongqawuse, and I wanted to say thank you for my tour.

I didn't say it, but I had a feeling that I might return one day.

My drive back to Mthatha from Qolora was relatively trouble-free, apart from a few protesters forming obstructive chicanes of burning tyres and glass on the main road back through Idutywa. I didn't pay them much attention, and found myself gravitating back to the topic of Nongqawuse's prophecies and the events surrounding the Great Cattle Killing. In particular, Carlos' comment about the Unbelievers spoiling everything kept coming to mind. I began to realise that if I were to continue my search for Nongqawuse and make genuine progress, I needed to alter my mindset. My mind, which had been fashioned by a British upbringing and education, needed a little retuning to start understanding 19th-century amaXhosa beliefs, priorities and sensitivities. In particular, I was struggling with the concept of returning ancestors and the fervent belief that they could rescue you long after they had passed away. Had the amaXhosa really expected their ancestors to rise from the sea to banish the European settlers and amaMfengu? Surely the dead were, well … dead? Apparently not.

I didn't know it, but fortunately help was just around the corner.

Near the mouth of the Gxara River on the Wild Coast, cattle cool themselves in the Indian Ocean.

4: MEET THE ANCESTORS

'The person who refuses to take advice hears by a hot wind.'

'Isala kutyelwa siva ngo lopu.'

Xhosa proverb: Rev. J.H. Soga, *The Ama-Xosa. Life and Customs*, 1931

The next day I walked up the potholed road in suburban Mthatha from my hotel to the home of my friends, Jane and Simon Mqamelo. I say 'friends', but in truth I'd yet to meet Simon, although I'd heard quite a bit about him. Jane was the editor of my first book, so I knew her through email correspondence, telephone calls and a conversation on her patio a couple of days earlier. Despite wrestling over the merits or otherwise of my syntax, grammar and spelling of isiXhosa names during the past few months, we seemed to get on well. So much so that she and Simon had offered to take me to Enkalweni for the weekend, their home in the country, about an hour and a half north-west of bustling Mthatha.

Our departure was delayed by a couple of hours as Simon needed to sleep in after arriving home from his workplace in East London at about 3 am. We introduced ourselves in his kitchen over tea and coffee, before loading a large red 4×4 Ford up to the gunnels. IsiXhosa was Simon's first language, but English was Jane's, so much to my relief they spoke English to me, and we were going to talk together quite a bit that weekend.

I took an instant liking to Simon and Jane. He was black and she white, in their fifties, with two grown children. With an inter-racial marriage, they were different from many people in South Africa. I felt invigorated in their company – I was going to have to look at the world through an alternative lens to keep up with them. Jane's views were greatly influenced by her Christian faith, which she shared graciously and sincerely. She also had a razor-sharp mind, aligned to a loyal maternal instinct. Simon, as I was about to find out, was greatly influenced by his Xhosa heritage, in particular his ancestors. Also, he'd been fashioned by apartheid – not just its severe prejudices, but the sharp end of the law. Amongst many things, it had restricted where he could go and live in his own country, the education he could receive, and whom he could marry. At the time Simon and Jane were married in 1992, the prohibition against mixed marriages had only recently been lifted.

Not far out of Mthatha, with mountains looming on the north-west horizon, Simon recounted that as a boy living with apartheid's segregation laws, he'd had to hide in the sheds and gardens of sympathetic white people in Cape Town where his father had been a gardener. As an intelligent black child, he'd been unable to get an education to match his talents. It had taken the illegal intervention of his father's white employers to nurture his intellectual inclinations and enable him to access higher education and graduate as a certified civil engineer. Now he held a management role as a water engineer in one of the region's water companies.

Not long before we turned off the main R61 highway, Simon casually pointed to the spot where he'd seen a spirit at about 3 am the previous night. A spirit? I was a little taken aback by such a seemingly far-fetched observation. He wasn't joking. This was not an aberration or unusual in any way, he insisted, and I got my first glimpse of his views; ones that were to help challenge my ossified mind and improve my understanding of Nongqawuse's prophecies.

No sooner had I been jolted by the prospect of spirits in the area than Simon pointed out a magnificent new road winding up the wooded mountains rising steeply in the foreground. In places, the road was suspended on concrete structures in mid-air above spectacular ravines and cliffs, giving us, as we drove over those structures, stunning views. The road snaked its way across the sheer slope of the mountain, at times skimming the tops of trees. We could have been in the Alps or Jura, with the engineering and scenery complementing each other in their magnificence and audaciousness. Even my fancy Nikon, with more pixels and digital nonsense than I knew what to do with, couldn't capture the grandeur of the views north, south, east and west.

While I was struggling to take it all in, Simon explained how he'd personally influenced the site and the building of this great engineering feat. He was extremely proud of that, and quite rightly so. This was no ordinary road, in no ordinary location. And so I listened intently, slightly mesmerised, as he described the long gestation and birth of his vision for a decent road that would link his birthplace with the wider world outside.

Within minutes, Simon had fluctuated from conversing about spirits and ghosts to state-of-the-art structural engineering. He seemed equally comfortable in both worlds. Jane beamed with pride at her husband's achievements. I, on the other hand, was disorientated. On we drove, reaching the summit of the mountain where the vista opened on to verdant grasslands, dotted with the occasional cluster of huts. A kestrel-sized falcon greeted our arrival at the top, darting off a wooden fence post. Herds of cattle came into view, and Simon wound down the window to point out which were his. Now the 4×4 came into its own, and we bumped and rocked our way up a coarse gravel track on the slope of a craggy hill to Enkalweni, his home village.

The home felt welcoming. A handful of rondavels (traditional round thatched huts) and a modest Western-style bungalow were set back from a kraal (a stone- and mud-walled enclosure). As the place where cattle and other livestock were retained for safekeeping, the kraal still held huge social and spiritual importance; traditionally, it was a place for men, not boys or women. Numerous mature trees, a field of maize and a sizeable vegetable garden adorned the homestead, which looked out over the rest of the village from a slight hill, backed by a rocky outcrop. Everything blended in beautifully. The sound of small birds, chickens and cows added to the natural ambience.

This had originally been the home of his father and family – and before that his grandfather, great-grandfather and so on for five or six generations. He and Jane had added buildings, trees and utilities. After their hard work and investment, they now had running water, flushing lavatories, electricity and, occasionally, the internet. In the midst of this idyllic rural setting, with a broad panoramic view of the Maluti Mountains on the horizon, I felt like I'd come on a retreat.

While I took it all in, Simon dashed off in the Ford to speak to his neighbour. He was concerned about the theft or loss of a couple of his cattle. By the time he returned a few hours later, the afternoon sun was giving way to low cloud and drizzle, and all three of us sat around a table in the middle of the hut, dimly illuminated by an electric light bulb. I was wearing my warm fleece jacket and my hosts were in jumpers. We could smell supper roasting in the oven.

And so began a long and varied conversation, one that I'll cherish for many years. We went on into the late evening and covered a lot of ground, mostly about amaXhosa traditions and perspectives of the world. At times I took notes. At other times I had to be on my toes to persuade Simon not to veer off to another topic. He seemed to like the fact that I was so interested in what he had to say that I took the trouble to gently stop him straying too far.

It became clear that at one level we inhabited a similar world and had a great deal in common. I called it the x + y = z world, and he chuckled, acknowledging the shorthand for rational western processes and facts. After all, that is why he was an engineer with a distinguished academic record, in a professional position of responsibility. And why I, as a trained scientist with a career in business, could relate to him. In fact, I came from a whole x + y = z family, consisting of engineers, scientists, entrepreneurs, compliance officers and bank managers. In that world, columns of figures had to add up, statutory regulations had to be adhered to and digital codes had to link together coherently to ensure computers on oil platforms worked.

Simon was more nuanced and interesting than that.

Over supper, in the muted electric light of the circular, ochre-coloured hut, it was abundantly clear that his ancestors played a huge role in his life. I'm not talking conceptually – I mean practically, every day. Through dreams and feelings, he listened to what his late mother, father and sister were telling him. He held them and their counsel in high regard, to the extent they were active influencers of his everyday life. One reason for his return from city life to Enkalweni almost every weekend was to be closer to them. As he pulled out a large roll of paper mapping the family tree, I felt I was being formally introduced to the extended Mqamelo family, going back many generations. He knew them all, using the word 'clan' to describe the whole group. Like many amaXhosa in this neck of the woods, they'd migrated here from elsewhere in southern Africa, particularly during the great ructions and mass displacement of the Mfecane caused by the Zulu expansion in the early 19th century. Simon's ancestors had come from Mozambique via Swaziland and Lesotho, where one of his great-grandfathers had died crossing a river.

Simon was the oldest of six siblings. His dead sister had been an *iGqirha* or *sangoma*, as he referred to her, a diviner and an ancestor, whom he held in very high esteem. As someone able to ward off witchcraft and heal with traditional medicine, she would have been held in high regard by the wider community, too. From beyond the grave, she now regularly influenced him through dreams, messages and signs. He pointed out her grave nearby, and I made a point of visiting it early the following morning in drizzle and fog, with only exuberant cockerels for company.

It would be fair to say that I like food, but our exploration of amaXhosa beliefs and the importance of ancestors was taking priority over supper on this occasion. My view of the world was being severely stretched and kneaded, like a well-worked dough. Apparently, x + y = z didn't always cut the mustard in the Mqamelo clan. Simon spoke of the spiritual world in matter-of-fact tones, without a shadow of doubt. He had a comprehensive picture of the cosmos that included God, Christ, spiritual beings both good and evil, ancestors, humans and humans yet to come. Life for him was a massive battle between good and evil, in which both sides warred for the soul of men and women. Evil forces could influence those who had passed on to the other side, but his prayers could nudge them closer to God – just as their intercession could help and guide him. His absolute confidence in the guidance he received infused him with an inner confidence and enthusiasm for life that I found attractive.

I reminded myself that spiritualism like Simon's, involving communication with the dead, had been practised a great deal in the western world in the 19th and 20th centuries. This had been the case after particularly major wars, when the bereaved sought solace by attempting to engage with their loved ones in the afterlife. Sir Arthur Conan Doyle, the famous author and creator of Sherlock Holmes, had been a major figurehead in the movement.

After some time, Simon asked me about my trip to the Gxara River and my opinion of Nongqawuse. It was becoming abundantly clear that whenever I mentioned Nongqawuse people wanted to know my personal opinion, but in truth I still wasn't

Big skies and verdant escarpments approaching Enkalweni (in Eastern Cape) where Simon Mqamelo was to introduce me to his ancestors.

sure. I was still attempting to formulate a view. After all, that is why I was exploring the region. I did not have enough facts yet, neither did I sufficiently understand amaXhosa traditions or the world of 19th-century British Kaffraria and Gcalekaland. So I talked about the great natural beauty of the Gxara River, the huge pressures faced by the amaXhosa in the 1850s and the fact that I wasn't sure whether Nongqawuse should bear the full weight of responsibility for the disaster. My waffly answer had all the intellectual rigour of a flaccid blancmange.

I sensed that Simon felt a mixture of shame, embarrassment and anger about the Great Cattle Killing. It was more than a remote historical event to him, and to be honest, it was starting to feel like more than that to me. A weird form of historical osmosis had started. My understanding of the facts was being infused with empathy and raw emotion. Although he listened to my inadequate answer, I sensed he really wanted to share his explanation of the events. He had strong views. The British, he insisted, were at the heart of this disaster – the governor of the Cape, Sir George Grey, in particular. Now I'd heard of this Sir George Grey theory before. The theory states that Sir George Grey himself or his henchmen, in the form of local magistrates, had either tricked the prophetess by disguising themselves as ancestors and speaking to her directly at the Gxara River, or by actively propagating the cattle slaughter message in order to accelerate the demise of the amaXhosa. Simon could see Grey's fingerprints all over the case. One way or another Grey was guilty.

I wasn't so sure. Perhaps he was right, but I wasn't here to have firm views yet; I was here to listen and learn. My informal education on amaXhosa traditions was still under way. But I felt I was making good progress. The school report might read *C+ for effort*, annotated with 'Treive must talk less and stop messing about so much'.

At about noon the next day, we'd loaded the 4×4 and were ready to return to Mthatha, when Simon and Jane walked off to one of the other rondavels adjacent to our living quarters. They asked if I'd like to join them, although I hadn't a clue why. Their body language was purposeful, so I tagged along. The atmosphere changed quickly. One minute we'd been coordinating space and weight distribution in a car. Now we were in a traditional round mud hut with none of the trimmings – the floor was made of solid, baked manure and the furnishings were sparse. In the middle of the floor was a shallow round indentation, into which Simon was placing a bundle of dry herbs. Jane knelt on one side, Simon and I on the other. We were silent. A few coloured candles burned, emitting a dim light. Neither of them told me what was going on, but I sensed it had something to do with the ancestors and prayer. I was right.

Simon lit the herbs, and a plume of fragrant smoke streamed upward to the apex of the grass roof, settling eventually and filling the cool interior of the hut. There was a deep calm, and Simon began talking out loud in rapid isiXhosa, his voice gathering pace and intensity as he knelt before the candles. His words sounded like prayer or poetry. He was communicating with his ancestors, offering thanks and good wishes for their wellbeing. After a few minutes he stopped, and Jane offered Christian prayers in English. I was flattered to be included in her despatch to God. Without a word we simultaneously got up, headed for the car and drove off to another rural village nearby. The same herbal ritual was performed here, this time in the home that had belonged to Simon's mother's family. Now that we had said our farewells to the ancestors we could hit the road.

At his home in Enkalweni, Simon explained the importance of ancestors in the everyday life of amaXhosa.

As we drove down the escarpment on Simon's magnificent road I reflected on my background and why I was wrestling with the notion of daily interaction with one's ancestors. In west Cornwall, where all my ancestors had come from, I did not sense much spirituality or reference to the afterlife with my lot; things were pretty straight up and down. There were regular pagan rituals out at the Merry Maidens, an ancient circle of granite stones near St Buryan. Up Padstow way they had the May Day folk festival with 'Obby 'Osses dancing in the streets, as part of a musical procession. For the most part, the Nicholas clan had been traditional Methodists, with a twist of Wesleyan thrown in for good measure. When members of my family had been lowered 6 feet underground in a wooden box, overshadowed by a grey granite chapel near Penzance, there had been little or no expectation of them returning. When you were gone, you were gone. The contrast between amaXhosa culture and belief in the ancestors could hardly have differed more from my Cornish family's Methodist beliefs and practices.

It was now becoming abundantly clear that to understand Nongqawuse, her prophecies and the dedication of tens of thousands of amaXhosa to the Cattle Killing movement, I needed to think much more like Simon. My cultural heritage needed to be put to one side for a moment. I had to accept that in the 19th century the desperate people of the Eastern Cape would have seen their ancestors as a perfectly plausible source of salvation. Why not? After all, ancestors would have been engaged in every other aspect of their lives. No one else seemed to be coming to their aid, and the suffering wrought by eight Frontier Wars with Europeans in less than 100 years cried out for a drastic and conclusive solution. Having seen Simon's reverence towards his dead sister's spiritual powers as an *iGqirha* or *sangoma*, I started to appreciate that prophetesses like Nongqawuse were seen to be special and could have real influence over their community. If I accepted these two notions, the prophecies and the Cattle Killing movement did not seem too difficult to understand.

My search for Nongqawuse seemed to be making progress, even though there was a very long way to go. This gave me some reassurance, as I flew out of Mthatha airport to start my journey home.

5: GRETA THUNBERG

'To stay in the darkness of redness!'

Elder in *The Heart of Redness* by Zakes Mda

I was greeted by reality not long after touching down at Heathrow. A nasty viral pandemic was causing alarm and confusion from Wuhan to Timbuktu, taking lives and disrupting life globally. All very inconvenient, but at least I wasn't holed up in hospital on a ventilator, like some people I knew.

Do you know that feeling when you think of buying something, and then you can't help noticing it all over the place? Consider buying a new pair of suede boots and before you know it, every Tom, Dick and Harry on the High Street has a pair. I believe this is called the Baader-Meinhof phenomenon.

It started to feel like this with Nongqawuse too. Much to my surprise, she was popping up everywhere. Was it that I'd just started looking, or had she been in front of my nose all the time if only I'd opened my eyes properly?

First, I came across an UK article called 'Beware the Tory cult that's steering Brexit' – from the *Financial Times* of all places. Simon Kuper, the journalist, was using the Great Cattle Killing and the division of Believers and Unbelievers to help describe the behaviour of certain politicians towards Britain's departure from the European Union. He thought some of them were rooted to the past and had a view of the world wholly different from those looking to a brighter future. He believed a type of Brexit cult was developing that would lead to self-destruction, a bit like the aftermath of the mass slaughter.

Not to be outdone, the *Sunday Times* in South Africa included the Cameroonian historian Achille Mbembe's reference to 'Nongqawuse Syndrome' as a suicidal tendency found in southern Africa at times of great stress. He saw the growth of populism, violence and millenarian movements as examples of this, in response to failures and disappointments felt by many post apartheid.

At the other end of the scale, on the StoryboardThat website I found a cartoon storyboard called 'Xhosa Cattle Killing' illustrating all the events from 1856 to 1857 in six Simpson-like images. Stiff cartoon images of Nongqawuse and Sir George Grey had speech bubbles coming out of their mouths with stilted phrases such as 'Kill the cows' and 'We're taking you to Cape Town, then'. I had to admire the brevity, and strangely enough it covered many of the key features.

A paper by Andrew Offenburger in the USA compared the Xhosa Cattle Killing movement to the themes of his favourite film, *Field of Dreams* (1989), starring Kevin Costner and based in Iowa. I couldn't quite make the connection, but Professor Offenburger had more letters after his name than I did, so I bowed to his superior knowledge and intellect. Besides, he described how he'd also met Trevor Wigley on his trip to the Gxara River.

Soon I found that the story of Nongqawuse and the Great Cattle Killing had been depicted in cartoon fashion, as well as by academics. (With permission of StoryboardThat.)

On the other hand Erik Bahre, a professor from Leiden in the Netherlands, had an altogether more academic take on things. *Greta Thunberg and Nongqawuse: Two Sixteen-year-old Women Challenging the World* suggested that the two young women had a lot in common, despite living more than 160 years apart and in different parts of the world. The learned professor thought they were both responding radically to major problems in male-dominated worlds because they were left with very little choice. Nongqawuse and Greta were 'exposing the impotence of society's leaders' by offering a 'radical break from the past'. He was flying the flag for young women when traditional male leaders were not up to the job.

It soon became apparent that comparisons with Nongqawuse went back further in time. Joan of Arc started to surface as a comparison more than once. I wasn't sure, but I think Joan was the illiterate French peasant girl who'd snubbed her nose at the English at a time when gallant folk rode steeds, wore armour and charged about with big flags claiming allegiance to Lord this and Baron that. It turned out that I wasn't far wrong. The Maid of Orléans, or Saint Joan, had in effect led the French to victory over the English in 1415, during the Hundred Years' War, after receiving messages from archangels and saints. Alas, she was captured by a pro-English bishop, tried as a heretic (mainly on the basis of her wearing men's clothing) and burned at the stake, her martyrdom now assured.

I wasn't quite so sure about the comparison between the two young women, but I could see why they might be mentioned in the same sentence. In short, when the

French and the amaXhosa establishment were staring down the barrel of defeat from a persistent external foe, each of these two had stepped forward to help. But unlike Saint Joan, a symbol of *la belle France*, Nongqawuse hadn't received much recognition nationally or internationally, as far as I could see. She seemed anonymous at best, or vilified by most people who knew about her, especially the amaXhosa.

Did you know that Mark Twain described Joan of Arc as 'easily and by far the most extraordinary person the human race has ever produced'? Very flattering, I thought. Quite the fan. He even wrote a novel about her.

On that score Nongqawuse, not to be outdone, can point to Zakes Mda's 2000 novel *The Heart of Redness*, which was about the Cattle Killing and way more. What a find! It contained fact and fiction, with two stories interwoven into one stimulating and provocative cocktail. And I consumed it like one, fruit slices and all.

The Heart of Redness describes not only the events and impact of the Xhosa Cattle Killing, but more importantly, the issues, beliefs, values and divisions caused by and arising from it. For example, retrieving self-identity had been a core theme, tested and explored throughout the narrative by characters from different centuries, some urban, others deeply rooted in rural traditions. In Qolora-by-the-Sea, where Mda's Nongqawuse had her visions, he situated two fictitious families, one living in the 1850s and the other in the late 1990s. The divisive theme of Believers versus Unbelievers, or traditionalists versus progressives, was vividly played out in both timeframes, with strong and credible characters in constant conflict. As Mda put it, modern-day Believers fervently defended the past and Xhosa tradition (or redness[1]) in response to the instability and challenges of post-apartheid South Africa. In contrast, the 20th-century Unbelievers derided tradition and strenuously promoted development, progress and modernity. Was this a reflection of modern South Africa's identity? Did the conflict in modern times mirror a similar tension that existed in 19th-century South Africa? Nongqawuse and the events surrounding the Great Cattle Killing offered Mda a credible platform to explore a whole panoply of thorny contemporary issues. It was a great read, and I felt I was back at the Wild Coast again.

A much harder-hitting read was *Mother to Mother* (1998) by Sindiwe Magona. The book's primary focus was an explanation of the background and circumstances surrounding a murder near her home. South Africa's troubled and violent past was a major theme. The story also introduced Nongqawuse and the Cattle Killing to convey how desperate previous generations of amaXhosa had been to rid their land of the unwanted strangers, the *abeLungu* ('the Whites'). It stressed the sacrifice made by the people in the Cattle Killing in order to reap the reward for getting rid of the European

1 Redness, in this context, refers to the reddish clay used for body decoration, with 'red' sometimes used as a derogatory term associated with backwardness.

settlers. As one of the main characters stressed, 'Anything. Anything to rid themselves of these unwanted strangers.'

In addition to literature, I learned that the Cattle Killing was depicted on the 126-metre Keiskamma Tapestry, now housed in the Parliament building, Cape Town. Inspired by the Bayeux Tapestry of northern France, and created by amaXhosa women, it depicted scenes in the Eastern Cape from the 1820s to the 1990s, and the release of Nelson Mandela from incarceration. In a manner of speaking, William of Normandy had been replaced by Nongqawuse of Xhosaland.

These articles and artwork confirmed that comparisons with and depictions of the prophetess ranged from the battlefields of 15th-century France to the cornfields of Iowa; from the pages of the *Financial Times* to a novel by Zakes Mda. So, Nongqawuse and the Cattle Killing were known by a wider audience than I had at first realised. Each depiction had its own take on the matter. It was all thought-provoking, if a touch confusing at times. I'm not sure what I had expected, but certainly not so many twists and turns in interpretation. After this casual peruse I felt vindicated in continuing my search, and threw myself into the task with greater conviction.

Amazon was the first and principal beneficiary of my renewed enthusiasm as I ordered numerous books, many out of print and coming from as far afield as Oregon, USA. I was soon on speaking terms with my local parcel delivery chap as he traipsed up our drive on a regular basis.

Courtesy of Mr Google, I was finding and printing off reams of newspaper articles, academic papers and PhD theses. Ring binders and Dropbox folders soon filled up. Messages to buy more space in the cloud reflected my growing library of Nongqawuse material. Once again, I was dodging domestic duties, to read. In my absence, elder and hawthorn bushes relaxed in the knowledge that they were unlikely to be cut back in their prime. The lawn shed its stripped crew-cut look and took on an erratic punkish appearance, while weeds and wildlife flourished.

6: THE PILGRIMAGE BEGINS

'Dawn does not come twice to awaken a person.'

'Ukusa akufiki kabini ukuvusa umntu'

Xhosa proverb: Rev. J.H. Soga, *The Ama-Xosa. Life and Customs*, 1931

Like just about everyone else on Planet Earth, including the labcoat-clad scientists, I did not anticipate Covid disrupting ordinary life for nearly two years. A few months of Covid disruption I could have understood – but really; two years! It soon became an unwanted guest. We've all had friends and family who don't know when it is time to leave. Was it Benjamin Franklin who said, 'Guests, like fish, begin to smell after three days'? That's how we felt about our uninvited viral visitor.

Any plans of resuming my search for Nongqawuse were reluctantly put on hold. South Africa seemed more distant than the 12,000 kilometres that separated us. With airlines and airports in a state of torpor, and international borders resembling the Berlin Wall, thoughts of finding the grave of the prophetess were put on the back burner. Instead of mulling over the intricacies of 19th-century amaXhosa history and the causes of the Cattle Killing, what brainpower I had left was spent playing endless games of Monopoly, chess and Go with my wife and our son, Oscar. Inside our intimate little family bubble, I held my own at Monopoly, struggled at chess and was humiliated at Go. Mealtimes, elevated in importance, became real highlights to break up the monotony of our Covid-secure days. Oscar in particular delighted in conjuring up exotic aromatic vegetarian dishes from around the world.

But man cannot live on chess and fried noodles alone.

I started to get fidgety with a Covid-induced form of cabin fever. After many months, I returned to my search for Nongqawuse, or my passion project, as Oscar called it. Passion project! I'm not sure I liked that catch-all phrase. It sounded like a sub-set of a midlife crisis. Would buying a Harley Davidson motorbike be called a passion project? Was it part of the millennial vocabulary that had passed me by, a one-line commoditisation of my interest? No, no, no – I wasn't keen on the pigeonholing of Nongqawuse. Passion project or not, out came the books that were by now way too familiar, harmoniously snuggled together on the new Ikea shelves. I'd even arranged my burgeoning but niche Nongqawuse-themed library using a spurious method of cataloguing that was so intricate it soon confused me. Entropy started to get the upper hand.

First to be raised from their slumber were those books I had previously graffitied with highlighter pens, HB pencils and biros in order to annotate paragraphs and borders with thoughts, expletives and opinions. Out, too, came a new cohort of books still exuding the intoxicating smell of printer's ink, knowledge and wisdom, all untarnished by my pen and pronouncements. As I leafed the pages of 19th-century African history, I was once again in the turbulent cauldron of the Eastern Cape, in the company of competing amaXhosa chiefs, zealous protestant missionaries, exotic prophets, callous military leaders, colonial die-hards and a stunning landscape soaked in the blood of all races and even more animals. I could hear the pristine waves of the Indian Ocean again, crashing against glorious stretches of Wild Coast beach.

In the depressingly clinical and isolating world of Covid, it felt reassuring to be back amongst the familiar people, places and landscapes with which I had developed a surreal and intimate relationship, even though we were separated by distance, culture and 160 years. Somehow, my relationship with this place and time felt close and authentic. Pictures on my office wall of Nongqawuse, Nonkosi, African bush and Xhosa *amakhaya* (beehive-shaped rural huts) added to the atmosphere of our reunion. In my small private world in Hampshire, rural Eastern Cape was, so to speak, within touching distance.

My reading was not confined to books. I had recently bought an all-singing all-dancing Apple Mac, with more computing power than the whole of the 1960s NASA space program, and decided to put it through its paces. With the aid of my new best friend, Google, I searched various South African historical websites and academic papers. Some were helpful, others less so. The Artefacts website,[2] with contributions by William Martinson, kept popping up, particularly with regard to historical sites associated with the Frontier Wars, Nongqawuse and King Hintsa. Progress. Here was a man who not only knew the history of the Eastern Cape but had a knowledge of the key sites where many seminal events occurred. Now to find and contact him. Despite my digital illiteracy, this task was easier than I had anticipated, and soon we were exchanging emails. William shared all sorts of historical titbits, and soon introduced me to other members of the Border Historical Society, based in the Eastern Cape. Quite by accident, I'd thus found a group of like-minded amateurs, with a mine of knowledge and experience related to the history of the Eastern Cape. Better still, these folk really seemed to know what they were talking about. They even sent me a copy of *The Coelacanth*, their periodical, containing members' local history articles going back decades. I'd struck a rich seam of gold. Instead of floundering around by myself, reading various tomes and trying to understand what on earth had happened around the time of Nongqawuse and the Cattle Killing, I now had some people I could refer to and ask opinions of, and who could help me fill in gaps in my understanding.

2 See Bibliography, under Anon.

It all snowballed from there. Once I mentioned that I planned a second visit to the Eastern Cape, this time to seek out the graves of Nongqawuse near Gqeberha (Port Elizabeth) and King Hintsa in Gcalekaland, offers of help hit my inbox. In fact, the itinerary of a mini-expedition was soon drafted – sites, drive times and background information. The enthusiasm for the trip was proving infectious, with some of the great and the good of the Border Historical Society wanting to join me.

I made a smart decision. I accepted their offer of help and hospitality, even though I was not quite sure what I'd accepted. I didn't even know them – but I was keen, they were keen and they certainly knew the Eastern Cape and many of its secrets and hidden stories. Perhaps I should throw caution to the wind. Besides, I didn't want a repeat of my previous car trip, crashing through mud and over boulders in my search for the Gxara River where Nongqawuse had received her messages from the spirits. The members of the Border Historical Society of East London sounded sensible, safe and welcoming. From the sanctuary of my home office, that was good enough, for the moment.

My desire to visit Nongqawuse's grave near Gqeberha (Port Elizabeth) was turning into a secular pilgrimage. The pull was strong, and the purpose spiritual as well as physical. Paying my respects and acknowledging her was becoming an important part of my endeavour. Unfamiliar as I was with pilgrimages, I bought a copy of Timothy Egan's 2019 book *A Pilgrimage to Eternity*. I thought there might be some lessons to learn, and indeed there were, despite our divergent objectives – his to find God and mine to find a 19th-century Xhosa prophetess. I was strangely reassured by his constant intellectual and emotional struggle. Wrongly, as it turned out, I had assumed he knew his mind and was on a long walk from Canterbury to Rome to reinforce his beliefs. Instead, his pilgrimage was shaped by a plethora of questions about his core beliefs and a constant challenging of his own and others' opinions. His pilgrimage was in fact a vehicle to exercise his beliefs, not contentedly embrace them. I wrote a mental Post-It note to myself to this effect. Also, I liked what he said: 'Movement is a pilgrim's oxygen.' That resonated with me. I definitely needed more oxygen. And I liked moving, too. It was nearing the time to put down my books and pick up my passport.

Now all I needed was for the travel restrictions to South Africa to be lifted. Unfortunately, the country was still firmly rooted in the bad boys' club, better known as the red list of unsafe travel destinations. Then the hokey-cokey started. Initially, UK government bigwigs changed it to a green list status, then back to the red list, and finally, by early January 2022, two years after my previous visit, back to the green list. Hallelujah. It was time to crawl into the loft, haul out the travel bags and dust off my neglected passport. Pounds were exchanged for rands, and I headed to Heathrow Terminal 5 for a rendezvous with BA flight 0042 to Cape Town.

'Normal' had resumed – well a new type of normal, involving pages of vaccination documents and QR codes, but it was certainly better than the previous months of grim statistics and dire medical pronouncements.

It was comforting and somehow reassuring to be back in Cape Town, nestled at the southern point of the African continent at the meeting point of the Atlantic and Indian Oceans. Southwards the seas stretched, like the world's largest tablecloth, to a distant non-existent horizon that eventually became the Antarctic. To the north there were the hazy outlines and silhouettes of mountains, hosting prestigious fruit growers and wine-making communities such as Paarl and Stellenbosch. On the False Bay side lay the flats, where hundreds of thousands of Cape people lived challenging lives in the shanty towns of Langa, Gugulethu and Khayelitsha. In the city centre, colonial buildings from the Dutch and British era stood resiliently cheek by jowl with assertive and precocious office blocks poking their angular heads skywards. Of course, there was the permanent and reassuring presence of Table Mountain, caressing the city and port. Often, cloud tumbled off the top, the white vapour contrasting with the fissured Cambrian sandstone. Almost as ubiquitous as Table Mountain was the steady clean breeze, keeping temperatures and humidity ideal for visitors like me from foreign and colder climes. I could have been on a Mediterranean island in early autumn.

Before heading off to the Eastern Cape on my pilgrimage to reacquaint myself with Nongqawuse, I spent the first five days working in and around the city catching up with old friends and finding new ones. I hadn't seen some for 42 years. Meeting in their homes, offices, coffee shops and restaurants, there was a palpable sense of relief to be seeing and touching each other in the flesh, without the digital warping of Teams and Zoom. Handshaking, hugging and smiling face to face took on a disproportionate significance, far exceeding the act of human comfort and friendship. We had permission to behave as humans again. Flesh replaced pixels.

Travel offers many frissons of excitement, none more so than meeting someone new and from a different culture. And so it was on meeting Jaco, my host from my business partners, who worked in the publishing industry. He collected me from my B&B in the Gardens district in his compact city car, and ferried me around for several days, introducing me to a range of bookshops, emerging businesses and South Africans of all races, who were mostly young, intelligent and with inquisitive minds.

Jaco and I quickly struck up quite a friendship. He came from a Cape Afrikaans background and my roots were Celtic, with a strong Cornish heritage. He was one of those annoyingly lucky people who looked younger than his years; I carried most of my life-inflicted knocks and bruises front and centre. He was exceptionally charming and diplomatic; I was a little rough round the edges and a touch over-enthusiastic. The fact that he lived near the old District Six part of the city and worked in the publishing industry indicated to me pretty quickly that he was probably from the liberal end of South Africa's social spectrum.

Much of our initial conversation focused on getting me to understand the new, evolving South Africa. What did the rainbow of the Rainbow Nation look like in 2022? This was 28 years after the first non-racial elections. Although I had visited the country many times during and after apartheid, I was conscious of how fast it kept changing and how many obstacles it had to overcome. He didn't sugar the pill, talking about the infrastructure challenges, massive unemployment, housing shortages, healthcare needs, crime, corruption and political shenanigans. It was quite a list. I really didn't envy Mr Ramaphosa, the president. He was ruling without the support of one of the country's principal spiritual leaders, Archbishop Desmond Tutu, who had stood as a conspicuous beacon of reason and hope during the apartheid era, and had died recently, at the venerable age of 90. As Jaco and I drove around, I could see numerous Cape Town buildings adorned with Tutu's image. 'Quite a man,' I found myself thinking. His personal balance sheet would have passed any integrity-based audit. I'm not much sold on the idea of heaven, but if there is one I hope he made it through the pearly gates more easily than I had got through Heathrow's Covid interrogation. However, I suspected that he'd find a cause to fight for in whichever new celestial neighbourhood he ended up. He was that kind of chap. One of the good ones.

As if to reinforce the challenges ahead for South Africa, an arsonist had set light to the Cape Parliament building just days before I arrived. Fire fighters were still keeping a vigilant watch outside. The large, incongruous statue of Queen Victoria in parliament's courtyard looked on, seemingly unamused. When Jaco and I drove by there was the distinct acrid smell of smoke. It was physically repulsive and depressing. The vile odour symbolised someone or some people trying to undermine the very democracy that so many people had literally fought for over decades – centuries in fact. Thousands had died, many shot in the back, for non-racial democratic representation. For me, a visiting outsider, the pungent burning smell emanating from the doors and windows of this seat of democracy was putting two nasty fingers up to the past and present voices of the majority, including Nongqawuse and other 19th-century amaXhosa whose lives I was trying to understand.

Jaco's first appointment for me was at the swanky and impressively named Century City shopping mall, north-west of Cape Town central on the N1 highway. It had all the accoutrements and blandness of shopping malls everywhere. A cynic might say that as malls are a ubiquitous commodity they're a barometer of the country's progress, and judging by the large crowds, bursting-to-full car parks and fancy bags full of stuff, things were improving here, at least for some.

After finding a table at Starbucks or a similarly branded coffee shop, Jaco introduced me to a young and dynamic manager from a large bookstore. They ordered coffees with names so long I struggled to understand them. To avoid a caffeine-based faux pas, I played safe and had a fruit juice instead.

The manager had a good reputation for understanding the local book market and using social media to promote the sale of books. He was just the person I needed to speak to, to understand how to write a book about Nongqawuse, King Hintsa and historical sites of interest in the Eastern Cape. But my bubble was burst almost immediately. When it came to books that sold well, he suggested that smut was popular. 'Smut!' I exclaimed indignantly to myself. He went on to explain that mummy porn was what kept his tills turning, not the history of a prophetess considered a failure and a liability by a whole nation. My disappointment was obvious to see. I explained candidly that I had read *Fifty Shades of Grey*, but I didn't feel qualified to write smut or mummy porn, nor did I want to. I wasn't finger-wagging and judging those who wanted to read smut, but it just wasn't quite my cup of tea. Moreover, I wondered what my wife would have said if I got home to declare I was abandoning travel and history writing for porn. (In fact, she'd no doubt have laughed a great deal and asked about the earning potential.)

By now, I was playing with the ice cubes at the bottom of my glass. It was time to leave, and we thanked him for providing an honest but sobering assessment. Besides, I'd had more than enough of polished floors, glitzy window displays and the excesses of 21st-century retail therapy.

While pulling out of the dark car park into the bright sunlight and the busy highway, Jaco and I chewed the cud and discussed the next day's agenda. Suddenly, I insisted that we do a U-turn at the traffic lights.

'Look – it's here!' I cried, 'We need to turn back!'

'What're you talking about? It's a busy road!'

'The Long March to Freedom Park – it's right opposite us,' I enthused, all mall-induced lethargy gone.

Sensing my urgency, Jaco relented without demanding further explanation, and we pirouetted nervously around the robots (traffic lights) and central reservation, dodging hasty trucks and suicidal taxi vans in the process, then came to a halt in a large anonymous car park sandwiched between several main roads. Nearby were the pristine edifices of Century City, and in the distance the omnipresent Table Mountain. Jaco looked confused. This was his town, and I was telling him where to go, and with no warning. I owed him an explanation, which I did while gathering my rucksack and hurriedly getting out of the car. I was a man on a mission.

At the Long March to Freedom Park I came face to face with dynamic statues of South Africa's indigenous leaders from the 17th to the 21st century.

'You know all those 18th- and 19th-century Khoisan and amaXhosa leaders I've been on about? Well, I'm about to introduce them to you. They're here, in statues of bronze. Come on – let's go!' I was just a scintilla short of being curt.

Unfortunately for Jaco, this sort of thing became the norm as we scooted around Cape Town for those five days. I kept him mesmerised (I fondly believe) with tales of Nongqawuse and Chiefs Hintsa, Maqoma and Sarhili, along with other 18th- and 19th-century Xhosa resistance leaders, and he seemed genuinely interested. Now, right here in front of us, was the Long March to Freedom Park, containing 100 or so bronze statues, icons of the liberation movement, from the 17th-century Khoisan leader Doman all the way to the 21st century, with the Mandelas, Sisulus and many others. I couldn't believe my luck. I'd heard about the park, but I'd been dubious about finding it.

The next thing I knew I was standing eye to eye with Oliver and Adelaide Tambo, dealing with my humility. Rapidly, my physical and emotional senses heightened, just as they had by the side of the Gxara River. It was one of those special moments life occasionally throws up, when you unexpectantly become strangely elevated and slightly dizzy. The glass pyramid at the entrance to the Louvre had triggered a similar emotion in me years earlier. Likewise, when I inadvertently found Caravaggio's enormous canvas of the beheading of Saint John the Baptist in Valletta Cathedral. I can't have been the only person disorientated by the spiritual intensity of the masterpiece and the sheer surprise of being confronted by it. Caravaggio asked questions of you, as did the Tambos now gazing at me.

The imposing statue of Chief Maqoma (1798–1873) at the Long March to Freedom Park. Maqoma was an outstanding Xhosa leader who offered stiff resistance to colonial expansion in the Eastern Cape during the 19th century.

Much as I admired Mr and Mrs Tambo for their commitment to the liberation struggle, I didn't have time to strike up a conversation, which is what they seemed to want. I insisted Jaco come with me as I rushed over the artificial grass to the far end of the park, some 70 metres away. This is where I thought we might meet the people of greater interest to me. We were soon joined by Walter Manganyi, a charming guide who seemed more than a touch curious about this bloke from out of town with a whirlwind of enthusiasm and a basic knowledge of Xhosa history. His day needed brightening up, and I was just the ticket.

My instincts had been right. Here, celebrated in dynamic bronze, were the icons I had come to find – and here was the man to fill me in on the many bits of their story I longed to know. To keep things interesting, I played a game. Instead of looking at the name plaques to identify the figures, I attempted to name them based on their features and persona. While Jaco was my audience, Walter was my judge; not only did he adjudicate on my identification of figures, he also corrected my flawed pronunciation of their names in isiXhosa. He was a tough taskmaster and an absolute stickler for correct pronunciation. Cs had to be expelled cleanly from my front teeth. My tongue had to click vigorously from the roof of my mouth to project the letter q, while x needed to be eloquently concocted from my cheeks. Rhythm, cadence and balance were taken into consideration, too. His linguistic stewardship was wonderful, and I revelled in the sounds of his corrective tuition.

'Here's Chief Sandile,' I declared confidently. 'His withered leg is the tell-tale sign.'

'Good – and what about this one?' said Walter.

'This must be Chief Maqoma, the warrior, brother of Sandile,' I replied, eager to please my teacher. Before pointing out my error, he corrected my pronunciation of Maqoma, and got me to repeat it. This time I had to accentuate the q into a rounder, louder consonant. It now sounded much more robust and confident, like the great chief himself.

'You're standing in front of Paramount Chief or King Hintsa. Chief Maqoma is over there.'

At the Long March to Freedom Park I came face to face with familiar names from the black liberation movement, including King Hintsa (1789–1835).

I stopped showing off and playing my facile 'who's who' game. It suddenly seemed inappropriate, perhaps a touch vulgar, for these two men of such fine standing in 19th-century Xhosa history to be the subject of my guessing game. Both Chief Maqoma and King Hintsa had done so much diplomatically and militarily to prevent the advance of European settlers from the Cape Colony into the land of the amaXhosa, in what is now the Eastern Cape. On occasion they had come within a whisker of defeating the British troops, aided by amaMfengu, Khoikhoi and Boer commandos. Chief Maqoma, in particular, had used the terrain – and British military dogma and incompetence – to inflict humiliating defeats. Several British military careers had been severely tarnished after brushes with Maqoma and his successors. This led to him being revered and feared by his enemy, the British, in the settler towns and army barracks.

In the end, both men were brutally crushed by the British machinery of Empire. As we have established, King Hintsa was shot, and his body mutilated, by Sir Harry Smith's men in 1835, and the news of his murder even unsettled the grey men in Whitehall. Chief Maqoma was grossly and unjustly humiliated in public, literally under the boots of Sir Harry Smith. British government ministers heard of this repulsive act, too. Repeated humiliation in front of his own people and failure to prevent the advancing European settlers drove Maqoma to the bottle allegedly, and ultimately to imprisonment on Robben Island to see out his final days.

So, in quieter and less exuberant fashion, I paid my respects to the two noble chiefs and carried on with my search. Would I find a statue to celebrate Nongqawuse and her contribution, failure though it was, to the liberation movement? She was not there – perhaps testimony to the way she is remembered as the harbinger of tragedy, even though she had acted, surely, in absolute faith and had been exploited by others in positions of power. When it came to amaXhosa prophets, I did find a statue of the legendary Makhanda Nxele, or 'the left-handed one' – Nxele for short. From a humble rural beginning, he rose all the way to the status of chief, and was regarded as both a prophet and a great military leader. His mixture of traditional beliefs, resistance and Christian teaching produced a heady cocktail of devotion and confidence that traversed hundreds of kilometres across the whole Cape region. At the height of his powers, in the Fifth Frontier War (1818–19) – just before mounting a fierce attack on the poorly protected settlement then known as Grahamstown, and now named Makhanda in his honour – he told his warriors that the British bullets would turn to water. Secure in this conviction of invincibility, Nxele's warriors charged headlong towards the colonial barricades and were mown down. And so a sure-fire victory turned into a disastrous defeat, and like Chief Maqoma, Nxele ended up on Robben Island. In 1820, while trying to escape, he drowned at Blouberg Beach – close, strangely enough, to where I stood in the park. For years, the amaXhosa believed that he would return and lead them in renewed battle against the encroaching Europeans. In fact, when Nongqawuse's prophecy began capturing imaginations 36 years later, many amaXhosa believed that it would be Nxele who would lead the returning ancestors to victory and the ultimate restoration of their freedom and independence.

I was quite mesmerised by now. It would not be an exaggeration to say that the Long March to Freedom Park had stirred my own imagination in ways that I could not quite account for. Walter and Jaco, noticing this, let me wander off on my own as I mentally introduced myself to many of the icons. Luis van Mauritius (1778–1830), a leader of various slave rebellions, caught my attention. He dressed dashingly as a pirate with a sword, gun, pistol, military jacket and large feather in his hat. Quite the swashbuckler.

Dingane, Cetshwayo and Shaka represented the Zulus. The Basothos were led by Chief Moshoeshoe, who had the distinction of seeing off the Zulus, the British and the Boers during his turbulent reign in the 1800s, by the judicious use of diplomacy, force and strategic thinking – no mean feat – and he went on to lay the foundations of modern-day Lesotho. I'd always held him in the very highest regard. As he prophetically told Governor Cathcart at negotiations in the 1850s, 'Peace is like rain that makes the grass grow, while war is the wind which dries it up.' Quite true.

The Long March statues are fluid, striding in full flow, gliding forcefully forward. Almost without exception these are not frozen statues, but people with a real purpose, people in a hurry with somewhere to go and things to do. With strong, upright backs they exude respect and integrity, but do not demand it. They look human, like us. Their hands are dynamic, too, either saluting or carrying something practical like a briefcase or a document. They have clients to see, world leaders to address. As they are only slightly larger than life size and rooted to the ground, I was able to make contact with them at eye level, leading to a strong sense of intimacy between myself and these liberation leaders. I'd read about Steve Biko; in fact, I remember hearing of his death on the television news back in 1977; led by Peter Gabriel and accompanied by several thousand other young people at Earl's Court in London, I had even sung about him. Now, I felt, I was shoulder to shoulder with the real man, in the here and now.

A large collection of bronze statues has the real potential to be cheesy or Disney-like, but here nothing could be further from the truth. I found it edifying and deeply moving. The collective kinetic force is way more than the sum of the parts. You have to ask yourself if these people came alive while we were all in deep slumber. They represent the unstoppable. I thought of the many great sacrifices they had made – the beatings, years of incarceration, family separations, career losses and deaths. They represent collective pain as well as celebration.

As I meandered deliberately up the park, mentally saluting these great people, I noticed Miriam Makeba, looking so full of life she might break out in a rendition of 'Pata Pata'. Since no one was listening, I broke out in song myself. Would her fellow liberation movement friend and diva Nina Simone be nearby? Unfortunately not. Perhaps the park is not big enough for two such huge personalities.

I nodded to Dr Martin Luther King, Mahatma Gandhi and Albert Luthuli, the ANC leader. I caught a glimpse of the diminutive South African MP, Helen Suzman, and Basil D'Oliveira, cricket bat in the air. Was that Julius Nyerere, former President of Tanzania, and Govan Mbeki, father of South Africa's second president? And Fidel Castro, too? Meanwhile, Robert Sobukwe, founder of the Pan Africanist Congress, and Chris Hani, leader of the armed wing of the ANC, seemed a little preoccupied, so I passed by.

It was a feast almost too rich to digest.

I was now standing in front of the Sisulus, the Tambos and Mandelas, celebratory and defiant as black liberation leaders, leading their distinguished cast on the Long March. I was humbled to the core. I had not expected to feel this way 20 minutes after leaving a ghastly shopping centre.

Walter and Jaco joined me. In an attempt to impress Walter, I repeated the names of the amaXhosa leaders, projecting the isiXhosa consonants as best I could. He said I was now quite good, but his eyes told a different story. There was still plenty of scope for improvement, so we smiled, acknowledging the progress I'd made. It was clearly 'work in progress'. I knew Jaco needed to get back to Cape Town, but I couldn't resist the opportunity to talk to Sarah Haines, the park's heritage director. Could I ask her 101 questions without incurring the annoyance of my wonderful host? I did not wait for his answer.

While eulogising about the park to Sarah, I mentioned that it seemed a little incongruous in its site just outside Cape Town, sandwiched between heavy traffic and Century City. I thought it should be a centrepiece, in a location commensurate with its stature and symbolism. Having seen the villages where Nelson Mandela had been born and grown up, and the Afrikaners' Voortrekker Monument, I thought the Long March to Freedom Park was of greater national significance, and ought to be a heritage site for all South Africans and tourists. She explained that the idea had come from Oliver Tambo's son Dali, who had visited his father's grave and came away wanting to honour his father for the many sacrifices he had made for the liberation movement. Later, he received a message from his father telling him, 'Don't honour me, honour them all.' This spawned the idea of a procession of statues to recognise their role in the struggle towards a fully democratic, liberated South Africa. The first display, of 20 statues in 2012, was in Bloemfontein, to celebrate the centenary of the African National Congress (ANC). Since then, the expanding phalanx has had to move around the country as various funding and political issues arise. Sarah was keen to find the 100 statues a permanent home, but that was proving tricky.

I expressed my disappointment at not seeing a statue of Nongqawuse; she was, after all, a liberator of sorts, certainly in intention. Surely, she deserved national recognition for her valiant attempts to remove the shackles of colonial rule and reinstate the independence of amaXhosa society? Were there any plans to introduce a statue of the prophetess? I wondered if I were stirring a hornet's nest, in light of how so many modern-day Xhosa people loathed and vilified Nongqawuse, making her almost solely responsible for the mass starvation, loss of life, cattle and land. Sarah deftly side-stepped the controversy, avoiding the politics of the teenage prophetess, pointing out that many different sections of the South African liberation movement were represented, including non-South Africans, such as Samora Machel of Mozambique. In particular, efforts were being made to better recognise the role that women had played. If I thought Nongqawuse deserved a statue, I'd first have to find about R500,000 or £25,000. That was more than loose change, and I promised to let her know if I won the lottery. I suspected that there might be one or two objections to my proposal. Anyway, that was a problem for another day.

With 'Pata Pata' still playing as an earworm, I thanked Walter and Sarah for their hospitality and saluted the fine men and women marching towards us. I was leaving their park a wiser and happier man. Also, I felt energised in my pilgrimage to find the grave of Nongqawuse. After meeting all these great people of the liberation movement, I was even more driven to pay my respects to the young prophetess at her place of rest. I was convinced that she had been the victim of circumstances and some very bad PR.

I could feel the pull of the Eastern Cape. It was time for my personal pilgrimage to truly begin.

7: 'TIME FOR A VAKASHA.' 'A WHAT?'

'Cattle are the race; they being dead, the race dies …'

Moni, Great Chief of the Bomvana

The 1,000-kilometre flight east from Cape Town to East London had spectacular views from the moment we took off. The geomorphology and Mother Nature painted vivid and uncompromising pictures whichever way I looked, and I was reminded of the time I'd flown over Namibia several years earlier. On that occasion I'd been mesmerised by the waves and valleys of rocks and red sand while listening to Radiohead's 'Bulletproof'. On this occasion all I had to accompany me was the white noise of Pratt and Whitney jet engines and fellow passengers in muted conversation.

With boyish enthusiasm I pressed my nose against the aircraft window until I left a sweaty oval signature on the glass. Now I could view the verdant Garden Route snaking up the coast in a narrow corridor between the sea and the sharp angular mountains to the north. A thin white line of surf hugged the seashore as the waves of the Indian Ocean fractured on the coast with powerful, metronomic frequency. Every now and again, gaping silvery river estuaries punctured the shoreline, the route of their sweet water meandering back into the interior and a source high in the mountains.

Hopping across the aircraft's central aisle to the vacant seats on the other side, I gazed at the panoramic view of the Little Karoo, landlocked by mountains and stepped escarpments. There was barely a birdbath of water in sight. It was visibly arid and flat, so static and dry, in marked contrast to the vast rhythmic ocean three aircraft seats to my right.

As we landed at King Phalo airport, I was disappointed to see that the pristine sun of Cape Town had been replaced by thick, low cloud. After collecting my luggage, I looked out expectantly over the car park for my host, but no one seemed to want me. Soon all my fellow passengers had dispersed, transported by loved ones and colleagues to homes and executive hotels. The temporary flutter of excitement after a plane's arrival soon dissipated in the balmy breeze. Now it was just me, a luggage porter and a couple of small birds squabbling over a fence post.

I used my time to reflect on King Phalo, whose name was written large on the utilitarian building. When he, the last chief of the united Xhosa people, had died in 1775, he could never have guessed he'd have an airport in East London named after him. For starters, East London did not exist in the 18th century. The city had mushroomed in size and importance since its establishment in the 19th century, a centre mainly intended to offer respite to the British army and new European settlers as they combated the climate, the terrain and the amaXhosa in and around Qonce (King William's Town) and the Transkei region to the east. I, for one, thought the king deserved the recognition, as the last monarch to rule a united people. After his demise, his jealous sons had permanently split the family into the Rharhabe and Gcaleka clans – and boy, was this to cause them major headaches in the following century. Successive waves of encroaching European administrators, armies and settlers found this division among the amaXhosa people useful, and exploited it during the 100-year Frontier Wars and at the negotiating table. Splits and divisions hardly ever strengthen anyone, and this was no exception.

As I concluded my reflections on the genealogy of the amaXhosa and on Phalo's status, my host – Dr Patrick Hutchison, or Hutch, as he preferred to be called – rushed over and greeted me warmly. It was a frenetic start to our relationship as he apologised for being late while pumping coins into a parking meter. We forfeited the ubiquitous formality of shaking hands or touching elbows, and I was only confident he was my correct host courtesy of a poor image of him on Google Images. I had also gleaned that he was an eminent doctor in the area, focusing on general practice. He was in his late fifties or early sixties, full of youthful enthusiasm, and breaking into a beaming grin from time to time.

We had never met before, but we hit it off from the moment the first coin hit the metal bottom of the parking meter. Our mutual interest in Nongqawuse and amaXhosa history in the Eastern Cape was an immediate and invisible bond. He asked me what my priorities were, but it was soon evident that he had organised everything already; an itinerary was drawn up and a vakasha had been prepared. I should say vakashas had been prepared – that is, not one but two – and I did not even know what a vakasha was. Hutch explained gleefully that this was the isiXhosa word for an expedition or adventure into the bush. I'd thought I was on a pilgrimage, not a vakasha, but I'm all for an adventurous pilgrimage. Along with other Border Historical Society enthusiasts, Hutch had arranged to take me to the important historical sites I had asked to visit – but, as he explained, they would likely as not involve plenty of adventure en route, since the sites might not be easy to find. How true that prediction turned out to be! He'd got everything organised – all I needed to do was pay for the petrol. We had a deal.

All being well, we were going to find the graves of Nongqawuse and King Hintsa, the memorial to the Cattle Killing and other historical titbits. I felt like a youth on a blind date.

It was still dark when we loaded up Hutch's Toyota Hilux the following morning, his two dogs scampering about excitedly and his wife, Julie, calmly managing our loading

Map 3. Vakasha No. 1, February 2022: Finding the grave of Nongqawuse and the Cattle Killing Memorial.

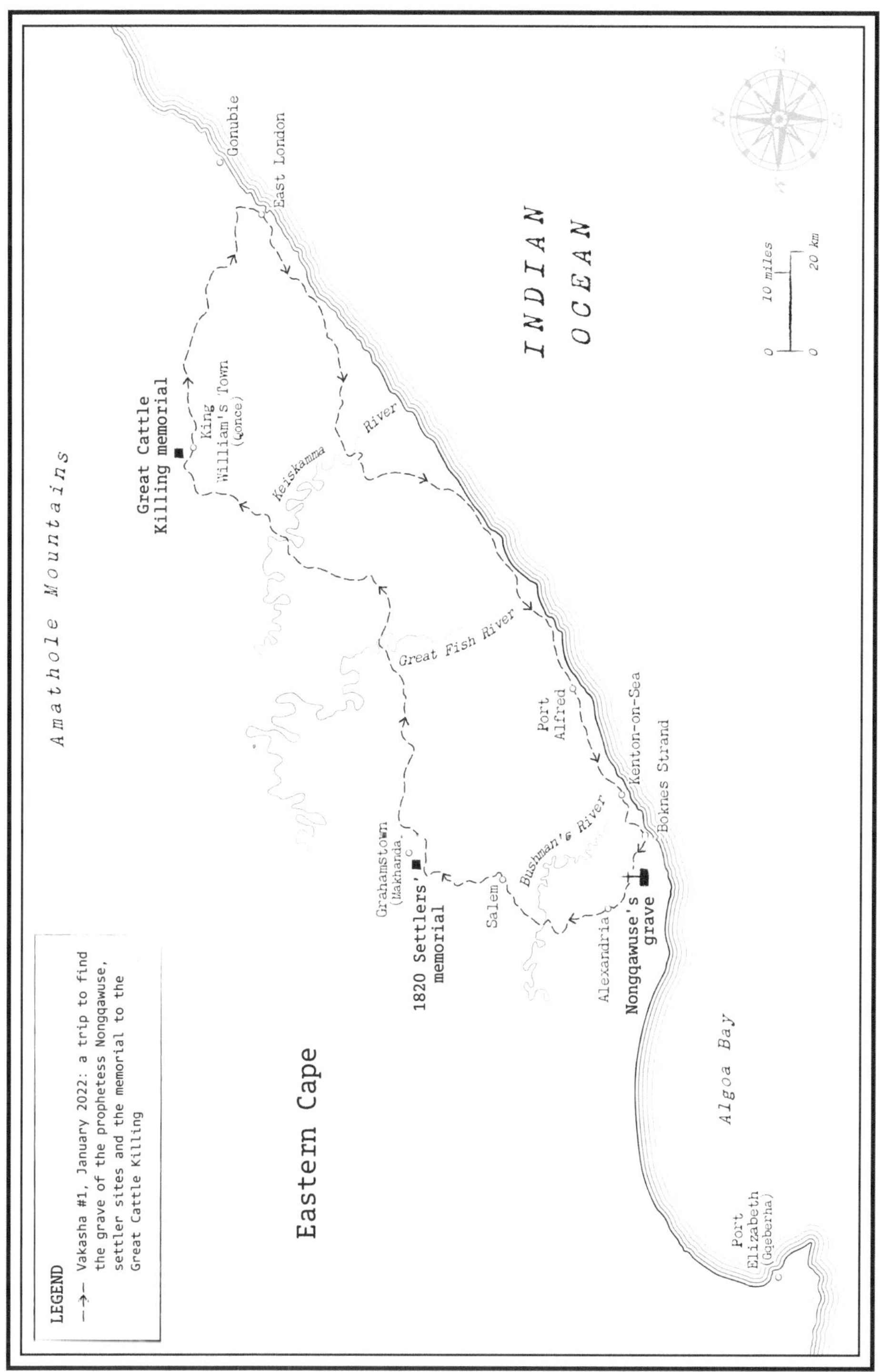

up and leaving. I was still a little bleary-eyed as I directed Hutch out of the garage. Into the melée arrived Mike Kenyon, a keen local historian and another member of the Border Historical Society. He was joining us for the day, which was useful as he actually knew where we had to go.

Mike had a touch of Che Guevara about him, a sort of ageing hippy, with greying shoulder-length hair, a goatee, casual T-shirt and shorts. His face was well lived in. He was tall and slim, and his manner laid back, in contrast to Hutch and me who were shorter, and both overly enthusiastic.

As we pulled out of the drive at about 6.30 am, I began to feel like a character in Jerome K. Jerome's novel, *Three Men In a Boat (To Say Nothing of the Dog)*. We weren't gliding down the Thames, and we did not have a canine companion, but during our 442 km, 11½-hour trip travelling together in sunshine, bucketing rain and swirling mist, we were to experience many of the laughs and tensions experienced by Harris, George and Jerome in the book.

East London was awake and stretching its limbs as we headed across town. Swarms of impatient white kombi taxis vied with each other like competing male antelope. They challenged the traffic lights, treating the red, amber and green as advisory, not mandatory. Impatient workers, huddled in small groups on the roadsides, jostled and raised arms to flag the kombis down, even though all vehicles looked at or near capacity. Dust and heavy exhaust fumes softened the light, but not the sound of aggressive revving engines.

Before escaping our urban orbit to reach the countryside, we passed the imposing Mercedes-Benz factory on the west side of town, the core to the local economy and an icon of civic pride. But I didn't have time to dwell on this 21st-century symbol of global commerce, as only minutes later we passed close by Gompo (Cove Rock), the site of one of Makhanda Nxele's last prophetic acts. The area sparked a great discussion among Hutch, Mike and me. Before he was taken away to Robben Island as a prisoner of the British, Nxele had prophesied that the ancestors would return to save the amaXhosa from European encroachment and violence. That was 1819 – some 21 years before Nongqawuse was born. In fact, he had been propagating similar ideas to the prophetess for some years, and, had fervently disseminated similar messages to his many admirers. It was becoming clear to me that much of what Nongqawuse promoted in 1856–57 was not new at all. After Nxele's death, very similar messages based on cattle killing and the subsequent resurrection of the ancestors were communicated by Mlanjeni the Riverman. Thus, the idea was already part of the zeitgeist when Nongqawuse had her visions. Resurrection, in particular, had been learned and embraced by the amaXhosa from the Christian teachings of missionaries and church leaders. Various prophets, picking up the theme, were already generating enthusiastic millenarian movements early in the 19th century, all of them featuring the triumph of the amaXhosa, with the help of their ancestors, over the British.

At Gompo (Cove Rock), in front of spectators, Nxele had promised to summon the ancestors out of the sea in order to drive the Europeans off traditional amaXhosa land. In addition, he said he would jump some distance from one large boulder to another, while the threatening sea swirled 80 feet below. It was to be a visible display of his powers in front of his admirers, whose longing to repel the British was so deep-seated that belief, and indeed absolute conviction, came easily. They even held a feast to celebrate the anticipated event. His stunt never took place, and soon afterwards he was captured by the British and died while trying to escape Robben Island. Nevertheless, his reputation remained untarnished. He had laid a foundation of hope and belief which Nongqawuse's vision simply echoed.

We passed Gompo (Cove Rock) without stopping, heading for Alexandria, near Gqeberha (Port Elizabeth), site of Nongqawuse's grave. The plan was to take in as many other historical sites as we could, including the Cattle Killing Memorial in Qonce (King William's Town), erected on the very site where hundreds of people had been buried after starving to death. Actually, the countryside we were traversing on the R72 was itself a memorial to the rich and tumultuous history of this area, so violently fought over by the Dutch, the British, the Khoisan and the amaXhosa from the late 18th century and through most of the following one. As we barrelled along with the Indian Ocean to our left and the undulating hills dotted with huts and small rectangular homes to our right, I felt history rising up to meet us.

***

Distilled to its simplest, the history of the amaXhosa was one of pastoralism and slow expansion south and west as they followed the grazing needs of their cattle, cultivating sorghum and maize, and organising their lives around local chiefs and a vibrant spiritual tradition. The verdant lands they occupied were rich and fertile – and, from the 17th century onwards, were highly desired by the Dutch and the British, who arrived first in Cape Town but soon moved east and northward. Clashes were inevitable, given the rapacious ambitions of the settlers.

For the most part, the amaXhosa people were physically strong and healthy. For centuries, they had held their own against the challenges of climate, disease and competing indigenous tribes such as the Khoisan and the Zulus. In the end, however, they were no match for the British, despite putting up a vigorous defence that lasted 100 years: the Frontier Wars. The Dutch, the British and other miscellaneous Europeans were covetous, arrogant and violent in their quest to take what they could – land, livestock and independence. At the instructions of successive Cape governors, civic leaders and army generals, the settlers were on a mission to destroy everything in the amaXhosa way of life that did not conform to European and Christian norms. The amaXhosa and all other indigenous people, such as the Khoisan, were to be controlled and harnessed for the benefit of Empire – global expansion, foreign revenue, evangelical brownie points and the like. To achieve this, the invaders were willing to use mass starvation, scorched-earth tactics, the latest ballistics and munitions, the Bible, duplicity, murder, humiliation, alcohol, deceit, hanging, deportation, enforced labour, imprisonment and social engineering. This list is only indicative, not exhaustive. A fuller list is depressingly long and even more disgraceful.

At times, when the British wanted to establish a firm boundary between the settlers and the amaXhosa, they designated rivers as barriers. We crossed the Keiskamma River and the Great Fish River, which had at one time marked the two boundaries of an area known as the Ceded Territory. It was thought that having this buffer zone between the settlers and amaXhosa would keep the peace; but, like most boundary pronouncements, it failed. Several treaties imposed by remote Cape governors and even more remote ministers of state in Whitehall were signed, established and then overturned, as new personalities, each with their own ambitions and insecurities, occupied the political hot seat. Seldom were treaties adhered to as colonial aspirations and pressures grew in the west and as anger and resentment fermented among the amaXhosa in the east. Frontier boundaries shifted between the Eastern Cape's major rivers in a staccato fashion west to east, east to west, but ultimately the shift was eastward, as the amaXhosa were driven further off their land and away from the settlers.

After each of the nine Frontier Wars, the amaXhosa population was compressed into an ever smaller territory. As they moved eastwards, traditional practices came under pressure, especially after the imposition of the notorious 'hut tax', variously paid in the form of money, grain, labour or stock. Their invaded land was parcelled up into unfamiliar squares and rectangles for new arrivals from Europe seeking to better themselves overseas. They brought with them sheep, new cattle breeds and a money-based economy. Property ownership began to usurp communal ownership. Emboldened Christians, particularly the zealous Wesleyans and Methodists, were often at the front of the finger-wagging queue, before shamelessly taking their slice of the pie.

The river boundaries set up by successive administrations merely delayed the macabre takeover. Today, they serve as physical reminders of yesterday's failures and countless lost opportunities.

***

In the Toyota Hilux our conversation shifted from a swapping of historical titbits to why I was so interested in Nongqawuse and how we were going to find her grave. On this and subsequent trips with Hutch and Mike, I was to learn that sites I considered of great historical and cultural significance in the Eastern Cape frequently lacked road signs of any meaningful kind. I had assumed that the new South Africa would celebrate its black history and promote some of the key figures from the struggle in the 19th century, such as the prophetess. Finding these sites, however, proved a labour of love, with a generous sprinkling of tenacity and eccentricity. Eccentricity, in fact, turned out to be a valuable asset on my pilgrimage.

We must have been getting closer to our destination, as under Mike's firm instruction Hutch suddenly took a sharp turn north off the coastal road and onto a dirt track that spewed out a trail of animated grey dust behind us. Casual chitchat ebbed as we concentrated on the task at hand. Mike had visited the site of Nongqawuse's grave before, so he was our navigator, eschewing the use of maps and GPS in favour of landmarks such as hills and trees. My excitement rose as we hurtled along the track with all the determination of a male moth tracking an invisible pheromone plume. Undulating grassy meadows surrounded us, with dense bush clinging to the gentle slopes of adjacent hills. Mike and Hutch kept up monosyllabic conversations to do with directions as I focused on the fields, hoping to see the grave or any other similar indicator just around the next bend.

My heart rate elevated with excitement, knowing I was close to consummating my pilgrimage. 'Not far now,' I kept saying to myself. 'Keep your eyes peeled!' I was glad to be making the trip in the company of my new companions. Alone, using creased maps and ropey GPS, I would have been lost and floundering by now, just as I was two years earlier, further north, when seeking the site of Nongqawuse's visions.

'There it is!' yelled Mike. 'I think that's the field – and there's the clump of trees.'

'You sure, Mike?' said Hutch.

'Yes! Look, there's the farm, down the slope. We'll need to get the owner's permission before visiting the grave, though.' He pointed down the gentle grassy slope at a large bungalow surrounded by outbuildings and trees. A blanket of low heavy clouds framed the agricultural pastures.

Mike's pheromone trail had worked.

We reached two rough yellow car number plates mounted on steel posts that were embossed in black lettering with 'Fick' and 'Glenshaw'. The farm was silent. I gazed up at a massive spreading milkwood tree. She had the appearance of an ancient flat mushroom, with near-perfect symmetry. Her modest and unassuming countenance belied the fact that she may well have seen her fair share of drama in this contentious landscape. She was clearly older than I, and would be here long after the worms had returned my own body to humus. She (I could not help viewing this stately, graceful being as a she) seemed an arboreal guardian, watching over the landscape where Nongqawuse had taken sanctuary here back in the late 1800s. Did she watch as the prophetess had been laid to rest in the adjacent field? I wondered what secrets were locked in her xylem and phloem.

As we milled about near the modern brick bungalow wondering how we might get someone's attention, the homeowner emerged – a stout Afrikaans man with a full head of silver hair, metal-rimmed glasses and sturdy limbs, dressed in the ubiquitous shorts and short-sleeved shirt, crocs on his feet. His name was Stephen Fick. Mike and Hutch greeted him in Afrikaans, but he soon switched to English to save their linguistic embarrassment. To lighten the mood, he joked that his first language had been isiXhosa, then Afrikaans and lastly English. In an understated way, he made an immediate impression. Before meeting him, I'd formed an unflattering stereotypical image of the Afrikaans farmer, brawn taking priority over brains. That prejudice was swiftly knocked into the long grass as it became apparent that Stephen had a sharp and dextrous mind, way superior to mine. He was delighted to hear that we wanted to see Nongqawuse's grave, seemingly taking immense pride in having her resting place on his land. His family, the Ficks, had lived here for generations. I got the impression that he lived quite an isolated existence and was pleased to have half-intelligent history enthusiasts to exchange ideas with. I didn't hesitate to tell him I'd flown some 13,000 kilometres to pay my respects to the prophetess.

Stephen Fick at Glen Shaw Farm was a proud custodian of the grave of Nongqawuse and her daughters.

With a little prompting from Mike and Hutch, he explained that his ancestors had arrived in 1698 or 1701 from Germany, and although they had farmed in and around Alexandria for generations, the 21st-century Ficks were focused on other careers. He, for example, was a chemical engineer, now running a consultancy. Inside his office there was a range of large computer screens displaying brightly coloured figures, a laptop, a modem, loose digital cables, multiple plug sockets, lever arch files, a physics book, a vice, a sleeping dog in a basket, a toolbox and a laminated sign saying 'Chemical engineers make it happen'. It looked like a digital nerve centre or an operational hub. This hi-tech backdrop juxtaposed our conversation about the plight of the amaXhosa in the 19th century and his family's personal engagement with Nongqawuse.

Stephen told us that after the Cattle Killing in the 1850s, many starving amaXhosa had fled their homes east and west of the Kei River, desperate for food. Nervous, weak and almost at the point of death, some had hidden in the vegetation around his great-

great-grandfather's farm, close to Alexandria. In response, the Ficks had cooked mielie meal[1] in big black pots, which they left outside near the hiding fugitives. When the farmers returned in the mornings, the pots were always empty. As a sign of respect and thanks, the local amaXhosa called the Ficks the Phekinkobe family, which translates into 'they cook mielies'. Stephen was clearly proud of his ancestors' compassion and the fact that the family had been given an isiXhosa name.

We lapped up his stories, plying him with questions and comments. As *de facto* guardian of Nongqawuse's grave, he knew a great deal of her personal history after the tragic events of 1856–57. After her failed prophecies she lived and worked on a farm owned by the Smith family west of Alexandria, in an area called the Kaba. She married and had a couple of daughters, living until her late fifties. I found this fascinating. After such a turbulent youth, rupturing a whole nation, reshaping the politics of the British Empire in this corner of the world, and in effect changing the history of the amaXhosa people, she went on to live a pedestrian adult life. One year she was the spiritual head of the amaXhosa, combating European encroachment with her uncompromising bovine-based visions; the next she was pottering around a colonial farm, doing menial tasks and raising a family. As she went about her domestic chores on the Smith's farm, did she reflect on her prophecies and their devasting impact on her followers near and far? I wondered if she had regrets. She must have believed her own message with the same fervour as her followers, and I wondered how she had felt when the devastating consequences began to manifest. Perhaps she felt the whole thing had got out of hand long before the devastation began. I wondered, too, if the Believers, the *amathamba*, had simply taken over her message, spreading and perhaps embellishing it in their enthusiasm to see decades-long hopes and prophecies fulfilled.

I suspect that Nongqawuse had, as we say in 21st century media parlance, 'moved on', the whole thing being too big and too painful to dwell upon. I remembered, too, that even today there are Xhosa people who believed the whole thing had failed because of the Unbelievers, the *amagogotya*. It is highly possible that Nongqawuse felt the same way. She may well have held onto a conviction that if only *everyone* had slaughtered the cattle and destroyed their crops they would now be living as free people, surrounded by plenty of healthy cattle and enjoying the company of their ancestors.

At this point Stephen produced a leaflet with the sub-title 'The Story of the Life of Xhosa Prophetess Nongqause: the suicide of the amaXhosa 1856–1857' with a photograph of the prophetess on the front page. This was not the first time the word 'suicide' had cropped up in relation to these events. I never liked that description. It was too blunt a word for such complicated and nuanced events – or was I just being an apologist for the disaster? The leaflet explained how, after the failure of her

1 maize porridge

prophecies, the young woman had been arrested by a farmer in the Cathcart district, many miles north from her home village at the Gxara River. Probably in Bomvanaland. When brought for questioning before Colonel John Maclean, the Commissioner of British Kaffraria (as that part of the Eastern Cape was then known) she apparently held fast to the vision, but blamed its spread on her uncle, Mhlakaza. It was he, she said, who had insisted on the veracity of the visions and propagated its widespread acceptance. As adviser to King Sarhili, the most senior amaXhosa chief, Mhlakaza held a position of extraordinary influence, and the idea is highly plausible. I pondered the idea: might coercion from her uncle have been a major factor – or might she in fact have been manipulated by the British administrator to implicate senior figures in amaXhosa society to press home the advantage of the British? Who would have been the manipulator here – her uncle, Mhlakaza or the British? Or both? Nothing to do with the Cattle Killing ever seemed straightforward. For every so-called fact or assumption there was an alternative explanation. True or not, the idea was an interesting addition to the jigsaw I was trying, but failing, to complete. For her own safety Nongqawuse was then sent to the infamous Robben Island off Cape Town. When released, she allegedly avoided her home district, where she was unwelcome, preferring to settle in the Alexandria district with the Smiths.

I'd read somewhere during my earlier research that she'd even changed her name to – of all things – Victoria Regina. What an irony.

Stephen had an enraptured audience, and so he went on to explain how a number of angry amaXhosa men had travelled a long distance to find Nongqawuse on the Smiths' farm, where she was working in domestic service. They had been aggressive and angry, and eager to punish the prophetess who had been responsible, as they saw it, for the mass starvation and disintegration of amaXhosa society. All caused by her colossal lies and deception. They wanted their revenge, their pound of flesh. With the appearance of the intruders at the farm gates, the Smiths hid the terrified young woman deep in a laundry basket and invited their unwanted guests to inspect the premises. She was not found amongst the dirty socks and trousers, but as a precaution she then went off to Gqeberha (Port Elizabeth) for a short while before returning to the farm to see out her days.

Our host had a great deal more to share with us, and invited us for tea or a beer. His warmth was touching, but we explained our packed itinerary and politely declined, eager to visit Nongqawuse's grave. As we took our leave, I noticed a blue visitors' book with handwritten entries dating back to 1963. What most surprised me was how few visitors there had been.

From the farm, Stephen pointed out a cluster of trees about a kilometre away, up a slope of undulating grassland, where the tops of the hills were capped with forest.

Vakasha No 1. The coppice near Alexandria where Nongqawuse and her daughters are buried.
I felt that my pilgrimage was making good progress.

Kilometres of wire fencing partitioned the vast landscape into a geometric patchwork. Stephen accompanied us up the dirt track to the field and tried to unlock a steel tube gate, but it would not open. So Mike, Hutch and I crawled underneath it, commando style, literally coming face to face with the red-tinged soil. At this point we thanked Stephen, and he returned to Glenshaw Farm.

I had arrived at the prophetess's modest grave to pay my respects.

The atmosphere changed slightly. Instead of being naughty schoolboys sneaking under a gate, our noses pressed into the grit, we were now visitors paying our respects to a significant figure in amaXhosa history. Our tone and volume reflected the gravitas of the moment. Hutch and Mike, knowing how important this was for me, insisted I approach the grave first. I was quietly grateful for their sensitivity as I walked slowly down the grassy incline to the low bushes and tall trees that marked the resting place of the young woman I had come to meet.

My four-year journey to find the prophetess was being fulfilled, and so with an unfamiliar mixture of anxiety and excitement I gingerly skirted the bushes protecting the oval wooded site. I attempted to temper my enthusiasm by reflecting on the significance of the moment. At the far side of the coppice, I came face to face with her headstone. I'd arrived.

The plain triangular slab of sandy-coloured rock reached the top of my leg. Coarse grass grew around the base, and persistent branches irritated the top. It was leaning slightly, so it was obvious that cattle roamed around at times. The location and the tombstone could hardly have been more modest, blending in almost perfectly with the land that had been fought over so many times in the 19th century.

A square metal plaque of brown and copper green, with the images of horned cattle in the top corners, was screwed into the headstone. It read:

GRAVE OF NONGQAUSE

THE XOSA PROPHETESS

WHO LIVED IN THIS VICINITY

AFTER THE CATTLE KILLING IN

1858

UNTIL AFTER HER DEATH IN 1898

ERECTED BY C.L. DEACON T.B. BOWKER I. MITFORD-BARBERTON 1963

My first inclination was to take photographs to capture this unique moment. But it felt trivial and vacuous, a hideous instinct – the kind of thing one might do at theme park. Yet an essential component of travel, even a pilgrimage, I guess. In the end, I bowed to convention and pulled out my cameras, consigning this precious memory to digital code. However, I was not on my personal journey in order to have a vicarious experience through the lens. Cameras were returned to their cases and placed a few metres away from the grave. It felt better to be devoid of the mechanical intruders.

Even though my companions and I hardly knew each other, they were wonderful, sensing that this was an emotionally laden moment for me. Standing graveside overlooking vast swathes of the Eastern Cape, we then intellectually shadow-boxed, vigorously discussing the events that Nongqawuse had precipitated and the devastation she had caused. More theories came to light. Many South Africans thought, as Simon Mqamelo had done, that the monumental tragedy had been caused by the devious governor, Sir George Grey, who had actually disguised himself as an ancestor – or had deputed others to do so – and then appeared in the reeds across the pond to convince Nongqawuse to spread the rumour of the great sacrifice required. On a misty day, and in the highly evocative setting of water, reeds and rocky outcrops, the subterfuge might have worked. Was it a plausible idea, an elaborate plot to break the back of the amaXhosa nation after umpteen Frontier Wars? I did not know.

On the other hand, had the desperate amaXhosa chiefs promoted the prophetess's vision as a vehicle to stir up their people to rise up and start another war against their enemies – the British, the amaMfengu and the Boers? The shorthand for this theory was the Chiefs' Plot.

Alternatively, the ordinary amaXhosa people of the 1850s may simply have been eager to usher in the promises that had long circulated as a result of prophecies about resurrection of the dead by the great Makhanda Nxele and Mlanjeni earlier in the century. Other strands of history played into this, too. The murder of King Hintsa at the hands of Sir Harry Smith in 1835 had sown especially deep seeds of anger and resentment among the amaXhosa, who may have been spoiling for a cataclysmic solution after decades of war, land loss and the humiliating murder of their king. Hintsa's death had also created an unplanned leadership change, causing cultural fracturing and societal disruption – fertile ground for extreme ideas like the Cattle Killing to germinate and spread. Would King Hintsa have been a wiser leader, able to exercise greater control than his traumatised son, Sarhili? Might Hintsa even have been able to prevent the spread of the madness and killing fervour? I thought he would have. If only we knew.

We could have been in a university tutorial, grappling with these ideas, acknowledging that the full truth of what had happened was unlikely ever to emerge. But we weren't in a lecture room being directed by a know-all academic; we were at the graveside of one of the principal players in indigenous South African history. This made the situation a great deal more edgy, more poignant. While it was entertaining to ask these searching questions, it was equally frustrating not to have real answers or even a consensus. If only Nongqawuse could talk to us from the grave! Could she resurrect herself either figuratively or literally? After all, she had prophesied the return of dead ancestors many times. Of course not. Our questions and conjecture were left hanging in the gentle morning breeze of the Eastern Cape.

Sensing I wanted another private moment at the site, Hutch and Mike walked back to the car, leaving me to a conversation I needed to have with the woman who had occupied my thoughts for the better part of two years. Now it was just her, me, the trees and a broad horizon. I felt a little awkward, not wanting to come across as an overzealous member of a fan club. Mentally, I reined myself in and steadied my breathing, but I addressed her nonetheless. It felt stupid, but I wanted to talk to her. So I did, only for a minute, nothing too much. I told her how I admired her efforts to resist the settlers and the European takeover at a time of extreme difficulty for the amaXhosa. At least she had tried to do something when most people had thrown up their hands in despair. I told her I had visited the site of her visions at the Gxara River. I started to mention the possible role of Sir George Grey and Mhlakaza in the drama that unfolded ... but then I stopped myself going too far. I was not here to interrogate

– I was here to pay my respects. She had been through enough. I said my goodbyes. It was time for us to part.

I had arrived expecting some sort of consummation or closure, and with the (in retrospect) ridiculous notion of finding answers to my questions. On that score I'd failed dismally. If anything, I had more questions. But it was comforting to know she had lived out a normal life with a family, and that she had escaped a lynch mob. All told, I was glad we'd had our – one-way? – conversation.

After collecting my photographic equipment, I had one last glance at the headstone, then I brushed past the dense bushes and headed up the open ground to join my companions. Mentally and emotionally I was still with the prophetess. This mystery had gripped me deeply. So I needed to shift gears to face the next leg of our vakasha – to Qonce (King William's Town) and the Cattle Killing Memorial.

8: THE INCREDIBLE TALE OF RICHARD GUSH AND THE AMAXHOSA WARRIORS

'The snake and the frog.'

'Inyoka ne-sele'

Xhosa metaphor: Rev. J.H. Soga, *The Ama-Xosa. Life and Customs*, 1931

My memory of the next leg of the journey is a blur of impenetrable scrub and grassland, ubiquitous clouds of dust, and shallow valleys merging into open veld. I was still too preoccupied with the events of the morning to engage much in chatting, but I caught snatches of Hutch and Mike's conversation about the British 1820 settlers who had emigrated to this area of the Cape, then known as Albany or the Zuurveld by the colonialists.

An hour later I was jolted from my daydreaming. It was nearly midday when the Toyota Hilux pulled up in a patch of what looked like rural England. In front of us lay a large oval cricket pitch. Heaps of lush clippings on the outfield and square suggested it was being lovingly attended to. There was even a heavy roller ready to chunter up and down the batting strip. Beyond the boundary were a couple of pavilions and a manual scoreboard, all framed by bushes and trees shaped like turrets.

Equally incongruous was the imposing 19th-century white church overlooking the cricket pitch. It seemed to be surveying the landscape, keeping a knowing eye on the goings-on. Framed by tall slim trees and a low white wall, the church conveyed solidity and permanence. Methodist or Anglican, I assumed, from my knowledge of such places, which had been formed mostly from the outside. Buildings like this featured large in my heritage, as I had believing ancestors, some of whom led rural congregations back in west Cornwall, near Land's End.

My companions were very animated, keen to show me around. We were in the village of Salem, one of the settlements of the 5,000 or so British settlers who had arrived in droves around 1820. 'Right … uh … I thought we were looking for Nongqawuse?' I mumbled to myself.

For the most part, our conversations that morning had been amaXhosa-centric, focusing on their history and culture, and the pressures imposed on them by 18th- and 19th-century Europeans expanding eastwards from the Cape. We had thrived on our different perspectives on amaXhosa history, discussing the roles of key figures such as chiefs Phalo, Hintsa, Maqoma, Ngqika, Ndlambe, Siyolo, Xhoxho, Sarhili, Sandile and

Salem looked tranquil, a far cry from the traumas of the War of Hintsa
(Sixth Frontier War, 1834–36).

Mhala, not to mention the prophets Nxele, Ntsikana and Mlanjeni. Cattle, communal land ownership, witchcraft, polygamy and battle tactics had all figured, too.

But here, at Salem, the talk changed. We spent an hour or so discussing the European immigrants to the Cape. As both Mike and Hutch could trace their ancestors back to the 1820 settlers, the subject took on a much more personal feel. Many of the themes we discussed around European colonisation were represented in some tangible form or another in the very place we stood, along with the adjacent graveyard. Searching questions arose – including why so many people would travel so far, on such a treacherous sea journey, to a place they knew almost nothing about save what they'd read in a few column inches of the newspapers. Why had the amaXhosa and these hopeful, intrepid settlers been literally thrust together in what was already a cauldron of conflict long before the settlers arrived? Salem, and the surrounding area, represented tectonic plates of cultural tension, with two proud and confident people butting up, grating, against each other.

***

Early 19th-century Britain saw the emergence of the Pax Britannica, with a growing population and high unemployment. Huge social and political upheavals had touched every county in the British Isles, including Ireland. The industrial revolution was getting up a full head of steam, literally and figuratively. Hungry new machines replaced the hungry men, women and children in factory towns up and down the country. To find what little work there was, families had to move from their own villages to the rapidly expanding towns and cities, where the air was often thick with smoke and the living conditions grim. Adam Smith, Edmund Burke and Tom Paine provided the era with its unshakeable philosophical energy and direction. Earlier, the Lunar Society and the paintings of Joseph Wright of Derby had illustrated the emerging – and exciting – new world of science, engineering and commerce – whose dark consequences were to be laid bare by Dickens and Social Darwinism towards the end of the century.

With the end of the Napoleonic Wars after 1815, many military men were surplus to requirements, while the land clearances in the Highlands of Scotland and the north of England left some of the most vulnerable homeless. Landowners prioritised land improvement – ie livestock and game and the consequent profits – over their tenants' welfare. In 1819, in the industrial heartland near Manchester, 11 people were killed and hundreds injured by charging cavalry when thousands of unarmed people met peacefully at Peterloo to protest their atrocious social and economic conditions. In addition, poor harvests and the Corn Laws added further misery to those at the sharp end of the social upheaval. At times the national atmosphere was oppressive.

It was into these unsettling and unpredictable times – accentuated by the wave of revolutions in Europe – that Earl Bathurst, the UK Secretary of State for War and the Colonies, suggested that selected British and Irish citizens be invited to settle in the Eastern Cape, where they could help alleviate several challenges faced by the Cape governor, Lord Charles Somerset. Unsurprisingly, he was enthusiastic too. First, new settlers would form a barrier between the Cape and the amaXhosa. There had already been five Frontier Wars; the last of them (the War of Nxele) had been from 1818 to 1819, and its embers, which might ignite another, were never far off. Besides, the conflicts were getting worse, longer and more intense, for both sides. John Cradock, governor to the Cape a few years earlier, conveyed both the ruthlessness of the various conflicts and the sentiments typical of British leaders of that time in a letter to Lord Liverpool, the British prime minister:

> I'm very happy to add that in the course of the service [i.e. the fighting] there has not been shed more Kaffir [amaXhosa] blood than necessary to impress on the mind of these savages the proper degree of terror and respect.

This was the first priority in bringing a new batch of settlers over – they would help to stabilise the area and keep the indigenous people at bay. Keeping a good distance between Europeans and the indigenous people was seen as essential to stabilising the frontier, particularly in the areas around the Zuurveld, the Fish River and the

Keiskamma River. This, of course, was not explained to the prospective settlers when they signed up.

Second, the settlers would help reinforce the local commandos and militia as and when conflict arose. Whether they liked it or not, they would have to help defend their communities – and, when necessary, attack. It was estimated that the amaXhosa in the region could muster 7,000–10,000 warriors if they needed to. As the British government saw it, the UK taxpayer should not foot the entire bill for the defence of the Cape. The settlers should handle much of it themselves. Hence, send more settlers over.

Third, the presence of a fresh contingency of British settlers would water down the influence of Dutch settlers, or Boers (also known as Afrikaners), who at the time exceeded the number of British in the country. The British naturally wanted their own values and administrative processes to prevail, and needed subjects loyal to the Crown and the Cape.

What was not foreseen were the consequences. Many disgruntled Afrikaners were to leave the Cape area in their thousands, heading north and east. Under new leadership, this huge train of disgruntled Boers became known as Voortrekkers. Their many hardships forged them into a distinct and resistant Afrikaans culture that was to have huge ramifications in 20th-century South African society.

Fourth, new British settlers would offer economic benefits by cultivating the land to grow produce suitable both for export and for supporting the Cape population. For the British treasury, a global Empire was proving expensive. So the Cape, after draining the coffers in London for decades, had to start paying its way and standing on its own two feet.

I have been unable to find any record of a discussion or agreement with the amaXhosa on the idea of importing 5,000 or so British and Irish settlers onto amaXhosa land. This is unsurprising; I think I know how such a plan would have been received by King Hintsa and his councillors. As Mike pointed out with a wry smile and acidic tone of voice, there was a great degree of irony in the proposed settler plan. In short, the displaced and land-impoverished amaXhosa of the Eastern Cape were being replaced by displaced and land-impoverished British and Irish souls. Both, he pointed out, had been brought to this state of desperation by the British establishment.

However, in the corridors of Westminster these proposals were well received. Parliament, led by Lord Liverpool, readily agreed to a budget of £50,000, and shortly after the offer of a 'new start' in the Cape had been advertised, the scheme was oversubscribed 20 times. Ships with the 1820 settlers started to leave in late 1819, when the Thames was frozen solid and strong winds immediately hindered progress. One ship even ended up marooned on a sand bar just offshore before a large wave sent it on its way. Over the months of 1820, the *Garland*, *Belle Alliance*, *Zoroaster* and further ships left the British Isles, packed to the gunnels with hopeful British families such as the Septhons, Trollips and Bowkers, off to make a new start in unknown territory. Spiritual leadership came from the likes of the Reverends William Shaw and John Ayliff. Passengers from all walks of life and strata of society were thrown together in crowded conditions, struggling to find their sea legs for the three-month journey to the Cape. On some ships tensions ran high, leading to fights among the passengers and with the crew. While some emigrants were excited and eager for new beginnings, many were in fact nervous, for themselves and their family. It was unlikely they would ever again see their relatives left behind. The unknown lands of the Cape were simply way beyond their comprehension, so remote from a rural Irish village, Scottish glen or English city. Thoughts of prowling lions and tigers were said to have brought some to tears. Others were upbeat, dreaming of a fresh start, a land with broad horizons and limitless opportunities.

Most landed at Algoa Bay, near Gqeberha (Port Elizabeth), in small boats, tenders to the big ships, striding out of the Indian Ocean surf and up the sandy beach to awaiting tents. Days or weeks later, carts drawn by oxen would take each party of hopefuls inland to the plots allocated to them, along with a few basic implements and some grain seed. Each man or family received 100 acres of land, which they were expected to cultivate in order to take ownership. It was an impossible start for many, as they lacked any agricultural knowledge, and when the first two harvests failed and flooding hit hard, some immigrants abandoned the land. In fact the most able, with their mechanical or other artisanal skills, abandoned their plots, ignoring the requirement for a travel pass, and gravitated to villages and emerging towns. This was how Salem was founded and grew, along with a surrounding community of farmers, in the area of the Assegai Bush River.

What of the amaXhosa, who had used this region as communal land for grazing their large herds of cattle? They must have felt very alarmed that the white people from across the sea never seemed to stop coming. More and more tall-masted ocean vessels were dropping off their human cargo every month, over several months. Besides, the new pale and exhausted figures did not look as though they were going home any time soon.

Initially, contact between the settlers and amaXhosa passed without incident. But in early 1821 amaXhosa started returning to a long-established clay pit in the settler area, to collect red clay for body decorations. Fairs were organised on a regular basis, where the two cultures could swap and trade goods. However, in September that year, underlying tensions and grievances violently boiled over when 48 head of cattle were stolen from a settler by amaXhosa raiders, and a boy tending the livestock was killed in the attack.

This was by no means the last conflict between the amaXhosa and settlers, Hutch was keen to tell me as we meandered among the simple, almost austere, headstones of Salem graveyard. Names such as Shaw and Penny announced the British heritage of those who lay beneath them. At the headstone of Richard Gush, we stopped. This was who Hutch had been looking for, a man of some distinction and very considerable bravery who came to prominence in January 1835, during the War of Hintsa. Conflict, I could not help noticing, was a theme in most conversations with Hutch and Mike, testimony to the tumultuous genesis of South Africa as a nation. We'll look more closely at the causes of the War of Hintsa later; suffice to say here that in late 1834 some 15,000 warlike amaXhosa streamed into territory that was theirs, but now occupied by thousands of colonial settlers. The principal victims were the farmers. The amaXhosa took the lives of the men, burned their buildings, and went off with tens of thousands of head of livestock, leaving the women and children to try and subsist alone. Unfamiliar with the cycle of frontier warfare, many settlers, on hearing about these attacks, ran for their lives.

In response to the rumours and panic, they congregated in Salem, forming a laager (fortified encampment) to defend themselves from the amaXhosa waiting on the hill opposite. The atmosphere would have been unbearable, with loss of life and property seemingly inevitable. Firepower, ammunition and prayers must have been on the minds of most – but not Richard Gush. He was a pacifist, a Quaker. He was not a man to sacrifice his faith and principles in the face of extreme adversity. Bold as brass, and accompanied by only one colleague, he went out unarmed to meet a group of amaXhosa warriors. Having established that the visitors were hungry, he made a deal. In exchange for food, the amaXhosa warriors agreed not to attack Salem. Gush returned to the village and collected bread, tobacco and pocket knives before returning to the visitors. True to their word, they left, with the inhabitants of Salem unscathed. Mutual diplomacy had prevailed.

***

Hutch was visibly proud of Richard Gush, taking a vicarious pleasure in his achievements. I was touched by this incredible story, a symbol of good and hope that occurred at a place and time when most of the history books are full of trauma and misunderstanding, ultimately leading to theft and bloodshed. I asked myself if the tale was fanciful, a legend distorted by time. I decided, on balance of probabilities, that it had the ring of truth. Occasionally, one person's actions can turn the tide, preventing the misunderstandings which so often cause or exacerbate conflict. Richard Gush, fuelled by his faith, had approached the amaXhosa as fellow human beings whose mood and intentions were not set in stone. His simple and human gesture defused what could have been a deadly incident.

At this point, tales of personal bravery, mass raids by amaXhosa warriors and the struggles of the 1820 settlers started playing second fiddle to our rumbling tummies. The tailgate of Hutch's car was dropped to form a platform for his mini gas stove. It was time for another brew. While we drank our tea, Mike concentrated on his box of hard-boiled eggs. For the second time in half a day, my colleagues deliberated hard on the oval packets of protein. As part of a bonding process they nattered on, and I mused on whether we would eventually adopt an egg-based motto for our vakasha – 'Have eggs, will travel', or 'One egg or two?' I kept my tomfoolery to myself, chucked the dregs of my tea into the long grass and vaulted back into the front seat. The sun was now fully up and strong. We still had a long way to go.

9: SETTLER OR INVADER?

'We are blue bucks of one forest.'

'Singama-puti ahlati linye'

Xhosa metaphor: Rev. J.H. Soga, *The Ama-Xosa. Life and Customs*, 1931

Within half an hour we were parked at the top of a hill with a panoramic view over Makhanda (Grahamstown, earlier known informally as Settlers' City). The site was dominated by a large, conspicuous brick building in a 1960s or 1970s European architectural style – the 1820 Settlers National Monument. Surrounding it, within the nicely manicured grounds, were other historical buildings and artefacts of significance to the history of the area. After the modest buildings of Glenshaw Farm and Salem it was a real contrast, and the view of the medium-sized town with its prominent cathedral steeple and low surrounding hills was quite impressive.

As we chatted, I got the firm impression that while this town and the imposing 1820s Settlers National Monument were important to both Hutch and Mike, this was for different reasons. I sensed that feelings and sentiments ran deep, but not in the same direction. In fact, the dynamic of our group changed slightly. A little edge, tinged with discord, was creeping into our conversation, indicating ideological differences between the two men.

Both of my companions could trace their family lineage back to the 1820 settlers. Hutch's family had arrived with several parties of English, Irish and Scottish origin. Mike's lineage was, however, from north Yorkshire and Manchester and, knowing him, I suspect they'd have been in or around Peterloo in 1819, when it had all kicked off.

It was soon apparent that Mike knew Makhanda (Grahamstown) very well, having lived there for some years. I realised, too, that he was pretty much an expert on the 1820 settlers, about whom he had opinions he was happy to share. Standing at the edge of the slope he surveyed the scene before us, pointing out places of interest such as Rhodes University (listing some of its distinguished alumni), the Cathedral of St Michael and St George and, at the far side of the valley, the new suburbs expanding over the slopes, representing the hopes and aspirations of many in the new South Africa.

Comfortable on his home turf, he started to express his deep loathing of European colonialism, particularly the British government and its associated establishments such as the military, the missionaries, the ambitious governors and the petty but influential local magistrates. Their decades of violence, and their contempt for and ignorance of the amaXhosa and Khoisan people, were foremost in his mind. His body language reinforced his words –shoulders and limbs opened out a little to reflect his more steely views. I began to understand why my new friend had served time in jail during the apartheid era. His sense of injustice still ran deep, his centre of gravity shaped by past and present wrongs. Here was a man standing before a large canvas, not afraid to tackle the bolder colours. The large monument celebrating the 5,000 settlers sent by the British government to permanently displace and control the amaXhosa did not sit well with him. His candid views, expressed with barely restrained emotion, were refreshing to me, taking us beyond the listing of historical dates and events. He had a knack for making things visceral and real. You couldn't smell the blood, but he made sure you could picture it.

Hutch, on the other hand, thought that a monument to the 1820 settlers was not an unreasonable thing. He was visibly proud; like it or not, the settlers were part of the history of the country, embedded in the landscape. Makhanda (Grahamstown), Salem and Gqeberha (Port Elizabeth) were just a few examples of their impact. Besides, the Voortrekkers had built a monumental edifice near Pretoria to commemorate the Voortrekkers and the Afrikaans people. Mr Mandela, the first black president of South Africa, was conspicuously remembered in cities, towns and villages by statues, museums and renovated buildings. Was, then, a monument to the brave 1820 settlers, who had suffered so much, really so unreasonable?

Hutch and Mike did not appear to be on the same page. Well, I know they weren't. I think Mike quite liked the disagreement – perhaps some measure of conflict was bread and butter to him. Too much consensus and he might have had to find an alternative, less popular, view. Hutch, however, was a bit pissed off with Mike, and told me so. Was I going to have to play piggy in the middle for the rest of the day while we were crammed inside the Hilux? I hoped not.

We made our way into the monument building and ambled about inside a massive theatre complex with an impressively cavernous interior adorned with huge abstract paintings and sculptures. A large metal statue at the entrance depicted a faceless man, possibly a miner, holding a hammer over his head. The figure conveyed the theme of toil and a strong work ethic. Overcoming adversity and resilience was conspicuously reinforced by a quote on the wall, 'We must take root and grow or die where we stand', by Henry Dugmore, one of the settlers; he had not minced his words about what they were up against. This was not some subtle flowery verse. No ambiguity here, I thought. But would you expect anything different from a man whose family had flicked the coin of life and were dealing with the harsh realities of frontier existence in 19th-century southern Africa? Of course not. Besides, he had been, like my grandmother, a no-nonsense Wesleyan Methodist.

Outside the monument there were other clues to the hardships the settlers had endured, and to the area's complex and confrontational past. The remnants of the star-shaped fortified walls of Fort Selwyn were a reminder of the Sixth Frontier War or the War of Hintsa. Built to protect the town in 1834–36, it would no doubt have witnessed the arrival of Harry Smith and Cape Governor D'Urban's first foray into the Eastern Cape. Both these loyal servants of the Crown were to change the course of amaXhosa history, significantly and irreparably, for the worse.

By now our collective appetite for history was wearing thin, and our appetite for a greasy burger was growing by the minute. We headed into the town centre to refuel at a Steers fast food restaurant. It was as sterile and unmemorable as any such restaurant anywhere in the world, except for the ambient muzak, which I found grating, particularly as I felt a little incongruous eating a cholesterol-filled fillet of gristle in a town exuding such history and academic excellence.

With a last slurp of our saccharin-sweet cola, we were out the door. Replete with junk food, we went down the bustling street to find Hutch's car. As we headed off into the drizzle and low mist of the Eastern Cape, I hoped that history-induced tension between my new friends had subsided.

10: THE CATTLE KILLING MEMORIAL

'One who perseveres meets not with misfortune.'

'Um-zingisi akanashwa?'

Xhosa proverb: Rev. J.H. Soga, *The Ama-Xosa. Life and Customs*, 1931

For an uneventful hour and a half, we headed north-east, crossing many of the rivers, valleys and escarpments that we had traversed near the coast at the start of our trip. That had been some nine hours ago, but it felt longer. Our early start was catching up with me. Between our intense in-car chats on amaXhosa history, discussing Mike's who's who of the Eastern Cape (he knew almost everyone of note) and our visits to various sites, we hadn't had much down time, and I felt myself waning. Besides I was getting restless to see the Cattle Killing Memorial. Would it conclude my search for Nongqawuse? Was it to be the site that drew many of the loose ends together? I certainly hoped so.

But as it turned out, the Cattle Killing Memorial was going to have to wait a while longer. Our mechanical workhorse seemed to be following its own nose through Qonce (King William's Town) as we parked outside the Amathole Museum, then all schlepped in. I wasn't quite sure why we were there. What did I know? I was only the rookie from out of town. I followed Hutch and Mike upstairs to the office of the museum's Curator of History, Stephanie Victor. It was a reasonable size, but it felt quite small and snug with four of us in it. It'd be unfair to say it was a little chaotic, but it was certainly busy with stuff, although I'm sure she knew where everything was. I recognised her style of filing.

Stephanie was a whirlwind of personality, a fission reactor of enthusiasm and interest who immediately shook off any lethargy I had from the drive. Within the first minute we learned that she was recently back from a Covid-enforced lay-off and waiting to hear if her thesis, *Xhosa Women of Royalty*, had earned her a doctorate. She was a mine of information, and as she, Mike, and Hutch caught up with one another (they'd all met before), I felt rather like a visitor at an ad hoc history buffs' tutorial. She was quite curious about the rookie from out of town and my interest in Nongqawuse.

No time to hang around, Stephanie was soon up from her desk, energetically trundling down the corridor and into some back rooms, chattering all the while. As the new boy from abroad, I was being singled out for the charm offensive, and it worked a treat – though I had to accelerate my intellectual and physical tempo just to keep up. The rooms, corridors and historical documents on display reminded me of Hogwarts.

By South African standards, the building was old, dating to the 1880s, and one of the books in the library dated back to 1642.

The walls displayed certificates with flowery handwriting from many decades, all vying for my attention – look at me, look at me! Old newspapers were laid out on angled wooden displays, impatient to be examined. Shelves were heavy with documents just waiting for some inquisitive soul to tease them open and reveal their time-bound secrets. Frayed leather-bound tomes snoozed under a polished bench, protected from the perturbations of modern times. It was all exciting and intense for me, this history larder – a nerd's paradise, storing yesterday's secrets.

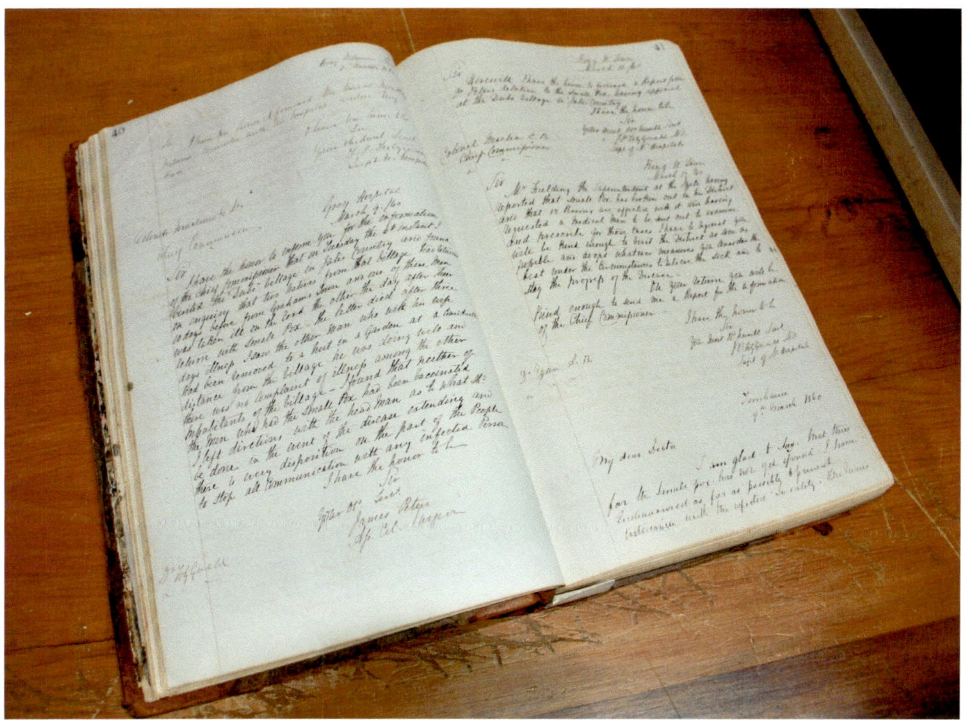

Dr Victor, the Curator of History, enthusiastically showed us around the Amathole Museum, where we got to see documents handwritten by 19th-century administrators and physicians.

Best of all, there was a direct window into 1860, in the form of beautifully handwritten letters by Dr Fitzgerald MD (one of Cape Governor Grey's personal appointees) to various local administrators, people whose names I recognised from the history books. These were the very people who had shaped the history of the Cape around the time of Nongqawuse – and here I was, touching the letters they had written or received! This was history coming alive. These people had not been passive bystanders during the stresses and strains of the 19th-century conflicts between the amaXhosa and Europeans – they had played a vital role, all of them, some good and some less good, though I am sure that at the time most thought they were working on the side of righteousness. More than 160 years of time and distance evaporated rapidly. From the yellowing pages and neat margins, I could feel the scratches and dried ink of their fountain pens. Fitzgerald's thoughts and concerns about a smallpox outbreak in the area had been earnestly conveyed in luscious black ink to lined paper. They were almost audible. In his looping rhythmic letter to Colonel Maclean, CB, the report was prefaced with the words

> *King W. Town*
>
> *March 10/60*
>
> *Sir,*
>
> *Herewith I have the honour to forward a Report from Dr Peters relative to the small pox having appeared at the Dubi village at the Jalii County.*

It terminated with a flowery salutation:

> *I have the honour to be*
>
> *Sir*
>
> *Your humble servant*
>
> *J.P. Fitzgerald MD*
>
> *Supervisor of N. Hospitals*

Dr Fitzgerald had been appointed as medical superintendent to Qonce (King William's Town) in 1856 by Sir George Grey, the Cape Governor. In 1859 Grey had a hospital built in the town, and named in his own honour, where the conscientious Dr Fitzgerald worked to the point of exhaustion doing what he could for the amaXhosa population. While most of Fitzgerald's efforts went to caring for his patients and operating a cataract surgery, he also expended a great deal of his energy and diplomatic skill in trying to win the support of the region's traditional healers, who were suspicious of the white man's treatments, and sceptical of their effectiveness. Some even suspected him of being an agent of Grey. I dare say that while their views of his treatments might in some cases have been justified, those who'd had their sight restored thanks to cataract surgery may have been a lot less sceptical.

During the mass starvation that followed the Cattle Killing, Dr Fitzgerald had written to Commissioner Maclean, the local colonial administrator, about the 'emaciated living skeletons passing from house to house'. Faced with this human trauma, Dr Fitzgerald joined the local Relief Society to raise funds, organise food distribution and administer medical attention to endless waves of suffering people. This benevolence met with the displeasure of Governor George Grey, and the Society had to be disbanded. Fitzgerald's long hours of hard work and conscientiousness took its toll on his own health, as he dealt with fatigue bordering on exhaustion.

Stephanie was now keen to show us other parts of the museum, so off we went again at whirlwind speed.

Downstairs we were shown a display entitled 'The Dead will Arise', explaining the Cattle Killing phenomenon, some of which I was already familiar with. I was struck by the startling statistics from the Population Return of 1857 for British Kaffraria, the area of the Eastern Cape between the Kei River and the Keiskamma River, excluding towns and the Crown Reserve. The tabulated numbers told the raw truth. In this part of the Cape alone, not including King Sarhili's vast Gcalekaland east of the Kei River, death from starvation and its associated diseases, plus mass migration to colonial works programmes and other employment on white-owned establishments, caused the indigenous population in 1857 to decline by 64 per cent – i.e. from 104,721 in January to 37,697 in December; a reduction of 67,0024. As a result of the Cattle Killing prophecies and Governor Grey's unsympathetic response to the misery and trauma, the amaXhosa population had been decimated. There is even evidence that some displaced people were auctioned as labourers. Even though I knew some of this, the fact and figures were jolting. It was another of those moments when I found myself gently shaking my head from side to side in disbelief.

By now, however, I wanted to get moving. I had flown 13,000 kilometres with the express purpose of visiting Nongqawuse's grave and the Cattle Killing Memorial. The memorial was within touching distance, only two blocks away, but the afternoon was drawing on, and I wanted to spend a bit of time there. 'Come on, guys, let's get going!' I thought to myself, and perhaps Mike and Hutch read my thoughts. We said our goodbyes to Stephanie and her historical treasure chest, and headed off to Edward Street, where the main object of my interest lay.

I had read about the memorial. It was situated on the site of a mass grave where some of the 40,000 amaXhosa who had died of starvation were buried. There they had lain forgotten for over 100 years, until a developer discovered their remains while laying the foundations for a new townhouse complex.

My proximity to this story had given me a deep sense of the suffering of these people. I knew that many survived at first on almost nutrition-less bark and roots, and had gnawed at the leathery hides or bones of the cattle they had slaughtered months before, now littering the countryside. As hunger progressed, they had huddled in their huts in family groups, most too weak to walk. Some resorted to cannibalism. Vultures circled overhead as bodies lay where they dropped en route to seek help, wherever it might be found. Those with enough strength managed to get as far as Qonce (King William's Town) or other settler communities seeking food and medical relief. Even then, survival hung in the balance.

Without fear of exaggeration, the scenes must have been dystopic in the extreme.

Having been to the source of the prophecies on the Wild Coast and the grave of the prophetess on Fick's farm, I felt that in coming to the memorial I was arriving at the natural conclusion of my pilgrimage. Here I would bring it all together and perhaps receive some answers to the questions swirling in my mind about the many strands of this calamitous story. But now I found there was just one obstacle in the way. The memorial was fenced off and closed, locked with a hefty chain and padlock that announced: 'This far and no further.'

I could hardly believe my eyes. Why on Earth would anyone want to prevent access to one of the region's most prestigious historical sites and a tourist attraction? In fact, why had I travelled so far to pay my respects at a site barring me with steel fencing and padlocks? Wasn't this an affront to those who had lost their lives fighting colonial rule? I was more than a little pissed off. There was not even a sign offering us an explanation or apology. An online search offered no warning or explanation, either.

From what we could see through the bars, the memorial sat innocuously in a quiet suburb of white bungalows and houses with brown-red roofs, in an area of about an acre or two. It looked like a cross between a park and a graveyard, covered with grass and with a handful of mature trees scattered about. Two sides of the open space were lined with headstones. An obvious centrepiece was the 3-metre statue hewn from a light grey rock, perched on a plinth of a darker grey. The statue was distinct and reflected the theme of the site. A sculpture consisting of a large pair of cattle horns draped in what looked like a blanket or scroll had, on each side of its base, reliefs depicting scenes from the Cattle Killing, including burial scenes and images of maize. Just below the horns was a black plaque with bold white lettering: 'Here rest men, women and children – innocent victims of the 1856/7 catastrophic cattle killing.'

However, Hutch, Mike and I were clearly not going to see much of this. We began discussing. The locked gate at Fick's farm had not kept us out – should we find a way around or over this one, too?

We scanned the tall steel bar fence in search of a gap or weakness. Nothing. Nada. Rien. This fence contractor had been mighty keen. No flies on them.

Next, we employed tenacity and eccentricity. First, Mike had a gentle attempt to climb the fence. Failure. I had an enthusiastic attempt. Failure. Hutch was our last hope. Success. With moves that might have been the envy of Spiderman, he somehow clawed his way up and over without any visible injury. Out of respect for the site, he was a little hesitant about going too far in. Besides, what should have been a short-mown lawn was actually tall grass and weeds, impeding his progress. I handed over my Nikon camera and asked if he could take a photograph of the centrepiece of the memorial. After clicking away, he scrambled back over the fence with Mike holding his feet and arms in support. It was inappropriately farcical for a historical site of such significance.

We had done our best here, but we had very little to show for it. Clambering over industrial-grade fencing at a major historical amaXhosa site had not been on our to-do list, and it felt like an anticlimax to a day that had seen us open doors to so many facets of the Cape's tortured history and seductive landscape. Our conversations about 19th-century amaXhosa personalities, settlers and Cape administrators had been lively, embellished with disagreements and challenging new perspectives. With the aid of Hutch and Mike, my knowledge, based on a modest library of amaXhosa history, had become animated and three-dimensional. Touching, feeling and smelling the soil of the Eastern Cape had helped me transform turgid texts in learned books into dynamic stories, where I could almost see and hear the tragic and avoidable events unfold.

With late afternoon gravitating towards early evening, we made a quick visit to the Grey Provincial Hospital, where in the 19th century Dr Fitzgerald had done his best under taxing conditions. The tarnished cream façade presented its unapologetic colonial brand of architecture to the world. Untrained vegetation growing vigorously out of the mortar prised open cancerous cracks in the entrance pillars. The structure looked precarious, ready to put a few more people in hospital. Outside, waiting ambulances emblazoned with high-vis chevrons reminded us of which century we were in, while agitated ibises and egrets perched high in the trees, audibly mocking our curiosity.

Despite the Cattle Killing Memorial being fenced off we attempted to get in by scaling the fence. Only Hutch succeeded.

Our journey had covered a great deal of ground, more than I had expected, so I had no regrets as we joined the N2 and headed back to East London. Although I had not seen the Cattle Killing Memorial up close, I had communed with Nongqawuse, in my own way, and been hugely enriched by people and place. This day's vakasha was at an end, but a new one beckoned – I still had the grave of King Hintsa to find.

11: REFLECTIONS

'The depth of a pool is tested with a long pole.'

'Isiziba siviwa ngodondolo'

Xhosa proverb: Rev. J.H. Soga, *The Ama-Xosa. Life and Customs*, 1931

Gallivanting about the Eastern Cape with Hutch and Mike, visiting numerous historical sites and interesting people, was a little more tiring than I'd expected. So I spent the next few days quietly perusing Hutch's personal library about local history. I was like a child in a sweet shop, sampling a bit of this and a bit of that, as though testing chocolate toffees and lemon sherbets. While I read and scribbled away taking notes, Hutch had patients to see in his surgery, attached to the house. I was full of admiration for my new friend. I met a couple of his patients and chatted to his reception team, and was touched to hear what high regard they had for him. Patients travelled long distances for his expertise and care. And it was clear that he really did care, way beyond the Hippocratic Oath. My admiration and affection for him grew the more I spent time in his company.

In between patients he would pop in to see how I was doing, directing me to various newspaper cuttings and handwritten reports, some dating back decades. His wife Julie made sure I was kept occupied, too. Before her late shift working as a pharmacist, she took me to the East London Museum, where I came face to face with a large coelacanth (*Latimeria chalumnae*). Now that's not a creature you hear about every day, but it's true, cross my heart. Caught by a local fisherman in 1938, the fish had been a major scientific discovery, a throwback to the dinosaur era, and described as a living fossil. Wherever I went in the region, the Eastern Cape seemed to throw up a surprise one way or another – whether in the form of stunning coastal scenery, mystical amaXhosa prophets or prehistoric fish.

Between coelacanths and history books I was doing a lot of thinking. Ruminating and digesting would be a better way of putting it. I had come on this trip mainly to learn more about Nongqawuse and the Cattle Killing, and to pay my respects. On first reading about the prophetess and her vision in Mostert's 1,300-page tome, I had been shocked and a little ashamed at not having heard about the surreal events of 1856 and 1857. In particular, I remember thinking how unjust it had been to heap all the blame on her for the horrendous tragedy. Had she really put the final nail in the coffin of an independent land for the amaXhosa? To my way of thinking, she had surely been a symptom, not the cause, of a disaster waiting to happen. I could not understand why she was so vilified in South Africa. Why, in the 21st century, was 'Nongqawuse' still used as a pejorative term? Did she really have to carry the can for the Cattle Killing? I felt it was an injustice, a gross distortion of events and an oversimplification of the truth. After visiting the source of the visions at the Gxara River, her grave near Fick's Farm and the Cattle Killing Memorial in Qonce (King William's Town), I was convinced that there was a fairer, more balanced narrative, one that did not justify the ridicule fostered by popular culture. Blaming a teenage girl for the Cattle Killing, with its huge loss of life and the break-up of the amaXhosa, was so unjust and simplistic, I felt, as to be untenable. Other players in this macabre theatre had questions to answer.

Let's go through a few of the possibilities.

The Grey theory

We'll start with Sir George Grey, the Cape Governor at the time of the Cattle Killing. In the eyes of many South Africans, he was and still is one of the principal villains. While Grey regarded himself as enlightened, telling the Cape Parliament he was out to 'instruct and civilize' with the aid of missionaries and settlers, he was viewed as Satan by many of the indigenous people. This led to the Grey Theory. I can see the appeal of making the British establishment responsible for manipulating a vulnerable young woman. But had Grey and his supporters really possessed the foresight and means to put ideas of a Cattle Killing craze into the head of a young woman in a remote part of the Eastern Cape, without that being noticed by the whole community? Did Grey sufficiently understand the amaXhosa's relationship with their ancestors to conjure up the idea of a resurrection, with the ancestors as New People rising out of the water to remove all European settlers? Most unlikely. And the notion of suggesting that black Russians were waiting offshore to help the amaXhosa fight the British would have been an idea too shocking and unorthodox for any servant of the Crown to contemplate.

Sir George Grey ('Satan' to the amaXhosa), Governor of Cape Colony (1854–61). Many South Africans think he instigated the Great Cattle Killing.
(With permission of the Western Cape Archives and Records Service.)

Besides, the idea of starting a Cattle Killing movement is not likely to have appealed to Grey's fastidious way of thinking. He was a man accustomed to using more conventional methods to defeat and control indigenous people in the Empire, such as military force, duplicity, the Church, schools, medical facilities, money and a rigid system of local administration.

However, that does not absolve him. As my friend Simon Mqamelo had keenly asserted, his dirty fingerprints were all over the crime scene. Grey was hot on controlling all affairs and being seen as the source of initiatives in the Cape in order to further his reputation with the imperial puppeteers in London. While I'm not aware of any solid evidence of Grey prompting Nongqawuse to start the Cattle Killing movement, he would not have been able to believe his lucky stars when the full tragedy unfolded; the millenarian cult of killing livestock and spoiling maize in 1856 and 1857 proved far more effective at reducing the amaXhosa population, breaking their culture and undermining the authority of their chiefs than any colonial military offensive would have been. In his words, 'We can draw very great permanent advantages from the circumstance, which may be made a major stepping stone for the country.'

The words 'very great permanent advantages', reflecting self-interest and self-promotion at a time of so much suffering and turmoil, are, from a 21st-century perspective, simply obscene.

In relation to the Cattle Killing, I think Grey is guilty on three principal charges. First, he represented the colonial system, which in the previous 50 years had taken, by various types of force and deception, land traditionally used by the amaXhosa for grazing cattle and expanding their families. As a result, the density of the indigenous population had increased significantly, since they were forced onto ever smaller pockets of land, often of lesser quality. The amaXhosa practice of transhumance, the seasonal movement of cattle to different pastures, for example, was not compatible with colonial rules on movement and the establishment of new settler farms.

Second, he undermined the amaXhosa's ability to manage themselves by removing much of the power of the chiefs; for example, the ability to levy fines. Grey and his magistrates cajoled the principal chiefs and their councillors to exchange judicial control of their people for a regular salary from the Cape governor. This significantly changed the power dynamic of amaXhosa society and the ability of the chiefs to control their people, particularly in relation to cattle theft. With their leadership compromised, it is likely that people began to disregard certain communal norms and practices that promoted loyalty and had held clans together over generations.

Third, and most obviously, he fully exploited the situation when thousands of starving amaXhosa, the Believers in the prophecies, turned to the colony for help. King Sarhili himself pleaded for help and forgiveness from the governor for the situation he had brought on his people by promoting the prophecies. After the Great Disappointment of February 1857, when the prophecies of Nongqawuse were not realised, Sarhili was desperate and wrote to Grey, via a translator, begging him to intervene. But it all fell on deaf ears. Grey went on to undermine the Relief Fund, set up by compassionate colonists in some of the frontier towns. Instead, he promoted his food-for-labour scheme, according to which only those who signed up for work on municipal works projects all over the Cape would receive assistance. The white-owned businesses, farms and works programmes were so desperate for cheap black labour that sales and auctions started up. Even though slavery had been made illegal in South Africa in the 1830s, by 1857 a price per head of £1–£5 was being touted in the Cape for amaXhosa labourers escaping the carnage of Nongqawuse's prophecies. People were so desperate that they even sold themselves to survive.

Equally repugnant is Grey's attitude to the Unbelievers, those people who rejected the Cattle Killing prophecies and kept cultivating at great risk to themselves. They had tried to prevent the disaster, warning and imploring others not to accept the prophecies. In the end they had suffered as much as anyone, their homesteads attacked and much of what they owned stolen. Despite repeated requests, Grey and his local magistrates refused to help or protect these people.

It is clear that Governor Sir George Grey had no compunction in refusing help to the Xhosa people, Believers and Unbelievers both, when they were at their most vulnerable. Despite his so-called humanitarian credentials and spirit of European enlightenment, at every turn Grey ruthlessly exploited the chain of events precipitated by Nongqawuse on that fateful day in April 1856. While I can see the appeal of this theory, I don't feel it stands up to scrutiny. While he ruthlessly exploited the traumatic events as they folded, I think he lacked an understanding of Xhosa culture sufficient to precipitate such a deep-rooted spiritual movement, based on cattle sacrifice and the resurrection of ancestors.

The chiefs theory

Was the whole Cattle Killing movement an elaborate attempt by the senior amaXhosa chiefs to stir their followers into war with the colony? It was possible that Nongqawuse and her visions fed into the chiefs' real agenda; to force their people by the depredations of hunger and loss of cattle to take up arms against the British administration. That is what Sir George Grey and some of his field-based agents on the ground believed, or said they believed. They read the tea leaves as best suited them. The fact is, Grey and his administration wanted to avoid another war at all costs, fearing a collaboration between the amaXhosa, Chief Moshoeshoe's Basotho and their neighbours, the abaThembu. It is possible that the amaXhosa chiefs sensed this – and knew, too, that the amaMfengu, their traditional enemy, might be persuaded to switch allegiance from the British to themselves, so that they would have a real chance of success. Thus the idea was touted that the chiefs had deliberately stirred up discontent to prepare their people for war.

It was a narrative that suited the scheming Governor Grey. Once again, he could paint a vivid picture of the Cape Colony and British interests as being at risk from the indigenous people. This would be justification for taking more amaXhosa land and removing the chiefs from their positions of power. All wonderfully convenient for Grey. Disastrous for the amaXhosa.

At the time, the British Empire was under severe strain in other parts of the world, most notably in India, where the 1857 mutiny was brewing. The suits in London were playing a geopolitical board game with the swift deployment of their metaphorical knights and castles. On the ground, this meant that military resources in regions of relative calm were being posted to hotspots of unrest. Grey was a shrewd operator, and more than familiar with this dangerous military game; by reporting on a possible insurrection in the Eastern Cape he could justify keeping his military resources, rather than sending them over the Indian Ocean.

To me, the chiefs' theory seems highly unlikely. You have to ask yourself whether the amaXhosa really wanted another war. They had already suffered greatly fighting the British army, the colonists and the amaMfengu. In the previous ten years they had fought two major wars, the Seventh Frontier War (1846–47), known as the War of the Axe, and the Eighth Frontier War (1850–1853), known as the War of Mlanjeni. Each time, it ended in stalemate or a reduction in their access to traditional lands and a further undermining of their authority.

The amaXhosa refuted this story by pointing out that starving people do not make great warriors. Even a colonial magistrate, Charles Brownlee, who had witnessed the Cattle Killing up close, with all its horrifying effects, reported to his seniors in August 1856 that 'starving people are not in a position to undertake aggressive warfare'. This was supplemented at another time with his observation that the 'movement seems peculiarly to have been one of the common people'. There may have been growing resentment towards the chiefs, as they were seen as a sort of pastoral aristocracy, with vast resources in the form of cattle. In short, the killing of cattle undermined the power and wealth of the chiefs.

Governor Sir Grey, of course, was not interested in these versions of events.

The prophets theory

To understand the role of the prophets, one must understand that the amaXhosa culture was (and is) a deeply spiritual one. The prophets were held in high esteem, especially during times of spiritual and physical stress. They occupied that hallowed ground between this world and the next; they were able to offer insights into the meaning behind everyday events, and to see into the future by listening to the gods and the ancestors. Prophets could be people of humble origins who possessed great charisma and promoted doctrines that spoke to all levels of society. Some, like Makhanda Nxele, had real physical stature and even reached the status of a chief, a most unusual occurrence for someone not born with the hereditary right. By contrast, the prophet Mlanjeni was more mysterious and spent hours submerged in rivers, eating a very frugal diet, so that at times he was too weak to walk. It is hard to exaggerate the influence of these men on the thinking and actions of people all over the Cape, extending for hundreds of kilometres.

There were also many minor figures making forecasts of tumultuous events. During the time of the Cattle Killing a young *amagqirha* called Nonkosi came to prominence as a seer at the Mpongo River in the Eastern Cape. Like Nongqawuse, she claimed to hear healthy cattle lowing and horns clattering just below the water's surface, ready to rise. These, she reported, would soon be joined by the ancestors, including King Hintsa. She even claimed to see the spirit of the late Mlanjeni while gazing into the water.

A common theme among many prophets was getting rid of the European colonists forever, restoring tribal traditions and returning to lands previously occupied by the amaXhosa. In different but broadly similar ways, they promoted the sacrifice of livestock to pre-empt the return of the ancestors and the restoration of their lands. The theme of resurrection, based on both traditional and Christian doctrines, often featured. Stories of Jesus Christ rising from the dead and the Christian teachings that someday all would rise as well were potent ideas, and fed right into the people's longed-for vision of the future. New beginnings with 'New People' is a notion that would have energetically resonated with many people at such hugely challenging times.

This was especially the case after lung disease, introduced from Europe, had decimated large swathes of the cattle population a year or two before the Cattle Killing. This had robbed all sectors of society of not only their wealth and prestige but also their source of nourishment. The people also had a strong emotional bond to their cattle, collectively and individually, so losses from disease or sacrifice would have been extremely traumatic. So it is unsurprising that notions of a new beginning – a cleansing and a fresh start, free of diseased livestock and crop infections – would have appealed to people desperate for better times. If humans, they argued, could be resurrected like the Bible said, why not cattle?

Knowing these traditions and the severe stresses caused by loss of land, cattle disease and drought, one can begin to understand how Nongqawuse's prophecies were well received. In a manner of speaking, the door was already half open. Many chiefs and ordinary people were receptive to her messages. They were desperate, and help from their ancestors conveyed through a quixotic young woman at the Gxara River fitted the bill. It was not such an irrational act after all, and certainly not a madcap idea propagated by a lone individual – an individual who deserves all the blame.

Would the instructions of local prophets prove more effective at resisting European colonisation than war or negotiated treaties? Over many decades both of those routes to freedom had failed.

One could argue that in light of amaXhosa tradition and beliefs the course of action taken was rational, or at least consistent. And herein lies the rub, as I see it. What had started out as a discrete prophecy made by one girl picking up the spirit of the times turned into a mass movement which was difficult, if not impossible, for anyone to control. I wonder if Nongqawuse should be seen merely as the one who inadvertently lit the touch paper or generated the spark that fell on to parched tinder, ready to combust? It is also worth remembering that she was only 15. How many 15-year-olds are wise, temperate and fully aware of the consequences of their actions? I know I wasn't; were you?

I doubt whether Nongqawuse could have known or understood how her utterances would be received and adopted. The pressures on her would have been huge. After the initial visions and prophecies, I imagine that from her point of view the idea seemed to take on a life of its own. It became woven into a people's uprising, a popular or nationalist movement, where individuals had limited influence. It all just snowballed. Chiefs, for example, sometimes had to check the mood of their own followers before deciding whether or not to promote the idea of slaughtering cattle and resisting corn cultivation. For ordinary amaXhosa people of modest means, the idea of new healthy cattle arriving from the underworld or rivers, the reduced need to cultivate corn, and promises of reuniting with their beloved ancestors would have had great appeal. As women undertook much of the agricultural labour and domestic chores, these prophecies spoke to a receptive audience. Life, they thought, would be less stressful, less back-breaking in their deeply patriarchal society.

What is more, the chiefs lacked means to punish ordinary people as they once had. As mentioned earlier, by taking the governor's salary they had compromised their own authority and become more impotent. In the word of the *Grahamstown Journal* of February 1857 'the chiefs, even if they had the will, which they do not, have not the power to restrain the people'. Colonial magistrates now held much of the power over law and order in amaXhosa life.

Even after the horrors of the Cattle Killing, other millenarian movements germinated and flourished in South Africa, including in the Eastern Cape, and endured into the 20th century. The theme of loss of human and animal life was common. Predictions of a better future, rescue from deprivation and the intervention of mysterious external powers such as God, or even a fleet of American aircraft, were recurring themes. As with Nongqawuse's prophecies, the root cause of these beliefs propagated by charismatic leaders was poverty and the erosion of the amaXhosa's political and social structures through imposed taxes, livestock disease, drought, lack of advancement and political disenfranchisement. Understandably, this fermented a loathing of white society and a desire to stand apart from the whites or to sweep them away.

The most famous of these millenarian movements were the Israelites, a breakaway from the Wesleyan Church, led by Enoch Mgijima. Sweeping the white man away was one of their main ideas, which made the political authorities particularly nervous. When about 3,000 Israelite pilgrims, devoid of all worldly possessions, congregated at Bulhoek, Eastern Cape, in 1921 to wait for the coming of the Lord, there was a long standoff with the police. The gathering was declared a rebellion, a threat to white authority. The Israelites insisted they did not answer to government authority and refused to move, waiting instead for God's message. Despite protracted negotiations and lots of toing and froing, patience ran out. The police resorted to the trigger, and so another tragedy unfolded as 200 of Enoch Mgijima's followers were mown down and killed. The date of 24 May 1921 became infamous for the Bulhoek Massacre. It was such a seminal event that Nelson Mandela mentioned it at the opening of his defence in the 1964 Rivonia Trial.

Earlier, in 1906, during a protest by Zulus against taxation, known as the Bambatha Rebellion, it was pig killing and the slaughter of white-coloured cattle that were promoted. Unlike the Cattle Killing, however, this did not lead to mass starvation.

In the late 1920s in the East Griqualand region of the Cape, another movement, known as the American Movement, was initiated and led by the mercurial Dr Wellington. He had acquired quite a reputation for his various and outlandish proclamations. Some called him an unscrupulous adventurer, others a bogus leader; perhaps he was just a flamboyant Garibaldi-type nationalist. He certainly caused one hell of a stir, drew a large following and made the authorities pretty nervous. Central to his philosophy was the idea of independence and self-determination for black people in Africa, largely derived from the teachings of the Jamaican leader Marcus Garvey. Dr Wellington proselytised liberation from European bondage by a black American army which would arrive in aeroplanes to save the people. Prosperity was guaranteed for all, with the development of new factories, greater personal wealth, and no taxes. When his prophecies failed, he promoted an epidemic of pig killing as a means of encouraging the American saviours. Despite his eccentricities and unorthodox methods – or perhaps because of them – Wellington and the American Movement gained appeal because the message spoke to the challenges, marginalisation and loss of hope felt by many ordinary black people. Like the Cattle Killing, the American Movement was a rallying point for hope of a better future at a time of despair.

Sarhili and Mhlakaza

Paramount Chief Sarhili, who succeeded his father, King Hintsa. Sarhili was a supporter of the Great Cattle Killing and visited the site of Nongqawuse's visions at the Gxara River to seek assurance. (With permission of the Western Cape Archives and Records Service.)

If Nongqawuse's visions were the spark that lit the tinder, there is a case for saying that it was her uncle, Mhlakaza, with King Sarhili, the paramount chief and most senior of all amaXhosa, who fanned the flames. Without their enthusiasm, encouragement and support, it is doubtful whether the Cattle Killing movement would have gripped so many people over such a wide area. I reckon that they, far more than Nongqawuse, deserve blame, because of the role they played in taking up the idea and vigorously spreading it.

Mhlakaza was quite a character, widely known, and present in the historical record long before Nongqawuse's visions. Years earlier he had been known as Wilhelm Goliat, and had accompanied Archdeacon Merriman as he wandered the Cape on foot, learning and preaching Christianity. Mhlakaza got to see a lot of the colony, learned Dutch, was baptised and received holy communion. Later, when he was snubbed and ridiculed by his host and his wife, he became disillusioned with Christianity and left, making his way to the area east of the Great Kei River known as Gcalekaland, where he became an adviser to King Sarhili. He also took on the responsibility of becoming a father to Nongqawuse, whose parents had probably died in the Eighth Frontier War (1850–53), or the War of Mlanjeni.

In reading various reports, you really can't help concluding that he was one of the principal conductors – or indeed *the* principal conductor – of the Cattle Killing enterprise. As a mature man, he would have enjoyed considerably more power and influence than a teenage girl. So when Nongqawuse shared her Gxara River visions and messages with her uncle, did he really and truly believe them, or did he see an opportunity to curry favour with those in positions of power, such as King Sarhili? It is possible that both possibilities were true. Allegedly, he was one of those who drew Sarhili's attention to his niece's visions and the radical message of sacrifice and a prosperous future ushered in by the ancestors. New times with New People were not far off, if everyone joined in. Over the months Mhlakaza preciously guarded where and when select visitors could meet the prophetess. It was a demanding and subtle business, managing Believers and Unbelievers of different rank, some of whom had travelled long distances to see her, with some acting as ambassadors for distinguished leaders of other tribal groups. He diligently kept certain visitors at a distance, allowing others a little closer, as Nongqawuse repeated what she had seen and heard in and around the Gxara River. Communicating with the ancestors in a manner unfamiliar to the anxious visitors, she would relay the spiritual message about the need to sacrifice more cattle and explain why the prophecies could not be fulfilled until the ancestors were satisfied.

Mhlakaza was therefore the conduit between the mercurial young prophetess and the outside world. If she was otherworldly, he was very much of the world. He had seen a great deal in his life and had learned about the effective communication of spiritual messages to sceptical audiences while preaching Christianity in the Cape. In a 21st-century context we might say that he was good at the PR; in today's world, he would definitely have a TikTok account or a YouTube channel, or both, plus a bit of an Instagram following. When the prophecies failed to materialise at the appointed times, after great sacrifices had been made by many thousands of loyal amaXhosa, he was quick to confer with his junior partner, and offer a plausible reason. The mantra they conveyed always centred around the ancestors' need for more cattle sacrifices. Better times were not far away for those who were committed. And so the fire was stoked and the bridges burned, and the wasteland of starvation materialised.

At this point you have to ask why King Sarhili allowed all this to happen on his watch. Stephanie at the Amathole Museum stressed that he was liked by his followers and was regarded as a fair leader, someone who considered matters carefully. His people and amaXhosa tradition were of utmost importance to him. When it all went so badly wrong in February 1857, he was absolutely distraught and angry at the scale of destruction and suffering – his kingdom and people were shattered. So, why hadn't the most influential man in the region stopped the Cattle Killing in its tracks, either at the start or over the following months? He had seen the warning signs; the prophecies had failed to materialise over many months and on several specific occasions. Although European magistrates repeatedly stressed the errors in his leadership and the dire consequences, he could not trust the Europeans. They had killed his father, King Hintsa, some 20 years earlier – and besides, they had even killed Jesus, the son of their own God. Who were the whites to offer advice on sensitive matters about life and death?

Sarhili would almost certainly have had his doubts – but month after month he endorsed the prophecies and urged on the lesser chiefs and their followers. So there came a point in late 1856 and early 1857 when there was no turning back. Too many livestock had been slaughtered, and it was too late in the season to sow the maize. Should the finger of blame be pointed at him, or him and Mhlakaza? Were they the principal instigators of the tragedy?

To tackle this Gordian knot we need to understand Sarhili a little better, so let's try to walk in his shoes for a moment. In modern parlance, we would say he had some issues. These would have clouded or at least influenced his judgement at this time of great stress.

Like many tragic historical figures, he had started life with a poor relationship with his father, King Hintsa, Paramount Chief of all the amaXhosa. Since Sarhili was the legitimate heir to the amaXhosa throne, the two patched up their differences – but early scars of rejection and disinterest run deep. In 1835, when only a young man, Sarhili was taken hostage by the British colonial forces. That was the point when Hintsa was seeking to muster 50,000 head of cattle demanded by the British army, and when Harry Smith and his men killed him, mutilated his body for souvenirs and dumped it on the ground. So young Sarhili came to the throne both as a direct result of his father's traumatic death, and at the end of another disastrous war against the British, the Sixth Frontier War (1834–36), or War of Hintsa. Being held hostage by the British added to his distrust and loathing of Europeans, the Cape administrators and the British army in particular. It is said that 'iron entered his soul'. This deep-seated feeling did not wane with time, and shaped many of his future dealings with the colony and his own followers.

During his chieftainship he saw the amaXhosa engage in three more vicious wars with the British, which resulted in the shifting of the Cape frontier boundary further east, all the way up to his territory on the Kei River. His geographical sphere of influence was declining rapidly, which placed enormous strain on his people in terms of freedom of movement and access to grazing. In addition, it was at that time that the Cape administration imposed restrictions on the chiefs that undermined their authority, in particular their ability to impose fines on clan members who transgressed. At a personal level he was wrestling with the sadness of not producing a living male heir, and his favourite loyal adviser, Bomela, had been 'smelt out' by a zealous witch doctor, leading to a slow, torturous death. And finally, as mentioned earlier all over the lands occupied by the amaXhosa there was a severe drought and a virulent lung disease among cattle, brought in, it was thought, by a Dutch shipment of diseased bulls. The sickness was moving inexorably east, causing deaths of a most gruesome kind that would have been painful for the people to watch, given the close relationship between the amaXhosa people and their cattle. I think we can quite safely conclude that Sarhili was in a tight corner, distraught at his circumstances and struggling to find solutions to numerous intractable problems in his personal and political life.

It was into these circumstances that he heard of Nongqawuse's visions at the Gxara River, virtually on his own doorstep. The location of these prophecies, offering as they did a better future and the restoration of amaXhosa tradition, must have been an encouraging sign. The news that his father, Hintsa, and great prophets such as

Makhanda Nxele would rise from the river with all the other amaXhosa ancestors and herds of fresh cattle must have been the one bit of good news he received at the time. Best of all for him was the news that the source of nearly all his problems, the Europeans, were to be driven into the sea and banished forever.

Initially Sarhili exercised caution. After the prophecies failed to materialise in the first few months, he personally visited the vicinity of the Gxara River, listening to and watching the river and sea for signs of the ancestors promising to return. Conferring with Mhlakaza and Nongqawuse, he was drawn in gradually, sometimes promoting the idea and at other times seeming more sceptical. At one point he was so worried that the prophecies were going to fail that he tried to take his own life. But he survived this trauma, and once again his pendulum of faith swung in favour of slaughtering cattle, eradicating witchcraft, destroying the crops and not cultivating any new maize. Despite several failures in the realisation of the prophecies on specified dates, Sarhili pushed on, leading from the front, insisting that the mass slaughter and corn-spoiling continue. As amaXhosa tradition demanded, his councillors, minor chiefs and followers were duty bound to follow. Loyalty and respect for the paramount chief were of the utmost importance.

The truth is, Sarhili knew that he shouldered the lion's share of the responsibility for the Cattle Killing, the subsequent suffering and the disintegration of amaXhosa society. He said as much after the Great Disappointment, when the sun had failed to turn red in mid-February 1857. And then, when the ancestors, the healthy cattle and the black Russians did not show up, as repeatedly forecast by Nongqawuse and promoted by Mhlakaza, Sarhili knew the game was up. His worst fears were realised. His faith had been misplaced, and he felt the pain and shame deeply. And so he escaped north of the Mbashe River, to the coastal forests of Cwebe, where he could elude the long arm of Grey.

***

After I had trekked around the Eastern Cape, I felt that my initial thoughts about Nongqawuse unfairly shouldering all the blame for the Cattle Killing had been vindicated. I did not derive much satisfaction from this conclusion, however, as the scale of the 1857 tragedy overshadowed questions of blame. But I was satisfied that it was not all her fault – not by a long chalk. It seemed to me that Sir George Grey, the previous Cape governors and the machinery of colonial rule had clearly played their part. They were the root cause of the circumstances, the many stresses, in which extreme notions could take hold and thrive. Her uncle, Mhlakaza, was partly responsible for fomenting the situation. With his connections to high power, he successfully translated the visions of a teenage girl into a message of hope and opportunity. Did a bit of personal vanity come into play, too? His standing and influence amongst the great and the good of amaXhosa society would certainly have been amplified as the excitement of the movement mushroomed. To a desperate and frustrated ruler like King Sarhili, the message from the Gxara River must have fallen on receptive ears. He was not a stupid or irresponsible leader – on the contrary, he clearly cared deeply for his people, the traditions of amaXhosa society, and their joint future. Although he did not enter into the Cattle Killing movement lightly or hastily, he was obviously convinced by the veracity of the prophecy. Once convinced of the mysterious voices and ambiguous figures in the distance, he led decisively, taking followers of high and low rank with him. Very little truck was given or leniency extended to the Unbelievers (*amagogotya*), who warned against the folly of the prophecies.

In the end, I believe, the disaster was a confluence of many factors, not least of which was the years of war and hardship the amaXhosa had suffered under the colonial invaders. Their arrogance and complete disregard for the traditions, way of life and social structure of the amaXhosa chiefs, and their confiscations of amaXhosa land over decades, gave rise to a pervasive sense of anger and resentment. Thus the amaXhosa people were primed to give ready assent to any message that offered hope. The message of huge sacrifice and resulting prosperity echoed the longings of their own hearts, steeped as they were in a spiritual understanding of the world and of absolute faith in their ancestors. It offered a solution – radical, risky and involving huge personal sacrifice. Such messages have appeal when the world seems to have lost its moorings.

And then there was a more immediate cause, one that still rankled after 20 years – the slaying of King Hintsa. The more I thought about it, the more convinced I became of the centrality of this heinous killing to the events that unfolded, and that for too long have been blamed on that single 15-year-old girl.

12: IN SEARCH OF THE KING

'Love your cattle; my people love me because I love my cattle. I therefore exhort you to love your cattle as I have done. Poor men will not pass by your place. They will stop with you. While you can respect the rich, you must not despise the poor.'

King Hintsa 1789–1835

In some ways, my physical and emotional pilgrimage to find Nongqawuse had partially satisfied my curiosity, and had vindicated my belief that the world had done this young woman a great injustice. To me, blaming Nongqawuse and using her name as a pejorative epithet seem wholly unjustified; others, I feel, were equally culpable, if not more so. Why could people not see that? I was puzzled by this easy scapegoating of a young girl. I guess simpler explanations are always preferred – makes the story easier to digest and retell. I thought that comparisons with Joan of Arc might be a little far-fetched, given that Saint Joan's mission had been successful (in the short term in any case) and that Nongqawuse's efforts had ended in tragedy, but at least the young prophetess had offered some resistance against the invading Europeans. She had attempted to be a liberator when others had not. After all, in the eyes of many she was validating the prophecies of other great amaXhosa prophets such as Nxele. If she is not to be celebrated, at least her good intentions should be acknowledged.

Among the many strands in this story that made it possible for the Cattle Killing to take place, the killing of King Hintsa stands out as a somewhat overlooked precursor to the tragedy. I thought it a particularly egregious death, cause of a festering physical and psychological scar for the whole of amaXhosa society. As mentioned earlier, he had been killed – or should I say murdered? – by Harry Smith and his troops some 20 years earlier, on 12 May 1835. In any society, killing the head of state is shocking. Blowing out their brains from a few metres away before cutting off their ears and stealing personal jewellery for souvenirs is barbaric in any culture. That had been the fate of Hintsa at the hands of his British captors – a hideous atrocity.

This single killing and mutilation caused seismic ructions that radiated rapidly and forcefully from the banks of the Nqabara River across Gcalekaland, the whole of the Eastern Cape, the hinterlands of the Western Cape and Cape Town, and up through the Atlantic as far as the creaking desks of colonial officials in London. Even the grey men in their dark frock coats were shocked. Some could be heard muttering that in the interests of Empire, heads would have to roll and career ambitions would be thwarted.

It was into this cauldron of anger and devastation that Sarhili succeeded his father as the most senior chief of the amaXhosa, or in effect, the king. There was, however, the immediate obstacle to overcome of Chief Sarhili being at the time a captive of the British, held hostage by Governor D'Urban and Harry Smith, pending Hintsa's return with 50,000 head of cattle as compensation for the amaXhosa cattle theft in the Cape Colony. But of course Hintsa would not be returning, as Harry Smith had abandoned his mutilated body on the ground. After negotiations and terms set for the return of livestock to the Cape Colony, Sarhili was released to take up his role as king and replace his father.

It is hardly surprising that the scars of his personal tragedy and national humiliation would never heal. Sarhili would never trust the European invaders – the administrators, the army, the magistrates, the missionaries, the settlers – nor their stooges, such as the amaMfengu. He would never accept their presence on amaXhosa land. The promises and treaties of his British enemies were to be treated with contempt and scepticism, not worth the paper they were written on.

The timing and circumstances in which Sarhili lost his father and acceded to the highest position in amaXhosa society contributed to his susceptibility to the prophecies of Nongqawuse, aided by Mhlakaza. He was a leader wanting – perhaps needing – retribution for the killing of his father, the paramount chief of all the amaXhosa. News from the prophetess of King Hintsa returning with other great ancestors and fresh cattle to drive the damned and bloody Europeans into the sea for ever must have seemed credible to Sarhili. A vindication, perhaps.

Even though the Cattle Killing prophecies failed in the 1850s, Sarhili would be found fighting his traditional foes as late as 1877 and 1878. This time it was the Wedding Feast War, the ninth and final Frontier War waged against the British and amaMfengu. Defeat followed for Sarhili. It was both terminal and humiliating, forcing him to flee to neighbouring Bomvanaland – almost, but not quite, beyond the reach of the victors.

***

After I had surveyed the landscape of the Eastern Cape, read heaps of books on amaXhosa history and visited the sites where Nongqawuse had had her visions and where she now rested, my mind remained restless. I found myself asking if Nongqawuse's visions and proclamations would have happened if King Hintsa had not been so ruthlessly killed and defiled by Smith's troops. Under Hintsa's stewardship, would the Cattle Killing messages have fallen on deaf ears? Or on receptive ones? Had he lived, would Hintsa have sided with the Believers or with the Unbelievers? So many questions, so few answers.

I had the feeling that if King Hintsa had survived and maintained his reign, the amaXhosa might well have doggedly persisted in their resistance to colonial encroachment, as they had done for so many years. They may have been worn out by war, but somehow King Hintsa would have navigated his people through troubled times without resorting to the mass slaughter of livestock at the recommendation of an unconventional teenager. His son, Sarhili, on the other hand, might well have been motivated by the need to avenge his father's death. I think the terrible news would have clouded his judgement, made him more receptive when the Cattle Killing vision first stirred in the Gxara River valley.

In 2020, when I first began exploring about the Transkei by myself in search of Nongqawuse and the Gxara River, I noticed a battered brown road sign pointing to the grave of King Hintsa, some 60 kilometres away. My hired car was too bruised, and time was running short, so I gave it a miss on that occasion, but filed it away in my mental 'must do' box. Now, two years later, with my Border Historical Society buddies for company, seemed like the right time to pay the site a visit.

And so, Vakasha No. 2, to find the grave of King Hintsa, got under way. But, like most trips in this part of the Eastern Cape, things took a little longer than planned. Well, to be perfectly frank, a lot longer. Google Maps, always an unreliable source of digital guidance for me, suggested that the 200-kilometre road trip from East London to the site of King Hintsa's grave would take just over three hours. Sounds simple, eh? As it turned out, rain (lots of it), mist, flooding (lots of it), historical distractions, the beauty of the Wild Coast, toyi-toyi-ing (protests, a ubiquitous feature of South African society) and navigational constraints challenged these optimistic estimations. Our round trip to visit the king's grave ended up covering 1,440 kilometres and took three days. On day one, despite driving to within a kilometre or so of the site, we failed to find it; the elements, the landscape and the dense vegetation conspired to defeat us. I am quite sure Google and their clever software engineers sitting in their trendy Californian offices failed to reckon on the Eastern Cape factor in their optimistic digital forecast. Of course they had. Bloody hopeless lot!

Hutch, Mike and I were joined by William Martinson, the chap I'd found online and who had introduced me to the Cape's Border Historical Society. Will was tall, slim, thinning on top, blessed with a boyish grin, and the quiet sort. However, when he did have something to say, which was not often, we listened. By profession he was an architect, and in his spare time he had a particular interest in the historical architecture of the region. He was our chief navigator for much of the trip, directing us with the aid of GPS and paper maps, while Hutch, who took the driver's seat, navigated by sight and memory. Both methods had their strengths and weaknesses, with the weaknesses pretty all-consuming when curtains of rain and a soupy mist obscured the road 5 metres ahead of us. At all times, the GPS was more than a touch temperamental, almost deliberately teasing, often failing just as we reached a critical junction or when the clouds thickened. The paper maps were so large they were difficult to handle in the back of a 4×4 as we jolted from side to side on rough tracks. They were impossible to fold, seeming to have

Map 4. Vakasha No. 2, February 2022: finding the grave of King Hintsa.

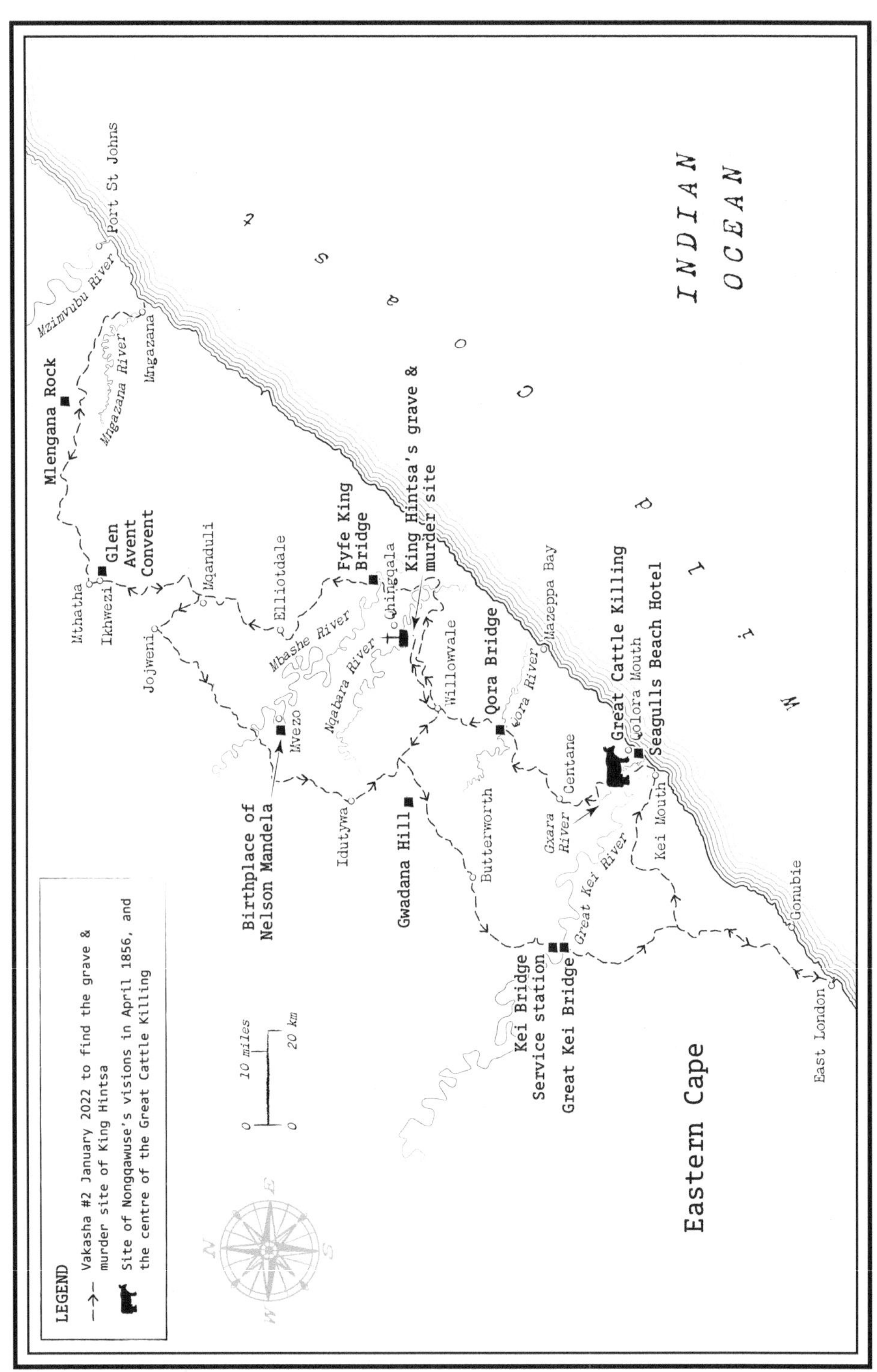

a life of their own, almost like a fifth character in the car, or a huge, unruly reminder of those Christmas morning scenes when all restraint is thrown to the wind. While they contained the nth degree of cartographic detail, in low light conditions it was nearly impossible to distinguish one river from another, and there were a lot of rivers – most of them angry and energetic, in full flood.

Leaving at 6.30 am, we were headed for the Great Kei River and the pontoon crossing near its mouth. We had decided that en route to King Hintsa's grave we would pay another visit to the Gxara River, where Nongqawuse had had her visions. Since we were so close to the spiritual fulcrum of the Cattle Killing, I could not resist asking the only other pontoon passenger what he thought of Nongqawuse and the prophecies. The well-dressed local gentleman, with beautifully polished black lace shoes, explained that he lived in East London, but was making a trip across the Great Kei to visit family members in Gcalekaland. He answered my questions in a forthright manner, insisting that the young girl had preached nonsense, that she was a liar and dangerous. In his words, it had been a lot of 'stupid stuff', and that contrary to the prophecies the ancestors would never be returning. There was no ambiguity in his words or room for doubt in the inflection of his voice. He knew his mind all right. Besides, he stressed that he was a Christian, as though that explained or justified his logic. I could not quite understand this. Perhaps he just wanted to terminate our brief chat.

Anyway, our pontoon soon nudged onto the shallow riverbank of coarse sand, and I thanked my companion for his time. Then off we sped in the Toyota, as another short, sharp shower tested the windscreen wipers.

On my first visit to the Gxara River, back in January 2020, I had been struck by an almost tangible spiritual quality in the calm, natural beauty of the river and its setting. My second visit reinforced that impression. It was all too easy to see how that gently meandering river, the sleepy lagoons, the rich and varied vegetation, the towering cliffs, browsing cattle and numerous birds and insects might give rise to the weird, wonderful and surreal, enabling one to slip seamlessly between the imagined and the real. The subconscious boundaries were blurred. I felt, again, that I was in one of Nature's holy cathedrals, where the alchemy of the past and present, ancestors and prophets might coalesce to project a picture of a different, better future.

I found myself commending Nongqawuse for choosing such a special location for her visions and her encounters with the ancestors. What a ridiculous notion – what was I thinking? Choice could hardly have come into the equation for Nongqawuse. Perhaps fate might be a better way of putting it. Yes, fate; now there was a thought; Beowulf's irrefutable comment that 'fate goes ever as fate must' sprang to mind. As I stood in the gelatinous mud on the edge of a pool in Nongqawuse's valley, with brackish river water lapping against beds of reeds, this sobering phrase about fate resonated deeply.

It had the ring of truth, to me, encapsulating so much about people, places and events in the world. How strange that a phrase from an Old English poem about Scandinavia bore so much relevance to the Eastern Cape and a small river somewhere near the bottom of Africa.

While I contemplated the role of fate in the affairs of humanity, the rain clouds parted with the aid of an ocean breeze, and patchy sunshine broke through. The sun can be intense in moist air, and Hutch put up his large umbrella for protection from it, as is common in the Eastern Cape on sunny days. The four of us ambled along the riverbank, taking in the beauty and atmosphere, saying very little. If we listened quietly, the site spoke for itself. It was a time to be reflective and respectful. Superlatives would have been inadequate or even a little crass.

I was so absorbed by the landscape and the spiritual significance of the place that I failed to look where I was walking. So when I stepped onto a flat wet rocky surface decorated with lichen, my legs shot out from underneath me and I hit the gnarly surface hard, attempting to cushion my camera equipment. Then I rolled a couple of metres down the side of the valley, where I was caressed by tufts of grass, flowers and miniature bushes. Ouch! My companions gathered around, concerned that I was injured from the fall, but the only damage was to my pride. What a way to come down from lofty thoughts. Had the ancestors, the so-called New People, out there just below the surface of water, seen me tumble? Was my fall caused by the intercession of the Gxara River's mysterious powers? Were they warning me off? More importantly, had my camera survived the combined forces of gravity and ancestral intervention? Indeed, it had. Fate, on this occasion, appeared to be on my side.

We met up back at Hutch's 4×4, parked a short distance from the river. The tailgate was put down and the gas stove lit for a fresh brew. It was only 8.30 am as we chewed the fat about Nongqawuse, her uncle Mhlakaza and the Cattle Killing movement. It was liberating to be talking about major events in amaXhosa history in the spot where the events had actually happened. We were not just interpreting words in big books written by clever people. Place had real significance, particularly in this tragedy. Here, over 160 years later, we could smell the same mud, hear the same leaves rustling, see similar cattle strolling the fringes of the lagoon. In light of the amaXhosa beliefs about their ancestors and the pressures on those 19th-century indigenous people from all angles, the idea of prophecies did not seem so fanciful. In fact, they seemed almost inevitable.

Over tea and sandwiches, there seemed to be a consensus that as likely as not, many of the senior chiefs, particularly King Sarhili, would in 1856 have been demoralised, in a desperate position, and ready for a radical solution to their many problems. I added into the mix my belief that the killing of King Hintsa some 20 years earlier had primed the situation for the prophecies to take hold and prosper. Ever-present, too, was the shadow of Governor Sir George Grey and his lackeys on the ground, discussing potential conspiracies against the colony.

After the tailgate was closed and the Toyota navigated out of Nongqawuse's valley, the weather gods made their presence felt again. For much of the day we had been exposed to alternating mist, drizzle, heavy rain, lightning and thunder. Hutch, Mike and Will had all been to the site of King Hintsa's death and grave before, many years earlier – in Hutch's case about 25 years earlier, which seemed to surprise him as much as it did his passengers. He was taking us on a cross-country route, which meant dirt roads, mostly. This way, we got to see much of Gcalekaland, including key towns, forts and topographical features. I have travelled thousands of miles on dirt roads, in various parts of the world – Brazil, Namibia, Morocco, Oman and Lesotho just to name a few – so I knew what to expect. Or I thought I did.

We reached the nearest town, Centane, without any difficulty. Much to Hutch's disappointment, we were unable to find the house where he had lived as a youngster. Where his house had stood, bushes and mature trees now flourished. He was slightly perplexed and visibly saddened. Memory Lane wasn't being kind to him. I couldn't help thinking what a reversal of the trend this was – trees now greening a space where once a building stood.

Will, on the other hand, was in his element photographing the architecture of buildings in the former colonial style. What I saw as drab old village halls and post offices were meat and drink to him. I relished his enthusiasm – and the enthusiasm of all my companions, bonding so easily over a shared curiosity for all things historical. Added to which, my Border Historical Society buddies had a huge breadth of knowledge about the amaXhosa and the European settlers, making the hours in the car, even in the midst of driving rain, utterly absorbing. Buildings, rivers, roads and mounds all generated lively conversation and debate, with everyone throwing in a few facts and opinions. And though we had a vague agenda for the day, there was no set order of places to see or timeline to adhere to.

As we left Centane, someone suggested we take a look at Fort Owen, built by the British army in the late 1800s, during the ninth and final Frontier War, the Wedding Feast War (1877–78).

***

It was here, and on the slopes surrounding Centane, that some of the final and decisive battles of the Ninth Frontier War had been fought, leading to the defeat of King Sarhili and Chief Sandile at the hands of the British army and their collaborators. Afterwards, both men fled capture, Sarhili across the Mbashe River, and Sandile to the Amathole Mountains. This battle was a seminal event in South African history, although few history books recognise it as such, in that it represented the end of formal military resistance by the amaXhosa people against European encroachment in the Cape during the 19th century. After that the amaXhosa had nothing left. What had started as skirmishes in 1779 between the Cape colonists and the Khoisan and isiXhosa-speaking people had flared into wars of increasing intensity and viciousness. Over the 100 years from 1779, few corners and few inhabitants of the Eastern Cape were not touched by theft, death, torture, kidnap, scorched-earth policies and starvation caused by armed conflict. Here, where I stood on the crumbling walls of Fort Owen, with Hutch, Mike and Will, was where that bloody chapter had effectively ended.

King Sarhili died impoverished in 1892, aged about 83, hiding pitifully in the forests and hills of Bomvanaland, north of Centane. Chief Sandile, the leader of the Rharhabe arm of the amaXhosa, fought to the bitter end until in 1879, when he was about 58 years old, he was fatally shot, to be found dead in a cave near the Amathole Mountains. What a woeful, humiliating end to such distinguished leaders after an intolerably intense period of military, political and social pressure, from external and internal sources. Starting life early in the 19th century, these two men and their distinguished families would have had little inkling of the wave of issues they would have to face in their lifetime. Their task of maintaining Xhosa lands and traditional amaXhosa livelihoods was unachievable in the end, the obstacles and multiple challenges almost insurmountable.

***

The four of us could not dwell on this depressing thought for too long, however, as the rain began bucketing down and we all made a mad dash for the Hilux. It was time to move on anyway, if we were to find the grave of King Hintsa that day.

Note for the inspired reader: If you're planning a trip to the Eastern Cape between October and April, the summer months, come prepared for afternoon showers and thunderstorms. Also come prepared for dirt roads, flooding rivers, gullies and culverts, precarious bridges and signage in various states of disrepair or non-existence. Nature decided to play games with us and laughed as we flailed about, driving in circles while wrestling rain, roads, thunder and lightning. Was this supposed to be some sort of deterrent? It sure felt like it.

The closer we edged towards the Nqabara River, the worse it got. From Centane, Hutch headed north-east towards Willowvale, ascending and descending several deep river valleys. The dirt road snaked and looped to cope with the rapid changes in altitude and deep curves of the major rivers. Distance, speed and height were challenging to judge in alternating rain and an obdurate mist. Fast-running streams ran down the middle of the road, some aggressively gouging the gritty ochre surface to form deep rocky gullies. Here the muscle power of our 4×4's engine and Hutch's considerable cross-country experience helped nudged us forward, metre by metre. Mike, Will and I swayed about in an erratic 360-degree motion as we might in a rowing boat on choppy waters. The smaller vehicles we encountered skidded and slipped towards deep ditches, one or two becoming wedged in. Passengers and curious locals stood in clusters, looking on with a mixture of concern and curiosity, protected by colourful umbrellas.

Vakasha No. 2. Struggling to find King Hintsa's grave in adverse weather, somewhere in Gcalekaland, Eastern Cape.

When we could get a glimpse of the scenery, it was quite arresting. It varied from an imposing wall of low thick thorn bushes and trees to open grassland liberally occupied by herds of cattle and round huts (*amakhaya*), mainly white, with pointed roofs. Fields of maize partnered the homes. At one point we caught sight of a mass of brown-tinged water, white in parts, as it rushed down a gully of boulders, through a blanket of dense bush.

Large parcels of flotsam and jetsam caught on the bridges' pillars and the riverbanks or tangled up in overhanging trees revealed how high and how strongly the muddy runoff water had swollen the rivers. Deposits of silt and sand formed swirling patterns on the surface of the bridges.

At one point we came to an abrupt halt at a river no more than 10 metres wide. In comparison with the other rivers we faced it was a tiddler. However, the water was so high and running so fast we could not see the bridge. It resembled a belligerent rapid. The river colour was dark, like an Americano with a splash of milk. As the bridge was invisible beneath the water, I assumed we'd have to turn back. To be honest, I was very nervous about attempting to traverse such a strong river current in the Hilux. It felt far too dangerous. What would happen if we got swept downstream? I wasn't in the mood for meeting my maker in a muddy river somewhere in the Eastern Cape.

Mike got out of the car and momentarily surveyed the submerged bridge before wading in, yanking his shorts up a tad on the way. Cautiously he shuffled his feet in the direction he thought the bridge went. To be honest, I was nervous on his behalf, but the flow of the water did not wash him away and he reached the opposite bank in one piece. Ever so slowly, Hutch followed Mike's lead, coaxing the Hilux to terra firma on the other side. A river in flood was not going to stop us from finding the spiritual home of the king!

I congratulated Mike on his brave move. He thought I was making too much of a fuss: it was nothing. I left it at that, but was grateful for his determination.

Finding King Hintsa's grave was proving to be a bit of an ordeal.
Bravely, Mike waded into a river to locate the flooded bridge.

As we doggedly pursued our goal close to the Nqabara River, the atmosphere in the vehicle changed. Hutch focused more on the shape of the horizon, trying to remember the Mbongo Hills and the bends in the Nqabara River in order not to miss a critical turn-off. There had been the occasional road sign to King Hintsa's grave on our travels, but all bar one had been useless; the signs were either bleached so white as to be unreadable, laid flat and upside down on the side of the road, or just missing from the post where they were supposed to be. Will valiantly juggled with the paper maps for a few hours, now and again validating or rejecting Hutch's route. Just as we needed a clear GPS signal for some digital assistance, it failed. Will held his phone at different angles and heights, but a digital map refused to download and come to our rescue.

Various expletives were muttered under our breath as we realised that our ambitions were thwarted – at least for that day.

We weren't lost, but we didn't know where we were. Nor were we getting any closer. One thing was for certain, we were not on the banks of the Nqabara River pondering King Hintsa's death, as we had planned to be.

Shit. I knew everyone was doing their best, but I felt disappointed. I had no right to, honestly, but I did. If the demise of King Hintsa had been a major contributory factor in the uptake of Nongqawuse's Cattle Killing prophecies, I felt that I needed to see his place of rest and feel the landscape where he had been killed. It was mid-afternoon, and we still had to get to Hutch's place at the mouth of the Mngazana River in Pondoland, where we were to stay overnight. Reluctantly and with a sinking feeling, I agreed that we should give up the search for the day, and we headed off to cross the magnificent Mbashe River.

Collectively, the weather gods smirked at our defeat. As we pulled into a craggy siding high on a ridge overlooking the mocha-coloured Mbashe River, the clouds parted, and for the first time in hours we enjoyed the warmth of full sunshine. The river below meandered like a huge python, twisting and curving purposefully south towards the Wild Coast. Further upstream the aquatic contortions are appropriately named the Collywobbles. Like the Great Kei River, it had symbolic importance as a major boundary. In this case it was a gateway to the lands of the amaBomvana, another distinguished isiXhosa-speaking clan.

After the long uncomfortable ride, we were relieved to sip a cup of tea fresh from the gas stove. Out came the ubiquitous hard-boiled eggs. While refuelling, we all gazed north and eastward, taking in the 180-degree panoramic view and the fresh air, still ripe with faint whiffs of petrichor and leached minerals. Will and Mike caught my attention and pointed into the broad valley at an arc in the river, constrained by a light grey cliff face. Still visible was the Fyfe-King bridge, which from the 1930s had served as one of the principal crossing points of the Mbashe. Now it was dilapidated, literally brought to its knees. Miscellaneous concrete slabs and pillars from the once proud structure were unceremoniously toppled and strewn randomly downstream, bullied and elbowed by large boulders from the riverbed. In this contest between humans and Nature, the victor was obvious.

A mere 33 kilometres away, as the crow flies north-west, was Mvezo, the village where Nelson Mandela had been born in 1918. Situated high above the proud river, Mvezo and the adjacent countryside offered the young Mandela spectacular views of Transkei, open grassy meadows in which to play and river pools in which to swim – a wonderful childhood for a man who was to enjoy little freedom in adult life.

The magnificent landscape of the Eastern Cape. Searching for King Hintsa's grave, we crossed the mighty Mbashe River in full flood. Only a few kilometres upstream was Mvezo, where Nelson Mandela had been born.

Fortunately for us, the new Mbashe River bridge was still passable, although liberally decorated with vegetation and detritus washed down by the high water. From here, we kicked on to Xhorha (Elliotdale) and Mqanduli, places I had known some 40 years earlier. Best of all, the rough dirt tracks were replaced by a metalled surface. No need for maps now. Hutch and the Hilux could drive the next section blindfolded. We rushed past Ikhwezi and Ngangelizwe on the outskirts of Mthatha, through the centre of the city and on to the R61 through Libode towards Port St Johns at the mouth of the Mzimvubu River. In 1980, I had hitch-hiked these roads for a weekend break at the Wild Coast. The narrow dirt tracks had been stony-rough and dusty, with unnervingly steep unprotected sides and cattle drifting about, frequently blocking the route. Forty-two years later I was whizzing along a smooth new dual carriageway, with carefree livestock now safely constrained by kilometres of fencing. The infrastructure of the region may have changed significantly with the passage of time and the dissolving of the homeland, or Bantustan, system in 1994 – but the scenery had not. Time had not altered the sculptured cliffs framed by dense bush and cultivated fields, the river valley, the rural homesteads and kraals. Once again, I felt privileged to view the natural gateway to the even more stunning Wild Coast.

By the time we reached Hutch's place at the coast, on the banks of the Mngazana River estuary, it was getting on towards 8 pm. Our 6.30 am start seemed a decade away. It was now dark – crow-black in fact – except for the occasional porch light puncturing the still undulating hills and valleys of Pondoland. As we left the sanctuary of the Hilux, we were greeted by an orchestra of intense insect and amphibian sounds. High-pitched chirps, resonating croaks and oscillating clicks imitated the strings, wind and timpani sections. An invisible conductor appeared to coordinate Nature's musical ensemble.

After being greeted by Hutch's friends and family, who had arrived earlier, we celebrated our vakasha with cold beer and game meat fresh from the flames. Despite our failed attempt at Hintsa's site, spirits were high. Hutch was unperturbed – we would have another go at finding King Hintsa's grave on the way back, weather permitting. In the meantime, he was excited to be in Pondoland. It was immediately clear that the house, the river and the coastline had a very special place in his psychological fabric. He exuded pride and excitement, in particular, starting with the way he enunciated Mn-gaz-ana.

The estuary of the Mngazana River overlooking Pondoland. Early in the morning I swam across to the other bank with Hutch. These were precious moments. (Photograph courtesy of William Martinson.)

13: PONDOLAND AND THE WILD COAST

'The sun does not set without some news.'

'Alithshoni linge-nandaba'

Xhosa proverb: Rev. J.H. Soga, *The Ama-Xosa. Life and Customs*, 1931

Although I was dog-tired from our challenging Cape excursion, and despite the rhythmic sounds of the Indian Ocean dissipating its breakers against the sharp rocks of the Wild Coast, I found it near-impossible to sleep. Will, my roommate, snored with the vigour of a Silurian reptile, teasing me with the occasional pause before restarting his guttural symphony. A few weeks previously, Will had just been a name I'd found on the internet, a history nerd in the Eastern Cape. Now I was sharing a bedroom with him. Besides his audible imitation of primordial creatures, I couldn't help noticing his feet sticking out, way beyond the end of his bed. Not that he cared. By now he was deep in la-la land, no doubt dreaming of 19th-century post office buildings and the architecture of military forts.

We both woke just after 5 am, with dawn gently tapping on the bedroom windows. Herds of large-horned cattle sleeping on the grassy slope outside partially obstructed our path to the beach. We nimbly tiptoed through the dozing herds and the very considerable volume of steaming manure, usually positioned strategically to match our next footstep. Flipflops were not an ideal footwear in these circumstances. From the seashore and with my toes in the warm ripples of the sea, the coastline revealed itself, much as a theatre stage does when the curtain draws back. A mackerel sky formed a proscenium arch as the sun poked through the clouds hugging the horizon, ushering in Mother Nature's sensual performance.

It is difficult to exaggerate the natural beauty of Mngazana. On one side of the river's broad sleepy mouth, grassy cliffs led down to stepped platforms of angular rock that tamed the regimented swell of the open ocean into messy waves. Dynamic white horses of foam reared upward and collapsed as the wind got up. The silhouette of a couple of young men fishing off the rocks framed the view of the tight bay. As the sun nudged higher, traditional and western-style houses became conspicuous, hugging the grassy cliffs. On the beach, a cave revealed itself.

North, on the other side of the Mngazana River, the coast was gentler, sculptured more by rolling sand dunes decorated with lush vegetation. Here the beaches were wider and the bays broader. In the distance, but still conspicuous, illegal sand mining scarred Nature's picture-postcard beauty.

In the midst of the curved bay of green slopes, rocky cliffs and rolling sand dunes, set back from the full force of the Indian Ocean, the Mngazana River estuary opened out, serene and majestic. At dawn, the light was powdery, as pockets of mist nestled into the shallow valleys and basins of the surrounding hills, imparting a delicate, diaphanous quality to the performance. Miles of flat mangrove served as the canvas on to which the slow, fat river ebbed and flowed with the tides. Welling up in rural Pondoland, the river seemed in no hurry to meet its saline destination. The vast expanse of water flowed in mesmerising curves that could have come from a Rubens masterpiece. A broad range of bird species, alone and in flocks, provided animated decoration to the scene, darting into the nervous waters to pluck out fish, or perching in high vantage points on the steep slopes.

At Mngazana I met Bongile Joseph, and enthused about the beauty of the river estuary and Wild Coast.

If I sound like I was seduced, I was. Well and truly. Hutch, recognising my vulnerability, insisted that we swim across the estuary to the other side before breakfast. Will declined the invitation, preferring breakfast only. At this point I should say that I have a handful of rules when travelling in rural Africa. High on that list is 'don't swim in rivers'. Besides the risk of currents and nasty microbial diseases, you never know what is lurking in murky water. The Mngazana River estuary was very murky, and large sharks were known to swim there. In fact, they're a constant feature of the Wild Coast. Hutch even admitted to having seen them in the river in the past. So my rational cerebral network suggested I decline his kind offer in favour of a coffee. But I was not in rational mode – not any more. I was more in seduced Mngazana mode, so accepted Hutch's offer. 'I can resist anything except temptation,' as Oscar Wilde said. Well, I was in that sort of territory. The temptation to swim that ravishingly beautiful river mouth was too great to resist.

We trekked down the muddy path, through the densely wooded slope to a homemade jetty and improvised boathouses. As I dropped carefully into the warm muddy waters, my eyes now at river level, the aquatic seduction was complete. Thoughts about large grey fish with dorsal fins slicing the water's surface and rows of glass-sharp teeth were sent to the recesses of my mind. After all, if they wanted to eat me, so be it. What could I do? Hutch and I chatted as we breast-stroked towards the huge golden sand beach

100 metres or more on the other side. By fixing our sights on one of the many cattle loitering on the sand bar we compensated for the current pulling us seaward.

My rule about not swimming in African rivers seemed like a trivial irrelevance as we stood on the rippling sand at the mouth of the Mngazana River. We had the best seat in the house, bar none, with a sensational 360-degree view of the estuary, the mangrove, the surrounding hills and the open sea. Occasionally, the sound of small fish fracturing the river's surface interrupted the gentle white noise of the Indian Ocean.

Hutch grinned a lot, a quiet picture of contentment and pride. His grin spoke volumes, even though we said very little. We did not need to. For a few minutes, time and tide slowed to a crawl. The cattle ignored us. These was a unique and precious moment – an experience you cannot plan for, and money cannot buy. Don't try looking for the Mngazana estuary excursion in your local Tui or Kuoni travel agents – likely as not you'll draw a blank.

When I had started my pilgrimage to find Nongqawuse I certainly did not expect to find myself basking in contentment on a sandbar. Ah … fate once more, directing me to enjoy every moment while I may.

With the push and pull of the tides and the inexorable flow of river water, our sandy island changed size and shape before our eyes. Our dry toes began to be nibbled by silty wavelets. So we ambled off our ephemeral vantage point, melted back into the brackish estuary waters and swam gently back to the jetty on the other side.

Over breakfast, with Mike, Will and me as his attentive audience, Hutch explained how he had been coming to this part of Pondoland since he was knee high to a grasshopper. Decades ago, his grandparents had run a trading station further inland. They had taken two days to travel to Mngazana for their holiday. In fact, he showed us an old black and white photo of oxen pulling a wagon along rough track, piled high with them and their stuff. The frozen grey figures offered a peep into different times and a very different world.

Hutch then recounted an event back in 1993, when, he now believed, local people in the Mngazana community had saved his life from someone or some group ready to murder him. It was shortly after the assassination of Chris Hani, the leader of the military wing of the African National Congress (ANC), known as Umkhonto we Sizwe (MK). A right-wing supporter of apartheid had killed Hani in the driveway of his own home as he returned from buying a newspaper. The killing greatly heightened racial tension in the country – riots broke out – and to prevent spontaneous widespread reprisals, Nelson Mandela addressed the nation, asking for calm. Some people, however, still took revenge, murdering Alistair and Glen Weakley, brothers on holiday in nearby Port St Johns. It was during this turbulent period that a local Mngazana man, previously unknown to Hutch, had insisted on providing him with protection by accompanying him out of the area; he knew exactly where and when Hutch was at serious risk of an attack. The threat was confirmed when they spotted someone hiding and acting suspiciously in the nearby bushes, just as Hutch's protector had suspected. Hutch did not want to believe that anyone would want to hurt him – Mngazana was his second home and he thought he had good relations with all his neighbours. However, faced with the circumstances and the facts, he concluded, he'd had a lucky escape.

Now, replete with breakfast, and the sun high, Hutch took us for a gentle hike to a grassy vantage point providing uninterrupted panoramic views across the hills of Pondoland, along the shoreline and south over the Indian Ocean. Here he held court. Gesticulating this way and that with his hiking stick, he recounted the high toll exacted on so many ships by the winds, currents, rocks and hidden reefs over that last 500 years. He explained that from the late 1400s the east coast of Africa, the Indian subcontinent and the Far East had lured the ships of monarchs, merchants and speculators along the Cape coast in search of geopolitical advantage, plus slaves, spices, porcelain, cloth and all manner of exotic cargo. The ships were mainly but not exclusively European, particularly from Portugal, the Netherlands, France and Britain. Decade after decade, however, the Wild Coast had no regard for rank or reason, as one vessel after another floundered and was wrecked, spilling its contents on the rocks and beaches. It was a coast that invited trouble. While many passengers and crew drowned before reaching the shore, some survived, literally dumped on the beach, struggling in that tentative zone between life and death while the grim reaper waited patiently. Their options were precarious and limited.

I found it curious that despite living so close to the ocean, the local tribes such as the amaMpondo did not have boats or engage in fishing. They remained firmly land-based, particularly attached to their livestock and gardens. But then the sight of large ships heading landward, with ruptured masts and flailing sails, would quickly come to the attention of the local chiefs, and the community would head to the shore to see what they could salvage. Metals, such as brass and iron, were particularly sought after.

The reception the survivors encountered along the Wild Coast varied. In cases where the amaMpondo and other clans had heard of cannibalism amongst the castaways, or where the survivors behaved aggressively towards local clans and failed to acknowledge their help, the indigenous population could withhold their hospitality and even be hostile. Some survivors headed off along the coast, north to Natal or south to the Cape, on hazardous journeys in search of help from European settlers. Many of these hazardous adventures failed spectacularly, sometimes ending in cannibalism or simply surrendering to the combined rigours of the terrain, disease, climate and indigenous hostility.

The Wild Coast at Mngazana. In past centuries many ships travelling to and from the Far East were wrecked here, spilling their human cargo onto the shore. Some integrated into local clans to form the abeLungu or 'the Whites'.

Some wreck survivors preferred to settle amongst the amaMpondo, marrying, raising families, tending livestock, cultivating crops and integrating into the community. To many, this life would have been considerably more attractive than a servile life back with their old masters. In fact, so many castaways settled into local communities on the Wild Coast that they formed a clan known as the abeLungu or 'the Whites'. Recent DNA and anthropological research in the region have revealed several other clans formed by desperate castaways. These include the amaIrish and amaFrance, named after their nationality, and the amaCaine and amaOgle, named after the principal survivors.

As Hutch was keen to explain, at one time during the 18th century, the abeLungu were prevalent in and around Mngazana, close to where we were surveying the landscape. If we wanted more detail, he suggested, we should read Hazel Crampton's *The Sunburnt Queen*. I already had (twice, in fact), and surveying the landscape of Pondoland – the ocean, verdant hills and valleys – I could sense the stories lifting from the page. It did not take much imagination to see ships smashed on the rocks, exhausted passengers scrambling up the beach and cautious amaMpondo watching from a safe distance, unsure of whether or not to welcome the visitors.

Collectively, we reflected on Bessie, the most famous figure in Crampton's abeLungu story. In contrast to so many historical stories about the Eastern Cape, Bessie's did not involve inter-racial conflict or aggression. Her remarkable tale begins in the 1730s on the Wild Coast, when at the age of seven she was found alive after the vessel in which she had been travelling was shipwrecked. She was adopted by the local community and went on to become the Great Wife of a local prince. This was the start of a dynasty that lasted many generations.

Buffeted by the warm but assertive sea breeze, we made our way down the hill to Hutch's place, ruminating about the abeLungu on the way. I reflected on what I might have done if I had been a castaway on these shore on the 1730s. Would I have attempted the long treacherous walk to a European settlement, or taken a Mpondo wife and settled down? A local wife sounded by far the more attractive option, assuming someone would have me. A few cattle, some crops and maybe a patch of *dagga* (marijuana) sounded quite appealing, if a little romanticised. Maybe I'd have become a member of the abeLungu. Who knows?

After we had been wandering about Mngazana for a day, swimming, walking and discussing the history of the Wild Coast, our attempt to find Hintsa's site seemed a world away. Over the embers of another braai and a couple of cold beers that evening, Hutch announced that we would have an early start the next day and make our second attempt to reach King Hintsa's grave. That was great news.

Better still, I got to sleep before Will started snoring.

As we were overlooking the Mngazana estuary, Hutch explained the history of Pondoland and the Wild Coast to Mike and Will.

14: BLOODY REGICIDE

'You cannot have two bulls in one kraal.'

African proverb

Early the next morning dawn sunlight nudged through the clouds, and fresh sea air flew off the Indian Ocean. As we loaded up the Toyota, the Wild Coast could not have looked more striking.

Boiled eggs – seven, to be exact, their shells already cracked – were lovingly placed in a Tupperware container and stored in the back of the vehicle with the rest of our paraphernalia. Hutch, Mike, Will and I had bonded into a tight little unit, based principally on our shared interests, although boiled eggs might have had the same effect, in a manner of speaking. I took a quick photo of my eccentric cabal of amigos before we headed off down Mngazana's narrow undulating track, patiently pausing for herds of cattle every few hundred metres until we reached the open road. Another 12-hour road trip lay ahead of us.

We made good time on the highway up to Mthatha. Here, we popped into the Glen Avent Convent so I could have a brief chat with some of my old friends and former colleagues resting in the cemetery. I introduced them to Hutch, Mike and Will, and recounted stories from 1980 when I had worked here. At times it was emotionally testing, but not as hard as on my previous visit a couple of years earlier, when I had returned after a gap of 40 years. I was grateful to my colleagues, who were sensitive to my enormous sense of pride and deep sadness associated with this place, and these magnificent, caring women. After a brief visit to my friends, Sister Raphael and Sister Dominic, the Mother Superior, we headed off in search of King Hintsa.

On the way from Pondoland, we called in at the Glen Avent Convent, Mthatha, to see my dear friend Mrah Buthelezi (Sister Raphael).

It was about 11.15 am, and Hutch was now a man possessed, determined to reach the banks of the Nqabara River on our second attempt. He employed his deep knowledge of the local roads, cutting this way and that to avoid the congestion of bustling Mthatha.

Down to Mqanduli, across to Idutywa, along to Willowvale and the Fort Malan road to the watershed of the Nqabara. The roads were not great and the signage dodgy at best – but the tracks were not flooded, the bridges were passable, and the visibility was excellent. Will still wrestled with the flaky digital map signal, and the large paper maps took up huge amounts of space on the back seat, but our collective spirits were high. We were making progress, mostly in the right direction. Hills and valleys, previously obscured by curtains of rain and mist, appeared large, prompting clipped, intense conversations among my colleagues about forks in the road and the possible destinations of various side tracks. At this point, navigation was king, although it was obvious that no one really had a firm grip of the compass, so to speak.

After several hours being tossed about in the Toyota Hilux, we actually reached the banks of the Nqabara River, not at the site of King Hintsa's grave, but somewhere a few kilometres away. It felt like real progress. Butterflies fluttered in my stomach. The riparian scenery was striking, particularly the contrast between the grey rocks of the cliffs, the impenetrable deep green bush and the fast-flowing muddy river. Conspicuous tyre tracks in large ovoid pebbles on the riverbank indicated that the ford was 15 to 20 metres wide in places. For the second time on this little adventure, Mike pulled up his shorts and waded in to test the waters. Could we drive the Toyota across? Was it possible after so much heavy rain? Hutch observed it carefully, calculating the risk. Nope, he said, not today. No one dissented. Too much water, too deep and too precarious. The Toyota was shifted into 4×4 mode and we returned to the main road, which was little more than a rough track.

'Which way, Will?' we all subconsciously muttered under our breath. We knew we were not far away. Just around the corner, a few kilometres away at most, lay our destination. The synapses of Hutch's antennae were fired up and twitching in high detection mode. He insisted that the shape of the surrounding Mbongo hills and the bends in the Nqabara River looked familiar – well, familiar-ish.

Fifteen minutes later and with little warning, Will yelled out, 'This is the right way!' There wasn't an iota of doubt as he pointed to a side track. If Will shouted loudly and gesticulated, while focused on an intermittent digital map, that was good enough for the rest of us. Mike and Hutch nodded their approval, and we headed off the main track to a single-lane grassy route, defined by parallel tyre tracks embossed in the grass and damp soil. Distinctly not a road. We descended quickly from the high ground to a spot close to the river, covered in coarse grass, some tickling our ankles, some flapping at chest height. Thousands of low thorn bushes were scattered everywhere, and by the bank of the river the bush was so dense it was intimidating. While the sight of the river was obscured by the thick wall of leaves, trunks and thorns, the sound of water tumbling over boulders and pebbles was a constant backdrop as we traversed the last bit of the journey on foot.

King Hintsa's grave on the banks of the Nqabara River near the Mbongo Hills, close to where he was killed. The site felt dignified but subdued.

We had arrived. One hundred metres across the grassy plain, right on the riverbank, I could just make out the plot of Hintsa's grave. Once more I was in a crucible of South African history. Here, where we stood, events had occurred on 12 May 1835 that significantly ruptured indigenous history, precipitating the rise of Nongqawuse and the Cattle Killing 20 years later. What would this part of my pilgrimage reveal? I did not know, and kept my thoughts to myself. The tone among us all was quiet and respectful. We were sensitive to the historical significance of the site and the knowing landscape. After all, the hills, river and thorny bush had witnessed what had really happened – they knew. The death of a king. Barbaric acts of mutilation and trophy hunting by the British. Nature's memory had not been corrupted by shallow imperial inquiries and biased military reports designed to save the careers and reputations of Harry Smith, Governor D'Urban and their entourage of scouts and officers. Time may have made subtle changes to the landscape, but the truth about the events of that day in May 1835 had not changed.

As we walked slowly to the grave I began to feel that we were at a real crime scene, and that we were detectives searching for a credible truth, including the roles and names of the killers and mutilators. Had the king been killed by accident, in self-defence, or had he been murdered? That was the big question. Even before we discussed the evidence, I sensed that my Border Historical Society friends leant towards murder. Wool wouldn't be pulled over their eyes too easily.

For 20 minutes, I put the detective work to one side and prioritised paying my respects at the grave. A highly polished dark granite grave and headstone stood prominently in a 10-square-metre plot, defined by crude wooden posts and steel wire. The grass was low, as though the plot were tended now and again. Large pebbles from the Nqabara River had been placed on the ground to decorate the site and to lead visitors from the rickety gate to the graveside. The sound of flowing water suggested the river was only a few steps away, behind a wall of impenetrable vegetation. A tourist information board explained the history of the amaXhosa and of Hintsa himself.

The burial plot was simple, and sympathetic to the natural surroundings. It had dignity and gravitas. The rectangular headstone exuded permanence and solidity, and was inscribed:

OLELE APHA NGU KUMKANI
U HINTSA WOHLANGA LWAMA XHOSA
OWAZALWA – 1790
WATSHONA – 1835
LE YINYANGO ESISIKHUMBUZO EGXUNYEKWE
NGAMAGCALEKA PHANTSI KOLAWULO LUKA
KUMKANI U XOLILIZWE SIGCAWU
NGONYAKA WE – 1985
AH! ZANZOLO

HERE LIETH KING HINTSA
OF THE XHOSA NATION
BORN 1790
DIED 1835
ERECTED IN HIS MEMORY BY THE
GCALEKAS IN 1985 UNDER PARAMOUNT
CHIEF XOLILIZWE SIGCAWU
REST IN PEACE

Simple and factual. All very businesslike. There was no mention of the circumstances in which he had died, but I still felt that we were at an amaXhosa equivalent to Ground Zero, the epicentre of a seismic event.

Scanning the plot and the lush surroundings, I allowed myself the luxury of drifting back to the turbulent Eastern Cape frontier of 1834 and the start of the Sixth Frontier War, the War of Hintsa, shortly before this death occurred. It was back to basics. How had this bloody killing happened?

***

At the time the amaXhosa west of the Kei River were in a state of high tension, hit by drought and antagonised by British raids on their cattle. So when Chief Xhoxho received a minor wound in a fight with a British patrol, the tinder was ignited once again. The amaXhosa from the Rharabe side of the amaXhosa, led by Chiefs Maqoma and Tyhali, were ready to fight, but first sought the approval of Hintsa, the Paramount Chief or King of all the amaXhosa. Hintsa played it safe, from the east side of the Kei River; the Rharabe could go to war against the British and the settlers, but he would not participate. However, he and his Gcaleka clan would take all the livestock they captured and hide it away, out of reach of the Cape farmers and the army, for safekeeping until the war was over. As the story unfolded, the hiding of livestock was to prove a catastrophic mistake.

In December 1834 Chiefs Maqoma and Tyhali led 10,000 or more amaXhosa warriors west over the Keiskamma River, through the Ceded or Neutral Territory, and over the Fish and Bushmans Rivers, coming to a halt by the Sundays River, and places like Salem, not far from modern-day Gqeberha (Port Elizabeth). You may recall the events at Salem, where a group of the amaXhosa warriors and Richard Gush had at great personal risk negotiated peace for food at a time of great tension.

Elsewhere, warriors descended on the settlements in huge numbers, killing only adult male settlers and sparing women, children and missionaries, in accordance with amaXhosa fighting etiquette, even though this would have led the women to survive as best they could without many of their menfolk. Farms were attacked and livestock driven east towards the Kei River and the safety offered by King Hintsa in the hills and valleys of Gcalekaland. Panicking settlers, hearing of the attacks, fled west in search of larger settlements, desperate for help. The European defence was shambolic, under-resourced and lacking credible leadership.

Enter Colonel Harry Smith, or more precisely, Henry George Wakelyn Smith. As you may recall, this is the bombastic British army officer referred to earlier. Almost more than any other single European, he shaped events on the frontier around 1835, not least the death of King Hintsa.

'Hurry Charge Wackalong Smite', as he was nicknamed, was a larger-than-life Victorian military man who had fought in the Napoleonic Wars, at the River Plate and against the Americans in the 1812 war. In the Peninsular War he, having rescued the young Juana Maria de los Delores de Leon from the fallen Spanish city of Badajoz, had fallen in love with her and married her. From all accounts, they became a devoted couple, rarely spending time apart – she even accompanied him on campaigns. When separated, they wrote each other passionate and intimate letters, sometimes in Spanish or in code. Later she would be known as Lady Smith, and the town of Umnambithi (Ladysmith) in KwaZulu-Natal, was named after her. You may be familiar with the town from its role in the Second Anglo-Boer War or the Ladysmith Black Mambazo band.

Unfortunately, Smith is remembered less for his inspired love than for his ego, absolute self-belief and the values of Empire, which included the need to 'civilize' everyone who was not British. As he put it, before sailing to Cape Town in 1847 on his second secondment to the region, 'If I can extend the blessings of civilization and Christianity in a distant land where, without any affectation of humility, I can say that some years ago I sowed its seeds, it will be a gratification to me beyond expression to do so.' He was no less bombastic when he reached Cape Town's Government House, where in response to concerns about trouble at the frontier he declared emphatically 'I am now the Governor and I *will be* Governor!'

He was known to flare up in a temper one minute, then lapse into humour and frivolity the next. He frequently humiliated his enemies in public, forcing them to kiss his boots or lie prostrate while he held his boot to their neck. Chief Maqoma knew all about that treatment. Smith revelled in staged displays of power by firing cannons, blowing up wagons and getting chiefs to openly declare their loyalty and love for him with the aid of his ridiculous ceremonial staffs of peace and war. All a macabre concoction of dangerous theatre and ridicule. Insensitivity was a core trait. He was completely blind to the nuances of amaXhosa culture, and at times during his two stints in the Cape (1825–35 and 1847–52) would declare himself the supreme amaXhosa chief. It seems too, that he mistook the chiefs' loathing for love and respect, being unable to empathise or read the attitudes of others. Overflowing with confidence and energy, in battle he caused the loss of many amaXhosa men, women and children and the destruction of their homes and crops, committing or allowing all sorts of other barbaric deeds. In pursuit of victory for himself and his colonial masters, he was ruthless. As a result, he became a hero amongst many of the strident settlers looking to expand the Cape frontiers and defeat the indigenous people, in particular the amaXhosa.

Overall, Smith's most enduring personal trait was hubris. Not an attractive trait, even at the best of times. But he was a man of his time, and hubris suited an expanding Empire just fine.

In January 1835, immediately upon arriving in the Eastern Cape he made his mark, by riding 1,000 kilometres in six days from Cape Town to Makhanda (then the colonial frontier town of Grahamstown), where he whipped the settlers into action, urgently organising a defence against amaXhosa raids in the region. Without drawing breath he then went on the offensive, retrieving cattle and attacking amaXhosa chiefs. Smith, the fighting man – who had spent too long pen-pushing in Cape Town – was now back in his element, organising armed men from the front and taking the fight to his enemies.

Colonial concern about the situation in the Eastern Cape was so great in the first few months of 1835 that Governor Sir Benjamin D'Urban soon arrived from Cape Town to assess the situation and exert his authority. D'Urban and Smith were very different characters. D'Urban was extremely thoughtful and cautious, a procrastinator to the point of dithering. By contrast, Smith was impetuous and eager for action, feeling far less need to think things through. A little tension, therefore, prevailed between the two men, but not so much as to detract them from their common goal – the defeat and control of the amaXhosa, particularly their principal chiefs, such as Maqoma, Sandile, Tyhali and King Hintsa.

King Hintsa, the senior Xhosa leader who was killed in 1835 trying to escape Lt Col Harry Smith and his men. (With permission of the Western Cape Archives and Records Service.)

Until that point, the Great Kei River had been considered a boundary, almost a backstop, between the Cape Colony and the lands of the amaXhosa, where King Hintsa resided. Despite the fact that Hintsa had declared his non-involvement in the Sixth Frontier War, D'Urban and Smith took the provocative step of marching troops across the river to Hintsa's Great Place near Gcuwa, which the colonists called Butterworth. In response to this serious escalation, King Hintsa at first made himself scarce, but eventually agreed to meet Governor D'Urban and Smith.

Arriving in his finery, the king made quite an impression. Smith admitted he struck a fine figure: 'a very good looking fellow, and his face, though black, the very image of poor dear George IV'.

The meeting was to prove a fatal mistake for Hintsa.

Invited as a guest of D'Urban and Smith, King Hintsa was then given a long list of the terms demanded of him to settle the war, including the return of 50,000 head of cattle and 1,000 horses to the colony. These were deemed to have been stolen from colonial farms in recent attacks and hidden in the woods and pastures of Hintsa's Gcalekaland. Hintsa's insistence that he was not involved in the raids by Chiefs Maqoma, Tyhali and others was not believed; from the British perspective, he was the king and he was in charge, so he had to remedy the situation and pay the penalties – immediately. It was not a negotiation, as the king had expected, but rather a presentation of unequivocal demands. Soon it emerged that King Hintsa, his son and heir Sarhili and the king's brother Bhurhu were caught in a spider's web of deception; D'Urban and Smith announced that they would be holding these men hostage until the terms were met. Things then rapidly deteriorated; Hintsa, Sarhili and Bhurhu were dragged to a tree, where nooses were placed around their necks as D'Urban and Smith taunted and threatened them.

At this point, D'Urban learned that Hintsa's men had been killing the amaMfengu, and became incensed. He was all for hanging Hintsa on the spot. The amaMfengu were a desperate group of refugees, displaced by Zulus, who had taken refuge amongst Hintsa's people since the late 1820s. When this renewed round of tension broke out, they had decided to leave, taking their possessions and Hintsa's livestock with them. In a scene slightly reminiscent of the Israelites' flight from Egypt to Canaan, 17,000 or so amaMfengu had crossed the Kei, leaving the Gcaleka in order to settle in the Cape Colony as British subjects. To stop this Biblical-scale exodus of refugees and all their highly valued cattle, Hintsa's men had begun attacking the amaMfengu as they fled. On receipt of this news, D'Urban had demanded that Hintsa stop this immediately. The king, indignant at the demand, was purported to have responded furiously with the famous: 'Why is there so much made of the Fingoes [amaMfengu]? Are they not my dogs? Cannot I do with them as I like?'

Now, however, with the noose around his neck, Hintsa agreed to stop the killings. Over the next few weeks, the amaMfengu ebbed away west in their droves towards an area of the Cape administered as British Kaffraria.

It was now early May and, although nobody knew it, the king did not have long to live. What is unclear about the ensuing action is whether or not Smith and his trusted Corp of Guides had planned to murder him at the very next opportunity, or whether the killing of Hintsa a few days later was an impulsive act or accident, born of frustration. Certainly, the British might have preferred him dead – his absence would be one less thorn in the side of the settlers. For the time being, however, D'Urban and Smith took down the nooses, and removed King Hintsa, Sarhili and Bhurhu to the British camp to remain hostages.

Shortly afterwards Smith and 500 of his troops set off to retrieve the 50,000 head of cattle demanded by D'Urban in return for ceasing hostilities and compensation. Hintsa was forced to accompany them to ensure the livestock were secured from his subjects in the adjacent countryside, known as Gcalekaland. After a couple of days wandering the landscape east of the Great Kei River, they had retrieved a few cattle, but nothing like the numbers they sought. Smith and his men grew frustrated and suspicious, believing that they were being watched from the dense bush by the king's people, who were in addition surreptitiously driving the cattle away out of reach of the search party. Tension was mounting and nerves were fraying amongst both captors and captives.

'What have the cattle done that you want them?' Hintsa asked Smith. 'Why must I see my subjects deprived of them?'

'That *you* know far better than I do,' Smith replied.

Scouts attached to the unit thought Hintsa was leading them a merry dance and planning an escape, so they were cautious and alert. Smith, too, was on edge, and apparently threatened to kill the king if he tried to escape.

On 12 May 1835 from the top of a hill, the taut wire of historical, military and cultural tension clean snapped. The tensile strength of amaXhosa tolerance to colonial humiliation could be heard to rupture in the thundering of hooves. King Hintsa broke free on his horse, galloping away as fast as he could. All hell broke loose in the British military unit – Hintsa was off, escaping at speed! The scene was frantic, and the stakes high for everyone involved. Lives hung in the balance.

Smith and his Scout Corp immediately took up the chase, shouting 'Stop! Stop!' as they galloped furiously over the rough terrain. In desperation, Smith attempted two shots at the king, but each time his pistol misfired. Although he nearly exhausted his horse in the chase, he eventually got alongside Hintsa and, still galloping, wrestled with Hintsa and hit him with his pistol. 'A devil could not have breathed more liquid flame,' is how Smith described this episode to his wife. Hintsa defended himself with *assegais* (short spears), but Smith somehow managed to shove him from his horse onto the ground. With his life now in the balance, the king ran down a slope towards the safety of the river with Smith's troops in deadly pursuit.

Struggling to bring his horse under control, Smith allegedly shouted to George Southey, one of his scouts, 'Shoot, George, and be damned to you!' Southey fired, hitting Hintsa in the leg, but the wounded king still got up and ran off. Once again, Smith bellowed, 'Be damned to you, George, shoot again!' This time one of the two Southey brothers – it's unclear which – shot Hintsa in the chest area. Although initially floored and struggling, the injured king scrambled further down the steep banks of the Nqabara River to hide amongst the boulders, bushes and flowing water. He was in a desperate situation, but probably hoping to reach some of his own people nearby.

The stage was set for a seminal moment in South African history – the killing of King Hintsa in the river, by George Southey under the command of Harry Smith. This seismic event has never been disputed, but much else was. Duplicity, obfuscation, contradiction, lies, conspiracy and complicity were hallmarks of the evidence later given by key actors in the tragedy.

King Hintsa, the senior Xhosa leader who was killed in 1835 trying to escape Lt Col Harry Smith and his men. (With permission of the National Library of South Africa.)

The official line taken by many of those searching in and near the river is that George Southey saw the king hiding behind boulders in the river armed with his assegais and, in self-defence, shot the king at close range, blowing out his brains and the back of his skull. Other testimonies gave evidence to the effect that Hintsa called desperately for mercy on being found hiding in the water, and that he represented very little threat to anyone. Was the heavily injured man trying to give himself up? Did men under the command of a senior British army officer shoot a king who was calling for mercy? Some of those caught up in the drama said they felt threatened by the amaXhosa who were watching and hiding in the bush nearby, but this evidence does not stack up. Figures watching from the bush do not detract from the fact that the king was badly wounded, allegedly asking for mercy and obviously no threat at all. Whatever the truth and half-truths, it is clear that he was hunted down, chased into the river and killed at close range.

Worse was to follow, although that seems hard to believe.

Not satisfied with the kill, the killers, like a pack of hunting dogs, went about mutilating the body and stealing his jewellery for trophies. His ears were cut off and attempts made to remove his teeth. It is alleged that parts of his genitals were even removed. Bracelets, armbands and other body decoration, as well as his assegais, were taken as 'trophies'. Some of these souvenirs even reached the streets of colonial towns, where they were snapped up. Literally and figuratively, there was a great deal of the king's blood on a great many hands as his body was dragged out.

Smith's men then left it lying on open ground. Smith insisted they wrap it, as some sort of gesture. Perhaps he knew there was to be an inquiry and that he had better make an attempt at respect. He claimed not to have the equipment to bury his adversary, and knew that news of the murder, and its circumstances, would not be well received in the corridors of Whitehall. Indeed, when Lord Glenelg, His Majesty's Secretary of State for the Colonies, heard of the killing, he was outraged.

Nonetheless, following this tragic episode Smith took his troops further into Hintsa's territory toward the Mbashe River and resumed the search for the missing cattle and horses. Their efforts were largely in vain as the local amaXhosa had assiduously moved their livestock out of sight and beyond reach. Most of the 50,000 cattle did not materialise.

Putting our 21st-century sensitivities and standards to one side, it is still impossible to view the events of 12 May 1835 with anything but revulsion, disgust and contempt. The settlers, the British administrators and the missionaries, one way or another, had over decades been preaching to King Hintsa's people the superior values of enlightened Europe, the Bible and so-called 'civilisation'. Even now I am left speechless. What can you say about the savagery heaped on the king and, by extension, his people? It flew in the face of everything the British claimed and believed about themselves, revealing a barbarism at the heart of all their talk. To follow up the killing of a king pleading for mercy by mutilation of his corpse – it really beggars belief.

Against this violent and horrendous backdrop, Hintsa's son, Sarhili, aged about 25, inherited the most senior position in amaXhosa society. Difficult times lay ahead, characterised by war, drought, cattle disease and the unresolved psychological scar that Hintsa's murder left across all of amaXhosa society. This included the rise of Nongqawuse's Cattle Killing prophecies only 20 years later. I couldn't help speculate that if King Hintsa had not been killed in these circumstances, he might have handled Nongqawuse and her sweeping prophecies differently; I think he might have been able to contain a local trauma and prevent it from becoming a national tragedy. Who knows? At any rate, I feel sure the reverberations of this tragedy had something to do with the many stresses and strains leading up to Nongqawuse's prophecies.

***

With difficulty, I traversed the slopes of the Nqabara Valley, trying to replicate the last footsteps of King Hintsa before he was shot by one of Harry Smith's men on 12 May 1835.

I left the grave and walked up the long grassy slope overlooking the river as I wanted to literally follow the footsteps of Hintsa, feel the final minutes of his life as he fled the pack of hunters. To my surprise, I found it necessary to stop several times on the incline to gather my breadth, and take in the bold sculptured landscape and lush vegetation. This wasn't history from a book, website or tutorial – I was attempting to re-enact the events *in situ*. How would a man shot in two places, carrying assegais, cope with the terrain I was encountering, assuming it had not changed too much with time?

Even without wounds or the threat of capture, I was amazed at how hard it was to descend the slope. The ground was very uneven underfoot, strewn with hidden gullies and mounds to trip over, the grass was chest-high in places, and thorn bushes necessitated frequent swerving to avoid nasty punctures. Soon I was visibly sweating and panting to keep up the pace. I imagined King Hintsa rushing down this terrain to escape his pursuers, the chilling shouts in the distance in isiXhosa and English, the crack of gunfire and the whistle of bullets in the air. Sparks and sharp metallic clicks might have highlighted the direction of fire as bullets ricocheted violently off rock and boughs.

Having slowly navigated my way down, I saw that the king would have had to rush across a piece of flat ground for 25 to 30 metres to reach the cover of dense bush at the edge of the river.

I concluded that the whole escape route would have been fraught with peril, even if the vegetation had been different 187 years earlier. Under the same circumstances, I doubted that I would have got as far as the river without being shot again. By the time the king waded into the river to hide, it is highly unlikely that he would have had much energy left at all, especially with seeping bullet wounds. He would have been a man desperately holding onto life by virtue of the adrenaline pumping through his veins and his pride as Paramount Chief of the amaXhosa.

When I joined my colleagues at the tailgate of the Hilux an ad hoc court had formed, and they were forensically evaluating the role played by many of the key people. At times they raised their arms and pointed their fingers across the crime scene to indicate likely directions of travel by Smith, Hintsa, the Southey brothers and a plethora of others. Then attention focused on motives and possible sub-plots amongst the various agents. Had the killing been agreed in advance, back at the camp? Had King Hintsa been murdered by Smith and his men, or was it self-defence, or was it an accident? Was this in fact a planned or pre-empted murder?

Doubt kept rearing its head in our minds – doubts that the British reports and investigations of this disgraceful episode had been honest and accurate. At the various hearings that followed the murder, Smith and his entourage had stressed the perceived threats to their safety from Hintsa's assegais and the hordes of his loyal supporters allegedly hiding in the thick vegetation. Self-defence was the principal pillar of their explanation: *his life or ours*. In a strident letter written at the time by Smith to a Captain Bain, he concluded with

> We shall be most happy to see you … I am now in the midst of a Mass of Papers and references and dispatches as to Hintza – Southey (George) will come off gloriously, it was an act of Self-defence.

At our own inquiry into these horrendous events, we decided that the multiple contradictions and refusal to comment by some who had been present smelt of a cover-up. In fact, it was a stench. Mike, in particular, spat out the words 'Harry Smith' with bile-laden contempt and loathing. Smith was not coming out well from his Nqabara judges. Our animated outdoor court concluded that it was unclear what had actually happened in the final minutes of King Hintsa's life, but more likely than not he was murdered at close range by George Southey, and that his body was mutilated by several men under Smith's command. As the senior officer in charge, Harry Smith had blood on his hands. Masses of it.

And so, in the end, our decision was unanimous. Smith had been guilty of regicide.

It was 4.25 pm when we packed up the mugs of tea and discarded the eggshells. Hutch muttered that he would not leave it another 25 years before he returned; then we all clambered into the vehicle and headed back up the slope to the dirt track and the main road to East London. Although we chatted further about historical events, we wanted the quickest route home, starting with the good road between Willowvale and Idutywa. That was not going to happen. Somewhere between the two towns we ground to a halt, forced, in a line of other cars, to wait while a toyi-toyi – protest – played out. I had encountered these a couple of times before and they weren't pleasant. In my experience, people were angry at the lack of basic amenities and jobs. Burning rubber tyres and other debris were strewn across the road. Flames and black smoke were visible, and acrid air seeped into the car. At first, young men just lingered around the obstructions, but then they picked up another rubber tyre and a bottle of petrol or the like, and started heading up the queue of cars. It was not hard to read the mood. The atmosphere was tense and could deteriorate quickly. Hutch knew the drill; this was not a time to hang around. He did a quick U-turn, heading off on a detour to Gwadana Hill and the N2 at Ibika.

It was 7.30 pm and dark when we pulled into Hutch's driveway, the dogs bounding out to greet us. Will embraced his wife, and then they scooted off back home, a handful of blocks away. Vakaska No. 2 was complete.

15: THE KING'S HEAD

'He did not want another Nongqawuse'

Paramount Chief Sigcau, *Daily Dispatch*, 1996

The next morning I intended to write up my notes from the previous days' travels. Hutch had patients to attend to, but before he shuffled off to his surgery he removed from the shelves various history and travel books that he thought might interest me. Once again, I was the proverbial child in a sweet shop, unsure which delight to sample first, the lemon sherbets or the pear drops.

The last thing he put on the dining room table was a scrapbook filled with newspaper cuttings pasted inside. Now, this looked exciting. The many articles were marked up in black ink. The first one I glimpsed was annotated by Hutch with 'D/D 29/2/96' – D/D being the *Daily Dispatch* newspaper.

'I presume you've heard of Nicholas Gcaleka?' Hutch asked in a mischievous tone.

'No. Never heard of him.'

'He claimed to have found the skull of King Hintsa. Caused quite a controversy. Have a read.' And with that Hutch sauntered off to administer health and healing, leaving me with a pile of books and two excited dogs.

Nicholas Gcaleka, King Hintsa's skull and controversy – what was Hutch on about? Was this another twist in the story of Hintsa's demise? This was new to me. Were his killing and mutilation not bad enough? Couldn't he at least be allowed to rest in peace? The king's grave at the Nqabara River had felt like a crime scene, and now here were a whole bunch of newspaper cuttings offering unexpected forensic evidence. All fired up, I skimmed through the scrapbook and quickly pieced together a bizarre, almost larger-than-life story involving South Africa, Scotland, President Mandela, the British royal family, *sangomas* / *iGqirha*, DNA sampling, fraud and a great deal else. Oh, I nearly forgot to say, Nongqawuse got a mention too. So, where to begin?

In 1994, the so-called Chief Nicholas Tilana Gcaleka claimed that he was a direct descendant of King Hintsa and that in his capacity as *sangoma* he had received visions, messages from the ancestors claiming that the skull of King Hintsa was in Scotland, and that he had to retrieve it. Nicholas Gcaleka was charismatic, by all accounts, and not shy about proclaiming his status and visions. As you can imagine, quite a brouhaha ensued as he came to public attention, insisting that the king's spirit would be restless unless his skull was returned to South Africa. A whirlwind of publicity was generated, as Gcaleka made bold claims and gave the impression of absolute certainty where in fact ambiguity and doubt abounded. To add an air of authenticity to his royal claims, he dressed lavishly in traditional attire, a leopard skin thrown over his shoulder. His hair was long and beaded, and on his head he wore striking headgear, all accentuating who he was and what he stood for. He cut a fine figure of a man.

Apparently, he caused quite a stir wherever he went, ruffling feathers along the way, all of which seemed to suit him nicely. The doubting Thomases, of which there were quite a few, would be proved wrong, he repeatedly proclaimed. He clearly subscribed to the principle that all publicity is good publicity. That's as maybe.

Gcaleka duly travelled to Britain where he recruited quite a following. Much as his visions had forecast, he did find an old skull in Scotland, near Inverness. Moreover, the skull had a hole in it, which he claimed was caused by the killer bullet from one of Harry Smith's men at the Nqabara River all those years ago. Gcaleka was triumphant, and he felt vindicated. Why not? Now he could return the skull to its rightful place in Hintsa's grave.

By this time the story of the king's skull was catching the attention of the British and

OUTRAGED: Chief Nicholas Gcaleka roars over the confiscation of the skull he brought from Britain claiming it was that of the last Xhosa King Hintsa ka Phalo.

Picture by PONKO MASIBA

Gcaleka wants Tutu, Mandela to decide

Daily Dispatch Reporters

BISHO — Xhosa traditional healer and self-styled chief Nicholas Gcaleka visited the Eastern Cape premier, Mr Raymond Mhlaba, here yesterday to discuss the contentious skull brought from Scotland.

Accompanied by a chief and three other traditional healers, Mr Gcaleka told journalists outside the premier's office the aim of his visit was "to see him about the confiscation" of the skull which he claims is that of the late Xhosa King, Hintsa ka Phalo, killed by a British soldier in 1835.

The much-publicised skull had been sent to a police mortuary for safekeeping in Willowvale on Thursday, at the instructions of paramount chiefs Xolilizwe Sigcawu and Maxhoba Sandile, at an imbizo held to decide its fate.

Unhappy at the turn of events, Mr Gcaleka said he would call on President Nelson Mandela and Archbishop Desmond Tutu to intervene.

"The government must intervene because that skull belongs to the nation," he said.

Should his pleas with the premier fail, he said, he would appeal to the nation, adding that the skull would be buried according to "the people's needs, not the few individuals'."

Mr Gcaleka said he did not recognise Contralesa as it did not exist in Chief Hintsa's day.

Meanwhile, the office of the British High Commission yesterday rejected claims made by Mr Gcaleka that British Prime Minister John Major and Prince Charles would attend a service to mark the burial of the skull.

Mr Gcaleka told the paramount chiefs of the Xhosas at Thursday's imbizo that Mr Major had telephoned him asking about the date of burial of the skull.

Mr Gcaleka claimed Mr Major had said he and Prince Charles would attend, and also promised to bring back Chief Hintsa's necklace which was in Britain.

"Prince Charles and Mr Major have no plans to visit South Africa," a spokesman for the British High Commission in Cape Town, Mr Andrew Noble, said.

Before its confiscation, Mr Gcaleka had planned to bury the skull on May 12.

One of the many articles in the *Daily Dispatch* for 1996 about Nicholas Gcaleka. He caught the attention of the world's media, politicians, and royalty in his quest for King Hintsa's skull. (Photograph taken by Ponko Masiba and used with kind permission of the *Daily Dispatch*.)

South African media. It had too many exotic, juicy ingredients to ignore. Stories involving kings, skulls, chiefs, visions and an exotic character like Nicholas Gcaleka were meat and drink to the news desks of television stations and the press. Gcaleka seemed to thrive on the attention and monetised his celebrity status, charging R180 to R300 per interview. He even got on Big Breakfast, a primetime BBC television show, where he rubbed shoulders with celebrities such as Robin Williams. Added to which, he took the opportunity to tell the British government and the royal family how the amaXhosa had been treated by the British in the 19th century. Now politicians were being pulled into the one-man vortex.

However, not everyone was being taken in so easily. Even while Gcaleka was in Scotland, a view was expressed that the skull was of Celtic origin and that the hole was not consistent with a bullet fired at close range. Did that perturb Chief Nicholas Gcaleka? Not a jot. Photographs appeared of him holding the skull high at arm's length and claiming to have been led to it by his ancestors.

When senior figures in the amaXhosa community and the Congress of Traditional Leaders (Contralesa), heard about these claims, they expressed extreme displeasure and refuted his status as chief and his links to amaXhosa royalty. Xolilizwe Sigcau, Paramount Chief of the AmaXhosa, referred to the 'self-styled Chief Nicholas Gcaleka'. In his view, 'Chief Gcaleka has no authority to allocate himself the right to deal with the issue as if it were his private property.' He went to say that that the royal house would thoroughly look into the matter. Interestingly, to stress his concern about the situation and the potential consequences, he said 'he did not want another Nongqawuse'. How telling. In 1996 Nongqawuse and the events of the Cattle Killing from the 1850s were being used as a reference point and a warning against matters getting out of control and causing difficulties to amaXhosa society.

Some people felt that, self-styled chief or not, Nicholas Gcaleka had raised an important issue; the British government had murdered their king and owed them an apology. A statement was made to this effect by the amaXhosa royal house, but no such apology was made, and the matter was dropped.

Meanwhile, the *sangomas* of the Eastern Cape Traditional Medical Practitioners Association were not impressed either; in their words, it all 'smelt a little fishy'. For a start, they did not recognise Gcaleka as a legitimate *sangoma.* In their eyes, he had no right to go about claiming visions about King Hintsa. Some were quite strident and accused him of playing with fire.

It was then revealed that Chief Nicholas Gcaleka was actually Mbambatho Tilana, a liquor distributor and salesman, not a chief. Nor was he a *sangoma*. As a result he was regarded as a fraudster and a charlatan, with no right to deal with matters of royalty and amaXhosa traditions. How dare he!

An obvious flaw in Gcaleka's claims was the fact that there is no evidence in any of the records that King Hintsa's head was removed from his body. His attackers had mutilated him by cutting off his ears and attempting to remove his teeth – but surely, if they had removed his head, this would have been documented? If he had been decapitated, the amaXhosa who buried him would certainly have conveyed the atrocity across Xhosaland. As there were numerous British troops at the site of the killing, it seems unlikely that decapitation of the king would have remained secret. One way or another it would have surfaced in one of the inquiries, whitewashed as they were, after the event.

None of this perturbed the indefatigable Mr Gcaleka, who demanded that the skull be returned to its rightful place and be buried with the king's body. The claims by his countrymen that he was a charlatan did not faze him, and he tried to elicit the support of Mr Nelson Mandela and Archbishop Desmond Tutu, as well as Prime Minister John Major and Prince Charles. This was the story that just kept on giving, as evidenced by the column inches and emboldened headlined in Hutch's scrapbook.

An *imbizo*, a chiefs' gathering, was called to discuss the whole issue, and the now infamous skull was removed from Nicholas Gcaleka, much to his annoyance. Some thought that bona fide *sangomas* should decide on the authenticity of the skull. Others felt DNA testing more reliable. The latter won the day, and scientists were called in to adjudicate. And so the story limped to a dull conclusion. Pipettes, bioassays and DNA matching revealed that far from being the skull of a distinguished amaXhosa king, this was in fact from a middle-aged European female. As others pointed out, the hole found in the skull was too small. George Southey's shot, at short range, would have caused a great deal more damage, not a small, tidy hole.

Things did not improve for Nicholas Gcaleka. Not only did his skull claims prove to be spurious, but back home he was hauled before a court in Mthatha on several counts of fraud related to liquor and mielies. He was, however, acquitted of the charges, and drifted away from the headlines until his death from cancer in 2019, aged 69.

So, despite Paramount Chief Xolilizwe Sigcau's earnest concerns at the beginning of this saga, a 20th-century Nongqawuse situation was averted. A mass movement ending in calamity had been avoided, thanks to some Xhosa diplomacy and the wonders of DNA testing. Added to which, Nicholas Gcaleka had travelled internationally and enjoyed the limelight for a few months.

In 2005 the bones of Sandile, another senior Xhosa chief, were exhumed and forensically examined by experts, as legend had it that his skull had been taken back to Britain by Lord Carrington after the Ninth Frontier War (1877–78). In this instance too there was no indication that the chief had been beheaded and the skull removed.

By the time I had explored this episode of local history, courtesy of Hutch's scrapbook, I wasn't feeling my best. In truth I was feeling more than a little rough. Much to my surprise, my Covid test kit gave a negative result. Hopefully, I'd feel better by the time I got home a few days later.

16: FABIENNE AND THE CURSE OF HINTSA

'The person who refuses to take advice hears by a hot wind.'

'Isala kutyela siva ngo lopu'

Xhosa proverb: Rev. J.H. Soga, *The Ama-Xosa. Life and Customs*, 1931

Touching down at Heathrow airport on 20 January 2022, I felt that I had covered a lot of ground on my Nongqawuse pilgrimage, which had expanded to include King Hintsa. Indeed, I had – more than 26,000 kilometres. I had seen and experienced a great deal in my trek between Cape Town and Pondoland, from the liberation movement statues in Century City to the sleepy rivers of Gcalekaland. New friends had been made, and I had eaten a great many more hard-boiled eggs than I was accustomed to. There was a lot to contextualise and digest. A period of reflection and rumination was probably in order, so that I could align my thoughts and draw some conclusions about the events in the Cape Colony of the 19th century.

That was not to happen. Once I'd emptied my suitcase of sand from the Wild Coast, washed a mountain of T-shirts and socks, and spent some time chatting with my wife, things took a turn for the worse. Thoughts about Nongqawuse and King Hintsa had to be relegated to the back drawer.

I had flown from Cape Town feeling a little under the weather. Back home, I started to run a high temperature, sleep 16 hours a night and sweat like a Swede in a sauna. Nausea was accompanied by extravagant bowel movements. It was not a pretty sight. Over an untouched bowl of cereal, we decided that an urgent trip was needed to Winchester Hospital's Accident and Emergency Department. I was dropped off with an expectation of returning home in a couple of hours. A couple of tablets would probably do the trick.

It was to be five days before I was discharged.

Triage was over in a jiffy, and I was swiftly shown to my own sterile grey-white cubicle, with a transparent plastic curtain and a bed to lie on. Electronic medical machines mounted on chrome trolleys and drips shared the space with me. The artificial light was bright, there was the clinical smell of disinfectant, and an enthusiastic quartet of monitoring machines, which sounded off beeps at 5- to 10-second intervals with an air of free-form jazz about them. Every now and again I could hear an elderly chap wheezing heavily in the next cubicle and a young girl sobbing somewhere, apparently nursing a broken arm. Medics in various coloured uniforms were dashing around with their bags of equipment, tending to patients and earnestly conferring with each other in low tones.

Much to my surprise, I did not have to wait long at all to see the doctor and nurse, who seemed delighted to have a patient who didn't have Covid or cut thumb. I explained that I had gone in search of Nongqawuse and King Hintsa in South Africa and returned feeling lousy. The historical significance of my trip did not appear to be of interest, so I showed them a nasty black scab from a bite on my shin and the discoloured flesh moving up my leg, and explained about the diarrhoea, which might be classified as a weapon of mass destruction if used in a theatre of battle. To help with the diagnosis I called Hutch to speak to the A&E doctor, who quickly recognised the symptoms of African tick fever. A suitable medicine was agreed upon. I apologised for all the fuss and assumed I could be discharged. No, no, no. I was going absolutely nowhere except the isolation ward. There were tropical disease protocols to follow. Protocols? A whole long list of them. Mandatory, apparently.

'Is this really necessary?' I thought to myself. The doctor enthused about treating a patient with tropical diseases, and she went on to explain that I probably had at least two other infections, including cellulitis, which was evidently travelling towards my groin. That could turn nasty. Stool and blood samples were required. Delightful. In the meantime, I had to remove my clothes and put on a hospital gown. Someone would come with a wheelchair shortly. A wheelchair – really? I don't do wheelchairs. However, it wasn't a point of discussion according to the polite but firm medic.

As I lay in Cubicle 9 dressed in an unflattering hospital gown, listening to pinging monitors and patients in pain, I must admit to feeling a little sorry for myself. I felt dreadful – hot, clammy, drowsy and out of control. The mention of sepsis and wheelchairs had not helped. Was this a curse by King Hintsa, punishing me for poking around the site of his killing and mutilation? Was I incurring the wrath of the amaXhosa ancestors for sticking my nose where I ought not to have? Was Nongqawuse part of the conspiracy too? I thought I had been respectful and courteous in everything I had done in the Eastern Cape. After all, my pilgrimage had been to better understand a turbulent period of amaXhosa history by visiting the places where events had happened on the ground. My motivation was to see and understand.

Who was I kidding? My predicament probably had nothing to do with a curse from Hintsa and much more to do with swimming in rivers at the Wild Coast, washing my hands in muddy ditch water and walking through long grass in shorts. I had broken my own rules about dos and don'ts in rural Africa and I was now paying the price.

Christ, I did feel lousy.

Lying in my cubicle, quietly waiting for my wheelchair to arrive, the atmosphere in the Winchester A&E started to change.

'I love you, honey. Everybody go *whoop, whoop*!' was being chanted by a patient in one of the adjacent cubicles.

There it was again: 'Whoop, whoop! Love you, honey!', only louder and clearer, and repeated now as a rhythmic chant. Next, she began adding French to her rant. '*Jamais, jamais, whoop, whoop! J'adore les fromages française. Entendez!*' ('Never, never, whoop, whoop! I love French cheese. Listen to me!'). By this time we could all hear her. Numerous medics rushed to the scene and attempted to calm the whooping patient, but to no avail. To the whooping were added various French expletives, and all of it getting louder and more insistent.

I assumed the poor woman was drunk or high. With another 'Hey, sexy baby, whoop, whoop!' she danced out of her cubicle to the central island where the A&E medics were stationed. Single-handedly, Fabienne (not her real name) turned a well-organised A&E department into chaos, as several of the staff tried unsuccessfully to coax her back to Cubicle 11.

It was both comedic and tragic. Her persistent 'Whoop, whoop, love you, honey. Sexy baby!' may have had many of the patients and staff laughing out loud, but we were probably watching a young woman's mind imploding. A psychotic episode was being played out in public.

When my doctor returned to send me off to my isolation room, I commented on Fabienne's tragedy and asked why she hadn't been given a heavy sedative to help. With a face that said it all, she confessed that the young woman had already taken sedatives.

On reflection my various ailments were perhaps not as grave as Fabienne's, although the pathology laboratory did find I was carrying latent tuberculosis, tick fever, cellulitis and shigella. Quite a present to bring back from South Africa. However, five days in isolation at the hospital followed by two weeks' rest at home soon had me on the road to recovery – I regained my strength and lost a few pounds around the midriff.

My friend Pete, or Pete McDad, as we affectionately call him, is sort of British and sort of Australian. None of us are quite sure and neither is he, not that it matters much. He's a large chap with generous features and a smart mind. Some might even say he's clever. He used to lecture in a university, I believe. Quite good by all accounts – well, his account. Nothing amuses him more than telling obscure jokes and taking the Mick out of people. I like Pete. He has a big heart and an appetite for recounting real-life stories, some of which may even be true. In his spare time, he shows tourists around Winchester Cathedral, explaining its rich and varied history. Before my South African jaunt, he'd extended an invitation to all members of our theatre group to a guided trip of the magnificent building. So, shortly after I had been discharged from hospital, my wife Clare and I accepted his invitation of a tour. A time and date were agreed upon, and in the meantime I started to collate my notes, photographs and thoughts from my recent trip. As far as I was concerned, that journey or pilgrimage was over.

Apparently not. Once more, fate played an unexpected hand. Right on my doorstep.

We were quite enthusiastic about Pete's free guided tour of the cathedral, and took the liberty of inviting my in-laws and my granddaughter. Opposite the ticket booth and before the tour started, Pete pointed out a polished limestone memorial entitled Roll of Fame, to commemorate 19th-century British soldiers from the local regiments. As the city has been home to army regiments for a couple of centuries, this was all rather unremarkable – until he pointed out a name about two-thirds of the way down. He thought it might be familiar to me. Indeed, it was. Chiselled into the masonry and decorated with blue ink I saw: 'Lt. Gen. Sir Harry G. W. Smith. 1860.'

I was extremely surprised to see Sir Harry Smith listed on a Roll of Fame in Winchester Cathedral. What was he doing here?

Harry Smith! What the hell was he doing in my home town? I had travelled great distances, often in some discomfort, to see and understand what he had done in Africa, and as far as I was concerned, it was mostly shameful and had caused a great deal of damage. Only a few weeks earlier I had seen evidence of his dirty work on the banks of the Nqabara River, in Gcalekaland. I had touched the headstone of King Hintsa, whom Smith's men had killed and mutilated. Now here he was, commemorated as some sort of hero on my doorstep.

Pete and the rest of the family could see I was rooted to the cathedral floor. Had he really, I thought in disbelief, been in one of the local regiments? I felt like I was being stalked. Or perhaps his appearance at this moment was just a thread in the rich tapestry of fate, in which case, Beowulf's 'fate goes ever as fate must' ought to console me. Fate or not, I was discombobulated. I had expected to marvel at Pete's explanations of stained-glass windows, Norman arches and Sir Anthony Gormley's statue, not wrestle with Harry Smith again. As we walked around, I tried to concentrate on Pete's words of wisdom, but my mind was elsewhere. I was not going to let this coincidence go unchallenged.

A few days later, I visited the local army museums. Winchester has a few. The last one I came to was dedicated to the 95th Rifles or Rifle Corps, Smith's regiment. At the ticket desk they knew very little about him or the Frontier Wars between the Europeans and amaXhosa. They were familiar with the Anglo-Zulu Wars of 1879, mostly because of the Stanley Baker and Michael Caine film of 1964. For once, I refrained from chitchat and hurried upstairs, scurrying past glass cabinets of guns and uniforms from battles fought around the world.

After skirting around a large mock-up of the Battle of Waterloo I came face to face with the man. There was no mistaking him. I couldn't avoid his haughty, steely stare from the wall opposite me. It was as though he were saying, 'Ha! You. I've been wondering when you might turn up.' It was only a portrait, but I felt quite adversarial.

Henry Moseley, the painter, had given Harry an air of gravitas and stern authority, with a dark uniform and a moody atmospheric background. A large silver medal on his chest projected his military achievements, and the deep scarlet lining of his coat reflected the passion and energy for which he was so well known by his admirers, of which there had been many. No expense had been spared on the picture frame, which was generous, gilded and extremely ornate, with flowery garlands.

Portrait of Lieutenant-General Sir Harry George Wakelyn Smith (1787–1860) in the museum of the 95th Rifles, in my home town of Winchester, UK. I sensed he'd been anticipating my visit. (By Henry Moseley, with the permission of The Royal Green Jackets (Rifles) Museum, Winchester 95th.)

Despite the formality of the painting and the frame, I was rather surprised at how human Sir Harry looked. This wasn't just a military bigwig, but a real person. It was a touch unnerving. I could barely take my eyes off him.

He stared back at me, his dark eyes following me as I inspected him from different angles. I kept thinking that although he might look all grand and authoritative there on the wall in a military museum, I knew some of his dirty secrets. That smart uniform and flamboyant medal might hoodwink most visitors, but not me. Did he really have to allow his troops to destroy so many amaXhosa villages and crops in pursuit of reprisals and territorial gains? How could he justify humiliating the amaXhosa chiefs in public – making them kiss his boots, standing on their necks, calling them dogs, and declaring himself their Great Chief or *iNkosi eNkulu*? He was blind to the anger, resentment and hostility his actions provoked. Could he not see he was helping foment more hostility, causing more loss of life, and creating more schisms across the Cape – and that these would have repercussions? Obviously not. Why of all things did he oversee the killing and mutilation of King Hintsa, one of the most atrocious acts in the

Cape's infamous history? His barbaric treatment of the king, his many acts of hubris and the greed with which the entire colonial project was carried out had created the conditions in which the Cattle Killing Movement could arise. Nongqawuse's prophecy was clearly an expression of desperation, an almost literal cry for help after decades of war and suffering. It is not the least bit surprising that King Hintsa's son and successor, Sarhili, had no trust in the Europeans, including the army, administrators, settlers and the missionaries, and that he longed for a solution that would rid his people of the Europeans forever.

I suspected that the man gazing from the painting before me would not have been too perturbed by my questions and accusations, and might have retorted with stories of his successes during the Napoleonic Wars and of suppressing the uprising in India. His self-confidence was well known, emanating from Moseley's portrait with just a hint of the superciliousness that defined his relations with the amaXhosa people.

The museum was quiet and almost empty of other visitors. There was a palpable tension between Smith and me. I was unsure how to terminate our meeting. I reflected on what had drawn me first to Nongqawuse and then to King Hintsa, and had brought me to the point of having such an emotional mental exchange with a man I had never heard of three years ago. The process had been organic. I had not gone looking for the Cattle Killing or the king's killing. I had simply read a book about the history of a country I had volunteered in 40 years ago – then followed the clues and joined the dots by visiting the sites where historical events had occurred. In the process I had become gripped – stirred to a sense of outrage, at times – by what had been inflicted on the amaXhosa people. To this day, South Africa struggles to shake off some of the effects of men like Sir Harry Smith, whose assumption of superiority coupled with brute force did so much damage.

Standing in the museum of the 95th Rifles in Winchester, gazing at Lieutenant-General Sir Harry Smith, I knew that my journey was not complete. There were too many loose ends. This man, I felt, had been central to the events I had been investigating, and I needed to know more about him. To me, he represented Empire, Victorian Britain and colonial suppression of the Cape amaXhosa during the 19th century. I had seen, smelt and listened to the landscapes that had shaped Nongqawuse and King Hintsa in the Eastern Cape. What, then, was the community that had shaped Smith? And where was it?

I resolved to find his roots. So my pilgrimage moved to Whittlesey, Cambridgeshire, a couple of hours from Winchester. No passport or Covid screening needed this time, just a tank of petrol.

17: A CEMETERY IN WHITTLESEY

'The teller's news is unsatisfactory.'

'Indaba ye-tyel' ayikoli'

Xhosa proverb: Rev. J.H. Soga, *The Ama-Xosa. Life and Customs*, 1931

My visits to the site of Nongqawuse's vision at the Gxara River, her grave on Fick's farm and King Hintsa's place of rest on the banks of the Nqabara River had all stirred within me a sense of excitement, a few butterflies in the stomach. On those occasions, I had come to pay my respects and to get a sense of the place, to hear and feel its history. Moreover, the site of Nongqawuse's vision and Hintsa's grave could be regarded as crime scenes from which death, mutilation and mass starvation had arisen; events that had shaped 19th- and 20th- century South Africa. As I drove along the flat straight A605 approaching the small town of Whittlesey, near Peterborough, I felt very different. Curious but hesitant. In a sense, I had already met Sir Harry, both on the banks of the Nqabara River, where he'd hunted down Hintsa, and at the army museum in Winchester. His presence had been hard to avoid. Now I was seeking some kind of closure, some resolution to the feelings of indignation my discovery of this man had evoked in me.

I pulled into the quiet town square, noticing the Buttercross and the local Wetherspoon's pub. All very nice. 'So this was the home of the great Sir Henry George Wakelyn Smith!' I thought.

Whatever my thoughts about Sir Harry, I needed to remind myself that at the height of his career in 1847, when he visited Whittlesey, Harry Smith was a superstar, a Victorian celebrity – and that is no exaggeration. Harry and his wife Juana were the number one billing. Each charmed in their own way. Although in 1835 Smith, having served his first term at the Cape, left under a cloud following the whitewash investigation into Hintsa's killing and mutilation, in 1846, while serving in India, he achieved the status of a national hero. During the First Anglo-Sikh War of 1845–46, the Sikhs had made serious attempts to wrest back control from the British. The grip of Empire on the Indian Subcontinent was being severely tested, and much hung in the balance. Would British rule be defeated? Under Smith's energetic leadership at Aliwal, heavy and significant defeats were inflicted on the Sikh army, thereby maintaining British power in the country. At news of the British victory, sighs of relief were audible in the corridors of government and the boardrooms of the mercantile elites. Their various interests were preserved, for now.

Overnight, Smith became known as the Hero of Aliwal. He openly used the title himself. Cannons boomed and bells rang on his return to Britain, and everywhere, from the rural pubs of the north to the House of Commons, the talk was of Aliwal and the great Sir Harry Smith. The Duke of Wellington, not known for exuberant praise, could hardly contain himself in the House of Lords, finishing off his speech with, 'I never read an account of any affair in which an officer ever showed himself more capable than this officer has in commanding troops in the field.'

Prime Minister Peel conferred on Smith a baronetcy. Cambridge University celebrated his achievement with an honorary degree. Queen Victoria, also part of the fan club, was not to be outdone and invited the Smiths to dine with her at Marlborough House. Afterwards she wrote in her journal, 'Sir Harry, a fine old man, was presented to me. He seemed so pleased at my praises'. In Whittlesey, 10,000 or so local people lined the streets to catch a glimpse of the Smiths on their way to a civic reception.

St Mary's Church , Whittlesey, where Harry Smith went to school, and close to where he was born in 1787.

My trip to Sir Harry's place of birth was a little less auspicious. No cheering crowds greeted me. Church bells were not pealing, and local dignitaries were not there to bestow honours. However, Sue and Ken Palmer were waiting for me at St Mary's Church just off the main square. They had kindly agreed to show me around the church where their local hero had gone to school in the 1790s. Apparently, I was not the only person who had come to Whittlesey in search of Sir Harry in recent years. I was struck by how large the building was, both tall and wide, with the steeple appearing to prop up the pewter bank of low cloud. A magnificent organ looked more than capable of belting out 'Jerusalem' when required. At the back of the wooden pews were colourful cut-out flags and words, probably the work of the Sunday School or something similar. It felt like a living place of worship, part of the community, and not all cobwebs and mothballs, like some churches.

Sue and Ken couldn't have been more helpful and were curious to hear of my trips in South Africa, so I politely and succinctly explained the Cape Frontier Wars, including the death of King Hintsa and the Cattle Killing tragedy.

It was not hard to find evidence of Smith. Mounted prominently on the wall was a white marble memorial comprising a distinguished bust of the local hero flanked by spearheads and drapes. The chiselled writing explained that it had been paid for by public subscription in 1862, and listed Smith's many military achievements from Spain to India over his 52 years of service. Below it, a framed poster from 1911 entitled 'Statement of the Services of Lieutenant-General Sir Harry George Wakelyn Smith' listed his army ranks, from ensign in 1805 to lieutenant governor in 1853.

Sue and Ken were particularly proud to show me one of Sir Harry Smith's ceremonial swords, still in its black leather scabbard with brass decoration. I was even invited to hold it. How strange, I thought, to be holding a sword held by Smith himself.

Ken then took me to see the modest end-of-terrace Aliwal House, where Smith had been brought up, the second son of 14 children. His father, John Smith, had been a local surgeon, but a man of limited means. At a young age Harry stood out for his athleticism, marksmanship and skill as a horseman, so a career in the army seemed likely.

Despite being right at his place of birth, where he went to school and later returned a national hero, I felt little connection with the man. I kept comparing Whittlesey with the Eastern Cape, particularly Gcalekaland. The flat agricultural fens, the neat brick buildings and the prominent grey stone church of Whittlesey were a world away from the verdant valleys of Nongqawuse's Gxara River and Hintsa's Nqabara River. These physical differences probably reflected the huge cultural and religious divisions between the crusading Europeans and the indigenous amaXhosa. What a shame, I felt, that those who left England to conquer the world could not appreciate the differences, but acted continually on an assumption of superiority. I wondered if they ever had an inkling of the riches in the cultures they vanquished.

Next, I drove over to the Sir Harry Smith Community College. Its website states, 'We pride ourselves in creating an ethos of respect, equality, tolerance and inclusiveness.' British values of democracy, the rule of law, individual liberty and mutual respect were also mentioned. I thought the ethos and values were wonderful, excellent moral pillars for a modern society, but I struggled to see how Chiefs Hintsa, Sarhili, Sandile and

Maqoma would have recognised those traits in their colonial adversary. Perhaps I was being unreasonable in comparing their perceptions of a 19th-century army commander with the 21st-century values promoted in the college. On the other hand, the colonial settlers, the missionaries, the military and every other Tom Cobley with a finger in the pie of Empire had nearly all been proselytising racial superiority along with their Victorian British values and Christian teachings.

I was mulling over these seeming contradictions in my car outside the school gates when two smartly dressed teachers came out, asking why I was taking photographs. They looked smiley but concerned. I explained my interest in Sir Harry and my travels to the Eastern Cape. More importantly, I showed them I was merely taking shots of the school's signage to help tell my story and show the links between the history of the Eastern Cape and modern-day Whittlesey. I couldn't help telling them that the last time I had been challenged for taking photographs was by security personnel in apartheid South Africa in 1980. We shared embarrassed smiles and I made my way to the town's cemetery for the last leg of my trip.

Ken and Sue's directions to Whittlesey's expansive graveyard and Smith's grave at the far end of it were spot on. It was a pleasure to amble through – calm, manicured and orderly. Now at last I felt I might get closer to the man, as I had not in the church, his home or his community college. Never in my wildest dreams had I imagined that my attempt to find and understand Nongqawuse in South Africa would end up with me at the graveside of Sir Harry and Lady Juana Smith, alongside vivacious flowering lilacs in the Fenlands of England. I started to feel some butterflies, mixed with solemnity.

The grave of Sir Harry Smith and Lady Smith, Whittlesey, England. My pilgrimage to uncover the story of Nongqawuse had finally come to an end in a quiet cemetery.

Here at the graveside there could be no more hubris – no more bombastic displays of cannon fire, no loud demands of obedience and standing on the necks of adversaries; no threats to kill and no bands striking up 'God Save the Queen'. Mass adulation was in short supply. A light grey raised granite grave surrounded by ornate black iron railings, at the far end of the cemetery, was his final resting place. The masonry inscription listed Sir Harry's many postings, and quoted the Duke of Wellington's words of praise from the House of Lords in 1846. All were weathered with a mottled patina of green by the chemistry of time and oxidisation. Harry had passed away from a heart attack in 1860, aged 72. Juana had joined him 12 years later, aged 75.

The themes of death and mortality stirring the bric-à-brac of my mind contrasted markedly with the sound of children playing in the schoolgrounds close by. Their frivolous shouts and laughter were a healthy reminder of youth, innocence and life, and I welcomed it. My mood, as moods tend to be around graves, was contemplative rather than gloomy. Before I became maudlin, they nudged my emotional dial in the right direction, as did the April sun creating fissures in the cloud.

My thoughts wandered to the other two graves I had stood before in recent months. Smith, Hintsa, Nongqawuse – two men of renown, each admired and feared in their day, and a young girl linked to each, whose prophecies had caused devastation that reverberates right up to the present. Each had shaped South African history, and yet death, the great purveyor of equality, had reduced all to worm fodder.

Feelings at gravesites are complex. So, too, are our motivations in visiting them. Only a few weeks before, in the company of Hutch and Mike, I'd stood at the humble gravesite of Nongqawuse, at the edge of a tiny coppice overlooking a vast open landscape of cattle pasture. I had been moved by her story and had come to pay my respects after a lengthy pilgrimage by way of textbooks, poems, academic papers, jet planes and my friends in the Border Historical Society. In my own inept way, standing at the headstone, I had shared my thoughts, explaining that she was not solely responsible for the Great Cattle Killing, the death of thousands and the ultimate rupture of amaXhosa society. I had longed to communicate a message to her in some irrational way – to permeate the soil with my thoughts, in a sort of terrestrial osmosis. I wanted her to know that I regarded her as part of the liberation movement, that I understood her response to the intolerable pressures she and her people had endured. She needed to know that she'd been unreasonably vilified and made the scapegoat by some who should have known better, and by others exploiting the circumstances. The disaster had many causes, not just her prophecies. I hoped she had been able to find some peace on the grassy slopes near Fick's farm.

At King Hintsa's grave I had felt a similar sense of respect and sadness at what had come to pass. His grave was also a crime scene. Here I had particularly felt the landscape trying to talk to us – if only I were not so deaf to the natural world! The secrets of 12 May 1835 were locked into the trees, rock faces and soil. They had seen what really happened in the final minutes of the king's life. Luckily for Smith, they could not speak at the court hearing in August 1836. I recalled leaving that site with the sense that the king's grave represented a huge injustice in 19th-century amaXhosa society. Regicide, arrogance, barbarism dressed up as Christian values – they cried out from the grave. Ripples from that death oscillated for decades, and were one of the many strands that gave rise to the tragedy of the Cattle Killing.

To be honest, standing at the far end Whittlesey's graveyard, I felt very little for Sir Harry and Lady Smith. I had thought I would, but I did not. It was impossible not to think of the loss of life, erosion of indigenous traditions and eventual subjugation to colonial rule that this man's actions supported. It was nothing short of brutal. I told myself that I was looking at things through the lens of a 21st-century perspective. Smith, I told myself, had been a product of his age. He was a Victorian hero, celebrated at home and by settlers in the colonies for doing what the Crown asked of him. Loyal to this cause, passionate in his dealings, no doubt believing in the rights and duties of Empire. All very true. But it all left me cold. I'd seen up close and firsthand the high price others had had to pay for his sense of mission and military ambitions. On too many occasions, he'd been the spark that ignited the tinder and spread the fire of destruction, particularly among the amaXhosa. He, as much as Nongqawuse, had a part to play in the Great Cattle Killing, though his role was more subtle and pervasive.

When something momentous happens it's always the last trigger that is remembered and gets the blame – or the glory. I remembered the shock I had felt at first reading the story of Nongqawuse, and the conviction that there had to be more to the story than is captured in the popular, condensed version. My journey to uncover the truth – or as much of it as we can ever know from such a distance of culture and time – had revealed that this instinct was right. Far from being the work of one girl, the Great Cattle Killing arose from causes many and deep. Colonial expansion, the utter insensitivity and brutality of men like Sir Harry, drought, cattle disease, the longing for liberation from everything the settlers imposed, the encouragements of Mhlakaza and King Sarhili – they all played a part. It had been a perfect storm of adverse events.

In my opinion, history had done Nongqawuse a great disservice by heaping the whole incident at her upon her.

As I left Sir Harry and Juana to their slumber, I hoped that in time a more fully rounded version of the story of the Great Cattle Killing would be told and known.

18: OH! NONGQAWUSE

'Words do not perish.'

Chief Mhala, 1857

While sharing the ups and downs of my pilgrimage to find a more nuanced and balanced version of the Nongqawuse story, I became acutely aware of how sensitive the Great Cattle Killing and its aftermath are in amaXhosa society. For some it remains an unhealed wound and a stone best left unturned. 'That stupid girl' or 'another Nongqawuse story' still trip off the tongue too easily from many people. Nowhere is this more succinctly articulated than the poem that begins

Oh! Nongqawuse

The girl of Mhlakaza

Who killed our nation

Hayi uNongqawuse

Intombi kaMhlakaza

Wasibulala isizwe sethu

From *The Dead Will Arise* by Jeff Peires

Guilt had been writ large. Judgement made.

To get under the skin of these 19th-century events I have attempted to shed many of my western assumptions and biases. In particular, with the help of the Mqamelo family, and others in the Eastern Cape, I've come to appreciate the everyday and cultural importance of cattle and ancestors to the amaXhosa. Ancestors were, and still are, fundamental to many of them, and it is front and centre to why the firm Believers were so committed to the message: 'sacrifice cattle, destroy crops, end witchcraft – and you shall be rewarded'. Difficult as the Cattle Killing movement is to digest, we must remain respectful of the beliefs that were so firmly entrenched in a deeply conservative culture, already traumatised by disease, weather, war and imperial expansion. Much that seems fanciful or incomprehensible to our 21st-century sensibilities fitted well into the 19th-century values and culture of amaXhosa society.

So, when sharing this tale with others, as I hope you will, remember to put it into context - the time, the place and the circumstances. Tread carefully, but don't be shy.

Which leads me to ask what you think about the role of Nongqawuse in these calamitous events of the mid-1800s. You've heard the evidence. Is it an open and shut case? Do you find her guilty on all counts? I hope not.

Alternatively, you may see Nongqawuse as a Joan of Arc or Greta Thunberg figure – a girl fighting for the survival of her people in a male-dominated world, facing colossal pressure from foreign settlers invading their space. Quite an appealing and relevant image in today's world.

Instead, do you lean towards the view held by many in the Eastern Cape that she was a victim of the Cape Governor Sir George Grey, or Satan as he was sometimes referred to? Perhaps the blame rests squarely at his feet for manipulating and deceiving a vulnerable teenage girl into promoting dangerous prophecies.

Conversely, are you of the opinion that the Cattle Killing movement was a wicked scheme dreamt up by the chiefs to drive their people into another war against the British? You wouldn't be the first to think they were stirring the pot and deliberately agitating their followers to fight back and take the conflict to the imperial power, once again.

Perhaps her uncle, Mhlakaza, put her up to it all in order to promote himself.

If you don't buy any of those narratives, then you might view these events as a sort of people's uprising, with commoners taking advantage of the chiefs as their power weakened in the face of colonial constraints. It is not too difficult to see the actions of Nongqawuse and her followers as a nascent black nationalist movement, with ambitions to rupture and overthrow both the indigenous and European power structures. Was it in fact a failed revolution or anti-colonial movement comparable to other 19th-century uprisings in the British Empire, such as in India? Is it too fanciful to compare it with any of the revolutions swamping European countries in 1848? History warns us that revolutions, once started, have a trajectory of their own, often very different from that of their inception. Is that what occurred near the Wild Coast in the mid-1800s?

During my pilgrimage to find Nongqawuse, I was often mindful of the observation by Professor Jennifer Wenzel in her book, *Bulletproof*, that perhaps the girl 'had the right motives but wrong methods'. Now there's a thought. If the tinder, so to speak, had been dry and sparks plentiful amongst the amaXhosa, perhaps other less drastic and self-destructive resistance may have precipitated a better outcome. Who knows? Pure conjecture. The notion still gnaws away at me.

If that is a perspective on the past, we shouldn't lose sight of the present and future. There must be lessons learned. According to Achille Mbembe, vigilance is required to avoid what he calls the 'Nongqawuse Syndrome', a suicidal tendency at times of great stress. And so in that vein of caution, I leave the last few words to a doctor friend of mine in general practice. Beside medical expertise, he has an in-depth knowledge and love of amaXhosa history.

> In the last three years I have gained a much better understanding of the Xhosa cattle killing through the response to Covid vaccinations. When humanity was faced with a global pandemic and formal medical science offered protection through vaccination it was felt at least 80% population vaccination was the best way to quickly achieve herd immunity.
>
> The medical evangelist mindset took over in GPs like me. We could make a difference and save the world!
>
> The most disconcerting experience of my entire career was to discover my practice constituting sensible likeable people who only consulted me because we are of like minds and no compunction, good friends of 30 years sometimes, held an alarming number of unbelievers. Here was a life and death matter affecting the globe, a millenarian event, and these wisecracks would not believe my professional advice. They instead would go to great lengths to help me to believe that vaccines were a plot to kill us all. Control us politically. It took me straight back to 1856, to Nongqawuse and the Cattle Killing Movement!

Of course, there are those who think the prophecies of Nongqawuse may still come true. Now there's a thought, but probably best left for another day …

Bibliography

Literature

Anon. *The Story of the Life of Xhosa Prophetess Nongqause: The Suicide of the AmaXhosa 1856–1857*. Leaflet at Glenshaw Farm, EC.

Anon. The Assassination of Hintsa? *The Phoenix Magazine of the Albany Museum*. Vol 8 Issue 1, 1995.

Anon. *This is Transkei*. Chris van Rensburg Press Ltd, 1978.

Alexander, J.E. *Excursions in Western Africa and Narrative of a Campaign in Kaffir-land on the Staff of the Commander-in-Chief*. Vol 2. Adamant Media Corporation, 2005.

Beattie, T.R. *Pambaniso, a Kaffir Hero: Or, Scenes From Savage Life. An Historical Kaffir Tale*. Sampson, Low, Marston & Company, 1891.

Beinart, W. *The Political Economy of Pondoland 1860–1930*. Cambridge University Press, 1982.

Biko, H. *Black Consciousness: A Love Story*. Jonathan Ball Publishers, 2021.

Blackman, M. The Murder of Hintsa. The Death and Mutilation of the Chief of the Xhosa in 1835 at the Hands of the British was a 'Barbarous' Deed, Concealed by the Perpetrators of a Web of Lies. *History Today* Vol 2 Issue 72, 2022.

Boxer, C.R. The Cape of Good Hope under the Dutch East India Company 1652–1795. *History Today* Vol 13 Issue 6, 1964.

Bradford, H. Framing African Women: Visionaries in Southern Africa and their Photographic Afterlife, 1850–2004. *Jnl of Cape History* Vol 30 Issue 1, 2004.

Bradford, H. *New Country, New Race, New Men: War, Gender and Millenarianism in Xhosaland. 1855–1857*. Oslo 2000 Conference: Session on Gender, Race, Xenophobia and Nationalism.

Bradford, H. Not a Nongqawuse story: An anti-heroine in historical perspective, in Nomboniso Gasa. ed. *Women in South African History: They Remove Boulders and Cross Rivers*, 43–90. Cape Town: HSRC Press, 2007.

Bristow, D. *The Hominins, Hunter-Gatherers and Heroes: Searching For 20 Amazing Places in South Africa*. Jacana Media. Pty. Ltd, 2019.

Brownlee, C.P. and Brownlee, W.T. *Reminiscences of Kaffir Life and History and Other Papers*. Bibliobazaar, LLC, 1896.

Burton, A.W. *Sparks from the Border Anvil*. Provincial Publishing Company, 1950.

Cosser, M. Pictures as Evidence. *The Phoenix* Vol 8 Issue 1, 1995.

Crais, C.C. *White Supremacy and Black Resistance in Pre-Industrial South Africa: The Making of the Colonial Order in the Eastern Cape, 1770–1865*. Cambridge University Press, 1992.

Crampton, H. *The Sunburnt Queen: A True Story*. Saqi Books. 2006.

Curtin, P. Feierman, S. Thompson, L. and Vansina, J. *African History from Earliest Times to Independence*. Longman, 1995.

Dall, N. The Cattle Massacre That Haunts South Africa. *The Daily Dose*, 1 November 2018.

Davies, S.B. *History in the Literary Imagination: The Telling of Nongqawuse and the*

Xhosa Cattle-Killing In South African Literature and Culture. 1891–1937. PhD thesis, University of Cambridge, 2010.

Davies, S.B. Raising the Dead: The Xhosa Cattle-Killing and the Mhlakaza–Goliat Delusion. *Journal of Southern African Studies*, Vol 33 Issue 1, 2007.

Diamond, J. Collapse. *How Societies Choose to Fail or Survive*. Penguin Random House UK, 2011.

Edgar, R.R. *Garveyism in Africa: Dr Wellington and the American Movement in the Transkei. Collected Seminar Papers*. Institute of Commonwealth Studies, 20, 1976.

Edgar, R.R. The Prophet Motive: Enoch Mgijma, the Israelites, and the Background to the Bulhoek Massacre. *Int Jnl of African Historical Studies*, Vol 15 Issue 3, 1982.

Egan, T. *A Pilgrimage to Eternity: From Canterbury to Rome in Search of a Faith*. Penguin Random House, 2020.

Elphick, R. *Kraal and Castle: Khoikhoi and the Founding of White South Africa*. Yale University Press, 1977.

Elphick, R. and Giliomee, H. (eds). *The Shaping of South African Society 1652–1820*. Longman Penguin Southern Africa Ltd, 1979.

Hofmeyer, G.S. Grey Hospital, King William's Town. *Sam J Deel* 70, 8 November 1986.

Hutchison, P. The Search for Hintsa's Grave. Border Historical Society *The Coelacanth* Vol 35 No.2 December 1997, 32-41.

Jefferies, A. and Voorwerp M. *The Absolute Border: The Ashamed Silence*? November 2021. Headline Printer KWT.

Jorgesson, R. Critically discuss the historiographical interpretations and debates around the Xhosa cattle-killing movement within a structured essay. History of South Africa in the 19th Century. Klopp, Carl Vernon's Lexicon of People & Places, 2015.

Laband, J. *The Land Wars: The Dispossession of the Khoisan and AmaXhosa in the Cape Colony*. Penguin Random House South Africa, 2020.

Lalu, P. *The Deaths of Hintsa, Postapartheid South Africa and the Shape of Recurring Pasts*. HSRC Press, 2009.

Lamar, H. and Thompson, L. (eds). *The Frontier in History: North America and Southern Africa Compared*. Yale University Press, 1981.

Landes, R. *Heaven on Earth: The Varieties of the Millennial Experience*. Oxford University Press, 2011.

Lehmann, J. *Remember You Are an Englishman*. Jonathan Cape Ltd, 1977.

Lister, M.H. *Journals of Andrew Geddes Bain*, Van Riebeeck Society Series 1 Vol 30, 1949.

Magona, S. *Mother to Mother*. David Philip Publishers, 2013.

Marks, S. South Africa – 'The Myth of the Empty Land'. *History Today* Vol 30 Issue 1, 1980.

Mda, Z. *The Heart of Redness*. Picador, 2000.

Mertens, A. and Broster, J. *African Elegance*. Purnell & Sons. S.A. Ltd, 1979.

Michener, J. A. *The Covenant*. Secker and Warburg, 1980.

Mkhize, N. Nicholas Gcaleka and The Search For Hintsa's Skull. *Jnl of Southern African Stds* Vol 35 Issue 1, 2009.

Mostert, N. *Frontiers: The Epic of South Africa's Creation and the Tragedy of the Xhosa People*. Alfred A. Knopf, 1992.

Nicholas, J.T. *A Nun and the Pig: Tales from South Africa*. Amberley Publishing, 2021.

Nienaber, W. Steyn, M. and Hutten, L. The Grave of King Mgolobane Sandile Ngqika: Revisiting The Legend. *Southern Africa Archaeological Bulletin* Vol 63 Issue 187, pp 46–50, 2008.

Nqandeka, H.M. *Don't Upset ooMalume! A Guide to Stepping Up Your Xhosa Game*. Jonathan Ball Publishers, 2022.

Offenburger, A. Millenarianism in Iowa and the Eastern Cape: Thinking Through Fields of Dreams and the Xhosa Cattle-Killing. *English Studies in Africa*, Vol 61 Issue 1, 2018.

Offenburger, A. Smallpox and Epidemic Threat in Nineteenth-Century Xhosaland. *African Studies*, Vol 67 Issue 2, 2008.

Offenburger, A. The Xhosa Cattle-Killing Movement in History and Literature. *History Compass*, Vol 7 Issue 6, 2009.

O'Loughlin, E. Quest For Head Raises Number of Skeletons In Museum. *The Irish Times*, 27 February 1996.

Opland, J. Xhosa Oral Poetry: Aspects of a Black South Africa Tradition. *Cambridge Studies In Oral and Literature Culture*, 1983.

Oppenheim, C.E. Nelson Mandela and the Power of Ubuntu. *Religions* 3, 369–388, 2012.

Pakenham, T. *The Scramble for Africa*. Abacus, 1991.

Pakenham, T. *The Boer War*. The Folio Society, 1999.

Peires, J.B. The Central Beliefs of the Xhosa Cattle Killing. *The African Journal of History*, 22 January 2009.

Peires, J.B. *The Dead Will Arise: Nongqawuse and The Great Xhosa Cattle-Killing Movement of 1856–7*. Indiana University Press, 1989.

Peires, J.B. *The House of Phalo: A History of the Xhosa People in the Days of Their Independence*. University of California Press, 1982.

Price, R. *Making Empire: Colonial Encounters and the Creation of Imperial Rule in Nineteenth-Century Africa*. Cambridge University Press, 2008.

Rogers, B. *Divide and Rule. South Africa's Bantustans*. IDAF, 1976.

Samin, R. Nongqawuse Resurrected: Legend and History in Zakes Mda's The Heart of Redness. *Commonwealth Essays and Studies*, Vol 31 Issue 1, pp 48–58, 2008.

Saunders, C. and Derricourt, R. (eds.) *Beyond the Cape Frontier: Studies in the History of Transkei and Ciskei*. Longman, 1974.

Scheub, H. *The Tongue is Fire: South African Story Tellers and Apartheid.* The University of Wisconsin Press, 1996.

Sleigh, J.C. *The World of the Dutch East India Company*. Tafelberg Publishers, 1980.

Smith, A. *First People: The Lost History of the Khoisan*. Jonathan Ball, 2022.

Smith, H. Moore Smith, G.C. (eds.). *The Autobiography of Lieutenant-General Sir Harry Smith, Baronet of Aliwal on the Sutlej G.C.B.* John Murray, 1902.

Smith, K. *The Wedding Feast War: The Final Tragedy of the Xhosa People*. Frontline Books, 2010.

Smith, K.S. *Harry Smith's Last Throw: The Eighth Frontier War 1850–1853*. Frontline Books, 2012.

Soga, J.H. *The AmaXhosa: Life and Customs*. Cambridge University Press, 2014.

Soga, J.H. *The South-Eastern Bantu: Abe-Nguni, Aba-Mbo, Ama-Lala*. Cambridge University Press, 2014.

Stapleton, T.J. Maqoma. *The Legend of a Great Xhosa Warrior*. Amava Heritage Publishing, 2016.

Stapleton, T.J. Maqoma: *Xhosa Resistance to the Advance of Colonial Hegemony. 1798–1873*. PhD thesis, Dalhousie University, 1993.

Stapleton, T.J. Faku. *Rulership and Colonialism in the Mpondo Kingdom c. 1780–1867.* Wilfrid Laurier University Press, 2001.

Stapleton, T.J. Reluctant Slaughter: Rethinking Maqoma's Role in the Xhosa Cattle Killing (1853-1857). *The Int Jnl of African Studies*, Vol 26 Issue 2, 1993.

Stapleton, T.J. They No Longer Care for Their Chiefs: Another Look at the Xhosa Cattle Killing 1856–1857. *The Int Jnl of African Studies*, Vol 24 Issue 2, 1991.

Tanne–Tremaine, P. *British 1820 Settlers to South Africa: A Reference Book*. Paul Tanner-Tremaine, 2019.

Taylor, S. *Shaka's Children: A History of the Zulu People*. Harper Collins Publishers, 1994.

Thompson, L. *Survival in Two Worlds: Moshoeshoe of Lesotho 1786–1870*. Oxford at the Clarendon Press, 1975.

Tropp, J.A. *Natures of Colonial Change: Environmental Relations in the Making of Transkei*. Ohio University Press, 2006.

Vigne, R. *The Transkei: A South African Tragedy*. The Africa Bureau, 1969.

Wenzel, J. *Bulletproof: Afterlives of Anticolonial Prophecy in South Africa and Beyond*. The University of Chicago Press, 2009.

Wilson, M. and Thompson. L. *The Oxford History of South Africa: I. South Africa to 1870.* Oxford University Press, 1969.

Wood, L.L.F. *Hintsa's Grave East Bank Nqabara River*. Unpublished paper, 18 June, 1997.

Online

Anon. A History of the Bulhoek Massacre. *South African History Online*.
Anon. *Brief History of the Xhosa People*. www.xhosaculture.co.za.
Anon. *British Values at Sir Harry Smith Community College.* www.sirharrysmith.cambs.sch.uk.
Anon. *Driving Whites into the Sea: History of the 'Great Delusion'*. www.nongqawuse.za/nongqawuse.
Anon. *King Hintsa kwaKhawuta of the House of Phalo*. www.nhmasa.co.za.
Anon. *King Hintsa's Grave*. www.artefacts.co.za.
Anon. King Sarhili kwaHintsa. *South African History Online*.
Anon. Nongqawuse. *South African History Online*.
Anon. *The Gush Family in South Africa*. www.1820settlers.com.
Bahre, E. Greta Thunberg and Nongqawuse: Two Sixteen-Year-Old Women Challenging the World. *Leidenanthropologyblog*, 7 October 2019. 2022.
Hayward, J. African Clans Descended From European Men. *The Naked Scientists, Science Features*. 16 October 2018.
Hirst, M. Sarhili's Grave at Tsholorha. *Imvubu* Vol 15 Issue 1, 2003.
Kuper, S. Beware of The Tory Cult That's Steering Brexit. *Financial Times Weekend*, 2 November 2017.
Mbembe, A. *South Africa's Second Coming: The Nongqawuse Syndrome*. OpenDemocracy, 14 June 2006.
Pitcher, G. *The Xhosa Cattle Killing*. Siyabona Africa.
Saul, N. www.xhosaculture.co.za.
Scott, T. Ancestral voices, prophesying doom. *West Country Voices*, 4 September 2020.